Cutting Edge Technologies and Academic Librarianship

universities. The research scholars surveyed seventy or 42% responded to the questionnaire. The research scholars surveyed were [illegible] (n=53) [illegible] + 9 (UR) [illegible] were 23% (n=16) (13 [illegible] UR) Arts & Humanities, [illegible] (n=17) (14 BV + 3 UR) Social Sciences, [illegible] (18 BV + 10 UR) Pure & Applied Sciences [illegible] Music & Fine Arts. The research scholars [illegible] university wise were, 69% (n=48) Banasthali Vidyapith and 31% (n=22) University of Rajasthan.

Three hundred and eighty six [illegible] self administered questionnaires [illegible] post graduate (PG) students of both the universities. The PG students surveyed one hundred and forty [illegible] responded to the questionnaire. The post graduate students surveyed gender wise were [illegible] female and 10% (n=15) male. The post graduate students surveyed university wise were [illegible] University of Rajasthan and 72% or n= [illegible] Banasthali Vidyapith. The post graduate students surveyed faculty wise were [illegible] (n=31) Arts & Humanities, [illegible] (n=65) Social Sciences, [illegible] Pure & Applied Sciences and [illegible] (n=23) Music [illegible]

[illegible] presentation of the collected data in the following [illegible]

- [illegible] information use [illegible] Faculty [illegible] research scholars and Post graduate Students.
- [illegible] between Banasthali Vidyapith and University of Rajasthan.
- [illegible] Arts & Humanities, Social Sciences, Pure & Applied Sciences and Music [illegible]

Library [illegible]

[illegible] understanding the need [illegible]

Cutting Edge Technologies and Academic Librarianship

Editor
Anna Kaushik
and
Nirmal Kumar Swain

Ess Ess Publications
New Delhi

Cutting Edge Technologies and Academic Librarianship

ISBN: 978-81-7000-713-5

₹ 1250/-

First Published 2014

Published by:
Ess Ess Publications
4831/24, Ansari Road,
Darya Ganj,
New Delhi-110 002.
INDIA
Phones: 23260807, 41563444
Fax: 41563334
E-mail: info@essessreference.com
www.essessreference.com

Cover Design by *Patch Creative Unit*

Printed and bound in India at Salasar Imaging Systems.

Contents

Preface

In the present era, cutting edge technologies are evolving at tremendous rate and being used in different kind of fields in order to systematize and gear the efficiencies of works with variant feasibilities in their respective fields. Libraries and information centers are known for providing valued information for users for variant purposes, nowadays, can't survive without technologies therefore libraries are very much using latest technologies into their services in connection to enhance the services in manifold formats. These technologies include bar-coding, Radio Frequency Identification (RFID), library 2.0 and cloud computing etc. These cutting edge technologies are helpful in proving prompt deliveries of services to the right users in minimal time. But, on the other hand, libraries and LIS professionals are facing various challenges and barriers in adopting, configuring, establishing and sustaining the cutting edge technologies into academic libraries. Therefore, it is sincerely felt to bring out a book on different issues associated with academic libraries using cutting edge technologies in to their services which make extensive platform of debate for library and information science professionals to exchange the various ideas, experiences, problems encountered and lesson learned during the using any cutting edge technology into academic libraries in real situation and proving possible remedies for cope the various problems related to using latest technologies in to the academic libraries as well encourage the LIS community for collaboration and to build a networks to resolve the issues encountered during successfully delivery of services day to day.

This book is consist of six sections such as Application of Cutting Edge Technologies in Librarianship, E- Learning and Academic Libraries, Digital Library, E- resources and services, Digitization and copy right issues and Miscellaneous and twenty nine chapters which mainly focused on diverse issues connected with various technologies in different academic libraries.

While inviting papers for this book, overwhelming response was received not only from India country but also from abroad countries and through this endeavour, editors discovered that LIS professionals have keen interest to adopt, link and widely use cutting edge technologies in the academic librarianship but LIS community want to share the problems encountering during the successful running the different technologies in to their respective libraries.

Editors of this book, sincerely extend their hearty gratitude and thanks to all contributors who were actively participated and contributed their worthy papers for this book well in time. Editors also thankful to those LIS professionals and family members for their encouragement, constant and salient support because without their support, it is not possible to start and end this journey successfully and shape this book. We are definitely ensure that "Cutting Edge Technologies and Academic Librarianship" book origin a platform for discussion the various issues related to use cutting edge technologies into academic libraries through which LIS community will really be benefited.

—Editors

List of Contributors

1. *Dr. Anna Kaushik*
   Deputy Librarian
   University of Kota
   Kota (Rajasthan)

2. *Surendra Kumar Pal*
   IISER LIBRARY
   Indian Institute of Science Education & Research
   Thiruvananthapuram Kerala, India

3. *Dr. Sasekea Harris*
   Science Librarian: Science Branch Library
   Adjunct Lecturer: Dept. of Library & Information Studies
   University of the West Indies (UWI)
   Mona Campus, Kingston 7, Jamaica WI

4. *Gopal Vipra*
   Librarian Offg.
   CE, RTU, Kota

5. *Mukesh Mangal*
   Assistt. Librarian, Central Library,
   Banasthali University (Raj.)

6. ***Dr. D. K. Shrivastava***
Divisional Librarian (I/C)
Govt. Divisional Public Library,
Kota, Rajasthan-324009

7. ***Dipendra Singh Sajwan***
(Library Assistant)
Institute of Human Behaviour and Allied Sciences (IHBAS)
Dilshad Garden, Delhi-110095

8. ***Dr. Parveen Kumar***
Librarian, S. A. Jain College,
Ambala City-134003 Haryana

9. ***Shweta Pandey***
Asst. Librarian
Central University of Rajasthan

10. ***Shri Ram Pandey***
Asst. Professor, DLIS
Mohanlal Sukhadia University, Udaipur-313001

11. ***Lakkho Singh***
Librarian
Govt. Polytechnic College
Kota (Rajasthan)

12. ***Chandresh A. Shah***
Library Assistant,
Junagadh Agriculture University, Junagadh (Gujarat)

13. ***Dr. Kanchan Kamila***
Librarian
The University of Burdwan
Burdwan -713104 (WB) India

14. ***N. Santhi***
Librarian,
Nadar Saraswathi College of Arts & Science,
Theni-625531. Tamilnadu.

15. ***Barada Kanta Mohanty***
Librarian, KIIMS, Cuttack.

16. ***Bhanu Partap***
Librarian
T.S. Central State Library, Sector-17, Chandigarh-160017

17. ***Abhijit Chatterjee***
University Research Fellow,
Department of Library and Information Science,
University of Calcutta, Calcutta

18. ***Mukesh Chand Bharti***
Librarian
SGT Medical College,Hospital & Research Institute
Budhera,Gurgaon (Haryana) 123050

19. ***Dr. Tabasum Maqbool***
Librarian, DIET,
Ganderbal, J&K, India

20. ***Ramveer Sagar***
Deputy Librarian, Manav Rachna International University,
Campus K Block
Delhi-Surajkund Road, Sec. 43, Faridabad, Haryana, INDIA

21. ***Dr. D. S. Thakur***
Documentation Officer,
NUEPA (National University of Educational Planning and
Administration, New Delhi

22. ***Anil Kumar Siwach***
Assistant Professor
Department of Library & Information Science
M.D. University, Rohtak

23. ***Sobhagyawati Gupta***
Assistant Librarian
Central University of Rajasthan
Bandarsindari, Kishangarh-305801
Ajmer (Rajasthan)

24. ***Madan Singh Rana***
University Librarian
HNB Garhwal University
(A Central University) Srinagar
Garhwal (Uttarakhand)

25. ***Vikas Asawat***
(Patent & Trade Mark Attorney)
3/183, Ganesh Talab
Basant Vihar Kota Pin 324009

26. ***Dr. Praveen Babel***
WISDOM Library,
Banasthali University – 304022

27. ***Dr. Fayaz Ahmad Loan***
Assistant Librarian,
Central University of Kashmir, J&K, India

28. ***K. Anuradha***
D. K. T. College of Education,
Amaravathipalayam, Perunthloluvu [Po],
Tirupur, Tamilnadu-641665

29. ***Shesh Mishra***
Assistant Librarian
Banasthali Vidyapith
304022 (Rajasthan)

30. ***Dr. Shabir Ahmad Ganaie***
Faculty Member, Department of Library & Information Science
University of Kashmir,Srinagar-190006

1

Adopting Cloud Computing in Libraries

Dr. Anna Kaushik

ABSTRACT

In present era, cloud computing is an emerging technology on the web. Libraries are adopting cloud computing technology in order to offer library services in most effective way so as to attract users as well as fulfill their information needs in utmost level. This article presents various barriers and issues for adopting cloud computing technology in the libraries. This article will able to serve as guidelines for those libraries which want to adopt cloud computing technology.

Key words : Libraries, cloud computing, adoption, guidelines, library services

INTRODUCTION

An adoption of new technologies in libraries is a long practice. Libraries adopt emerging technologies time to time for variant purposes or on the basis of technologies merits and demerits. There are some reasons behind adopting cloud computing technology for libraries such as due to changing demands of the users, development of new platforms and providing library services promptly with their own work places and leisure time. For instance recently web 2.0 applications adopted by the libraries and now libraries are shifting over their services on cloud based environment by using cloud computing applications and services.

Cloud computing technology comes up as a virtual revolution in information communication and technology sector. The cloud computing term basically refer as marketing term that is also known as utility computing through which services delivered through various platforms and models to the customers. In cloud computing, hardware, software, functionality and platforms installed and run in a local environment and performed on the network in internet cloud that re-usable, constantly update and have compatible to couple with web enabled technologies. Libraries are using some cloud computing services since long time especially online databases and large union catalougue but nowadays cloud computing appeared with variety of services models and deployment models. National Institute of Standards and Technology (NIST) defined cloud computing as "cloud computing is a model for enabling convenient, on-demand network access to a shared pool of configurable computing resources (such as networks, servers, storage, applications and services) that can be rapidly provisioned and released with minimal management effort or service provider interaction[1]". Among various service models of cloud computing technology, three service models viz cloud infrastructure as a Service (IaaS) used for data storage, Platform as a Service (PaaS) used for application deployment and Software as a Service (SaaS) used for software hosting widely accepted and used in cloud computing technology connected services. Likewise deployment cloud service models such as Public cloud (open to all), Private cloud (developed by individual organization), Community cloud (developed by a community (people)/many organizations) and Hybrid cloud (a mixture of more than one deployment models of cloud computing) also widely adopted by the users. Cloud computing technology also offering various good advantages for libraries such as cost saving, ease to implement, flexibility, scalability, sustainability, energy saving, easy to upgrade, reliability, continuity and show case for libraries.

RELATED STUDIES

Kim et.al[2]study highlighted issues such as outage, security, performance, compliance, private clouds, integration and cost regarding adoption of cloud computing and also provide a market prognosis. Romero[3] conducted a study on cloud computing benefits and drawbacks in the light of library automation and suggested some measures to be considered while adopting cloud computing in library automation purpose. Many studies were carried out in the cloud computing need of adoption in universities perspective, Sasikala and Prema[4] explored the factors wok behind the necessity of cloud computing in university which include costs increase, students success, institutional performance and competition in development. Katz et al.[5] study claimed that universities found as an early adopters of cloud computing services in comparison to other sectors such as commercial and governmental. Katz et. al.[6] also pointed out the issues such as policy and control issues, new services that will move above campus before older self-operated services, using an accidental strategy formed around consumer choice for using cloud computing in higher education. Nirmala and Sridaran[7]raised the various challenges and possible solutions at the design and implementation level of cloud computing for users. Sanchati and Kulkarni[8] explored security issues like surrounding data location, mobility and availability in cloud computing using for digital and university libraries. Goldner[9] study shows that how cloud computing is different from other computing technologies and discussed how cloud computing solutions may be beneficial to libraries. Patel and Patel[10] highlighted the various issues, opportunities and challenges in cloud computing. Hence there is no study found on the adoption of cloud computing in the libraries.

IS REALLY NECESSARY TO ADOPT CLOUD COMPUTING IN THE LIBRARY

Before entering in cloud computing environment libraries should ask following questions themselves through which libraries will able to judge the really needs of cloud computing services in the libraries:-

- Will cloud computing services able to achieve the objectives of the library and meet the information needs of the users?
- What guarantees do the cloud computing providers give to libraries through the service level agreement (SLA)?
- What procedures cloud computing vender follow to protect library data from unauthorized use/access?
- Is there any mechanism cloud computing provider has in respect of data backup if any disaster take place?
- Is it possible to move easily form one cloud service to another cloud services?
- What types formats and standards cloud services provider currently using?
- What is the experience a cloud service provider has with regard to libraries?
- What is the cost involved at the initial and long term level while a library go for cloud computing services?

BARRIERS TO ADOPT CLOUD COMPUTING SERVICES IN THE LIBRARIES

Security

Security is a main barrier to adopt cloud computing services in the libraries which related mainly to privacy of library data to be stored on cloud .Though none technology is ensured 100% security but in a cloud computing environment security issue must raise. There is no control over the data to be stored on cloud or one cannot know that where library data is available .It is possible for data can be stolen using side-channel attack and male ware also attack on client server machine. Less control over security by handing over library data to a provider could lead to providers mining that data to sell to other companies. According to the cloud security alliance, provider often are not transparent about their hiring practices and what protocols have been established regarding libraries access to data. Access granted to the wrong people could lead to data mining or disclosure of confidential data. Security issues mainly concern with XML signatures, browsing security, flooding, reputation fate sharing, side channels, control over library data, dispense of the internet. The security measures that Amazon Web Services employs may serve as a model for other cloud service providers.

Performance

Another barrier is performance of cloud computing services that deals with communication time between the client computer and the web server in the cloud. The problem becomes critical when number of simultaneous users increased and transferred of data form cloud increased. The physical distance also matters. Due to above problem some time, organizations also feel with regard to increasing the bandwidth for the communication purpose just after the adopting cloud computing services.

Interoperability

In cloud computing environment there is lack of universal standards and interfaces of communication as each cloud services used its own standard and interface to connect the users with their cloud services. Therefore, one library may have problem to shift over their data and services from one cloud service to another cloud service and a significant risk is always occurred.

Control

Control mechanism over user always varies in different cloud computing services. As such no significance control attached with cloud computing services therefore this is also a barrier to adopt cloud computing in the libraries.

Reliability

Another key barrier is reliability through which trust somewhere connected. Any library must concern with reliability issue of any technology as their valuable data was shared by the adopted technology. Cloud computing technology has lesser reliability indicators in comparison to other web enabled technologies. Many cloud computing services are using commodity hardware that may collapse unexpectedly.

Cost

Cost is very important barrier to adopt cloud computing in libraries as libraries have many time less budget and demand of user regularly increasing. The balance of library budget and users demand is not match many times. Hence libraries are moving towards significant technology which may be helpful to satisfy the information needs of the users. Nowadays, cloud computing services are available in various payment modes. Some cloud computing services start with free service and then move to paid mode and many cloud computing services are started with low price and after some time their price increased high. Thus the cost of cloud computing services are varies greatly. If libraries continue to trend toward shifting their data to clouds, what is the controlling mechanism for cloud computing services providers with regards to hike prices.

DISRUPTION OF CONTINUITY IN SERVICES

Continuity in services of cloud computing is the level of service priority. If the capacity of the cloud is strained during the peak usage, a client's level of service may decrease proportionately with the service fee the pay for.

FAILURE OF CLOUD SERVICE PROVIDERS

Instability of the cloud computing service providers is also critical barrier in adopting cloud computing in the libraries. In this regard, libraries should ask some questions form themselves before selecting cloud computing service provider. These questions may include what will happen if cloud provides company goes to out of business or is bought by other company, will your library data is secured, will your library is able to recover the data and what will happen if you unable to recover your data in a timely manner.

ISSUES TO BE CONSIDERED WHEN ADOPTING THE CLOUD COMPUTING IN THE LIBRARY

- In depth study of cloud computing applications and services that currently being used in the different libraries and matching the requirement of users and objectives of the library with adoption of cloud computing services and applications.
- Libraries must diligent in terms of security, customer support and corporate integrity while selecting cloud computing service provider especially connected with library data.
- Security and privacy issues must be clearly demonstrated with regard to library data storage, technical and other legal implications should also identify prior to adopt the cloud computing services. Security in cloud computing can be maximize through standardization of security levels in which all participative organizations should follow that standards of security. Server would enforce specific security measures depending on the level assigned. This standardization would allow users to designate specific security levels to different information. Provider of cloud computing could change more or less base on the security requirements for the data that it is housing for the user. It is also suggested that a user never login through a third-party sources.
- Develop a proper strategy to adopt cloud computing services in the library. The steps which may be considered for making an effective strategy incorporate developing the knowledge about cloud computing, evaluating the present stage of the library from the point of view of the IT needs, information needs, structure and usages, experimenting the cloud computing services, choosing the best cloud computing services, and implementation and management of chosen cloud computing services.
- Prior to decide the payment modes for cloud computing services each library should undertake an in-depth analysis to choose most suitable payment mode. There are different types

of payment modes are available for cloud computing services:

Pay-as-you-go is the most popular payment mode for cloud computing services. Most of cloud computing users use this payment mode to get cloud computing services. In this mode a user pay only that amount what he/she used.

Another mode is "Subscription", in this mode user make payment for potential user of cloud computing hardware and services on the basis of certain period of time that may be a month, year and so on. This mode also used as different ways such as number of users, functionality wise, flat rate (unlimited users and resources) etc. However it is suggested that a library should diligently make estimates for payment mode for cloud computing services as per their suitability choice and users.

- The cost of increasing scalable storage options in cloud computing environment should be judge in advance. Many providers offer very competitive price of cloud services at initial level but then successively increase their rates very much. A cloud services provider which at first seems less economical future might actually turn out to be cheaper one if the initial cost is compensated in the future. Therefore it is better to pick out that vender of cloud computing services whose future rates are low rather than whose original rates is very low.
- It is very essential to make remote access policies of cloud computing services very much clear through which users of libraries must be able to use the services from anywhere with many flexibility. For ensure this practice, the access levels assigned to each user must be clearly defined so that clear policies can be created.
- Energy saving is the key feature of the cloud computing technology. As less energy consumption is used in the cloud computing services rather than traditional IT infrastructures. Hence library should use those technologies which reduce the energy consumptions.

- Identify the opportunities and benefits for switching from existing computing infrastructure to cloud computing.
- Development of benefit and risk evaluation framework to support decision when, where and how we can adopt cloud services.
- Develop a roadmap for optimizing the current IT environment for adopting of public and private cloud services.
- Identify the secure in-house competencies that will be required to manage effective adoption of cloud services.
- Assess the technical challenges encountered during moving from any infrastructure into a cloud environment even a private cloud and various services (internal and external) in order to identify where the problem may arise.
- Ensure that the networking environment is really ready for adopting cloud computing services.
- Data ownership also be clearly defined in terms of access complete data of their libraries, re-use and if changing the cloud computing at any stage in future.
- A library must know that the services are truly open as in services oriented architecture libraries is to shift the use of internal technical expertise from maintaining software and services towards innovative uses of cloud services in their local environment.
- A dynamic Service Level Agreement (SLA) is required so that libraries may get optimum Return on Investment (ROI) for adopting cloud computing into their services. Service Level Agreement (SLA) is a very crucial juncture through which all services are governed during entire period. Libraries must be very carefully checked the Service Level Agreement (SLA) of cloud computing service provider before signing or agreeing with the SLA that made between cloud service vender and a library as its effect the entire cycle of cloud computing adoption practice. For this reason, a library should negotiate a well-defined Service Level Agreement (SLA) that specifies services

and disasters recovery procedures and all kind of guarantees. A strong SLA will able to address many concerns and allay fears about switching to cloud computing services. Service Level Agreement (SLA) is a document which describes the certain performance criteria, promises remedial actions, penalties, legal implications etc., made between service provider and user. An SLA contains service level objectives (SLOs) that define objectively measurable conditions for the service. The SLA describes the Cloud Service, documents Service Level Targets, and specifies the responsibilities of the Cloud Service Provider and the Customer. Service level Agreement (SLA) has two kinds one is infrastructure SLA- the infrastructure provider manages and offers guarantees on availability of the infrastructure, namely, server machine, power, network connectivity, and so on. Another is application SLA, in the application co-location hosting model, the server capacity is available to the applications based solely on their resource demands. A strong cloud related Service Level Agreement (SLA) may contains key elements such as server uptime, persistent Storage, network performance, load balancing, cloud storage, location of the data, access to the data, portability of the data, server reboot, support response time, domain name Services, security / privacy of the data, process to identify problems and resolution expectations, change management process, dispute mediation process, 7 x 24 x 365 supports and service termination. The life cycle of SLA is rotated in five phases such as contract definition, publishing and discovery, negotiation, operationalization and de-commissioning.

- Libraries should examine the compatibilities with regard to switch over on cloud service to another cloud service at any time or in future so that no problem may be taken place in this task.
- A reliable cloud computing services provider may contains proactive security protocols including monitoring, processes to limit exposure to threats, shift reaction times and multi

layers to protect data and provide sound customer support around the clock with zero-hour response time to any security threats a client may face. For entering the integrity of cloud computing provider library may contact the other libraries / organizations which currently using their services and get feedback about the cloud computing services as well as respective vendors.

- Libraries should make a strong and detailed back-up strategies including information about secondary clouds in place, any other redundancy measures to address server failure or disruptions in the cloud services and network connectivity must be considered while adopting cloud computing services in the libraries.

CONCLUSION

Cloud computing is an emerging technology through which libraries have good opportunities to improve their services easily. Cloud computing technology is offering many benefits to libraries such as minimize the efforts, hardware, software and total cost of managing library services, resources and enhancing the both user's experience and library staff workflows. Cloud computing also take care all kind of transparency of library data and users. The vision to adopt cloud computing in libraries is to delivery of library services, resources and expertise at the right time within users' workflows and in effective manner. The cloud computing models encourage libraries and their users to participate in a network and community of libraries by enabling them to re-use and socialization of information. Cloud computing also creates powerful platforms for libraries on the web and provides their users to access library's resources and services at local, collaborative and global level. Hence cloud computing technology gives different future to libraries to explore their services and resources at ultimate extent.

REFERENCES

1. Mell, P. and Grance, T.(2009). Effectively and securely using the cloud computing paradigm .http://csrc.nist.gov/organizations/fissea/2009-conference/presentations/fissea09-pmell-day3_cloud-computing.pdf (accessed on 2 November2012).
2. Kim,W., Kim,S.D., Lee,E., and Lee, S. (2009). Adoption issues for cloud computing. In *Proceedings of the 11th International Conference on Information Integration and Web-based Applications & Services* (iiWAS '09). ACM, New York, NY, USA, 3-6. (DOI=10.1145/1806338.1806341 http://doi.acm.org/10.1145/1806338.1806341)
3. Romeo, N.L.(2012). Cloud computing in library automation: benefits and drawbacks. *The Bottom Line:Managing Library Finances*, 25(3), 110-114.
4. Sasikala, S. and Prema, S. (2010). Massive centralized cloud computing (MCCC) exploration in higher education, *Advancesin Computational Sciences and Technology*, 3(2), 111–118.
5. Katz, R. N,, Goldstein, P. J. and Yanosky, R (2009). Demystifying cloud computing for higher education, *EDUCAUSE*, available at http://net.educause.edu/ir/library/pdf/ERB0919.pdf (accessed on 2November 2012)
6. Katz, R.N., Goldstein, P.J. andYanosky, R. (2010). Cloud Computing in Higher Education, *EDUCAUSE*.available at http://net.educause.edu/section_params/conf/CCW10/highered.pdf (accessed on2 November 2012).
7. Nirmala, A.P. and Sridaran, R.(2012).Cloud computing issues at design and implementation levels: a survey. *International Journal of Advanced Networking and Applications*, 3(6),1444-1449.
8. Sanchati, R. and Kulkarni, G.(2011). Computing in digital and university libraries. *Global Journal of Computer Science and Technology*,11(12)Ver,1,1-7 available at http://globaljournals.org/GJCST_Volume11/6-Cloud-Computing-in-Digital-and-University.pdf (accessed on 3 November 2012).
9. Goldner, M.(2012). Winds of change: libraries and cloud computing. *BCLA Browser: Linking the Library Landscape*,4(1) available at http://bclabrowser.ca/index.php/browser/article/view/362 (accessed on 3 November 2012).
10. Patel, H.B and Patel D.R. (2011). Cloud computing: issues, opportunities and challenges. *International Journal of Engineering and Social Science*, 1(2), 64- 76.

2

Cloud Computing and Library Services : Challenge & Issues

Surendra Kumar Pal

ABSTRACT

Cloud computing can help libraries collaborate with each other in a facile manner. Every library has its own electronic data resources. If all electronic data resources are put together in a single place which may be accessed by a group of libraries, the whole electronic data base will become huge. This space which contains all the electronic data can be some cloud, say, a library cloud. This library cloud will contain the digitized data of different libraries and hence, will help libraries integrate their data. The need for maintaining and backing up the data will be no more the responsibility of the libraries since all the data will be stored in the cloud which shall be managed by some cloud provider. It will also help the libraries in scaling up or down their data capacity whenever required. This scaling up or down is purely a function of need. Hence, the libraries would be consuming exactly the required space. As a result, libraries will not have to predict their future needs and buy space and infrastructure beforehand. This is co adjuvant effort of the libraries will not only increase the overall efficiency (since the data will be shared) but also open doors for innovation, make libraries a lot more scalable and help save money as well. This model would let libraries maintain more control over the applications and data stores that contain sensitive, private information about patrons. Provisioning and maintenance of infrastructure for Web based digital library present several challenges. This paper discusses the Cloud Computing concept in libraries, how make effective library services by cloud computing, Issues, challenges and benefits of cloud computing also.

Keywords : Cloud Computing, Cloud Computing in Libraries, Library Services through Cloud Computing, Digital Library.

INTRODUCTION

Cloud computing is a new computing paradigm, involving data and/or computation outsourcing, with Infinite and elastic resource scalability, On demand "just-in-time" provisioning, No upfront cost ... pay-as-you-go. That is, use as much or as less you need, use only when you want, and pay only what you use, Cloud Computing is a completely new Information Technology and it is known as the third revolution after Personel Computer and Internet in Information Technology. As it is still an evolving paradigm, its definitions, use cases, underlying technologies, issues, risks, and benefits will be refined in a spirited debate by the public and private sectors. According to the definition of NIST (National Institute of Standards and Technology), Cloud Computing is a model for enabling convenient, on-demand network access to a shared pool of configurable computing resources (e.g., networks, servers, storage, applications, and services) that can be rapidly provisioned and released with minimal management effort or service provider interaction. To be more specific, Cloud Computing is the improvement of Distributed Computing, Parallel Computing, Grid Computing and Distributed Databases. In other words, by collecting large quantities of information and resources stored in personal computers, mobile phones and other equipment, Cloud Computing is capable of integrating them and putting them on the public cloud for serving users. Digital library is a development-oriented hardware and software integration platform, through to technical and the product integration, each kind of carrier digitization, carries on the effective deposit and the organization, provides the network the effective service. After Digital library technology popularization, provided the high grade information service but simultaneously also to expose all sorts of questions unceasingly, because the zones of different the current economic condition limit presented the development.

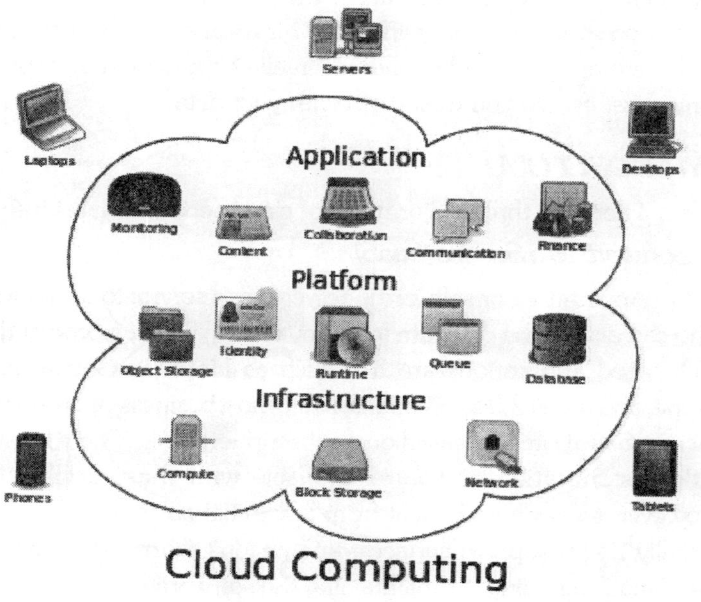

Fig. 1. Showing Cloud Computing

WHAT IS REALLY A CLOUD COMPUTING

Cloud Computing as a computing model, not a technology. In this model "customers" plug into the "cloud" to access IT resources which are priced and provided "on-demand". Essentially, IT resources are rented and shared among multiple tenants much as office space, apartments, or storage spaces are used by tenants. Delivered over an Internet connection, the "cloud" replaces the company data center or server providing the same service. Thus, Cloud Computing is simply IT services sold and delivered over the Internet. Cloud Computing vendors combine virtualization (one computer hosting several "virtual" servers), automated provisioning (servers have software installed automatically), and Internet connectivity technologies to provide the service. These are not new technologies but a new name applied to a collection of older (albeit updated) technologies that are packaged, sold and delivered in a new way. A key point to remember is that, at the most basic level, your data resides on someone else's server(s). This means that most concerns (and there are potentially hundreds) really come down to trust and control issues. Do you trust them with your data?

TYPES OF CLOUD

There are three major types of cloud services available[4]:

1. Software as a Service (SaaS)

Applications or software is delivered as a service to the customer who can access the program from any online device. Some of these Web-based applications are free such as Hotmail, Google Apps, Skype, and many 2.0 applications, while most business-oriented SaaS, such as SalesForce, is leased on a subscription basis. There is usually little customization or control available with these applications. However, subscribers benefit from low initial costs, have access to (usually 24/7) support services, and needn't worry about hosting, installing, upgrading, or maintaining the software.

2. Platform as a Service (PaaS)

With PaaS, a computing platform is provided which supplies tools and a development environment to help companies build, test, and deploy Web-based applications. Businesses don't need to invest in the infrastructure required for building Web and mobile applications but can rent the use of platforms such as Windows Azure, Google AppEngine, and Force.com. Applications which are built using these provider's services, however, are usually locked into that one platform.

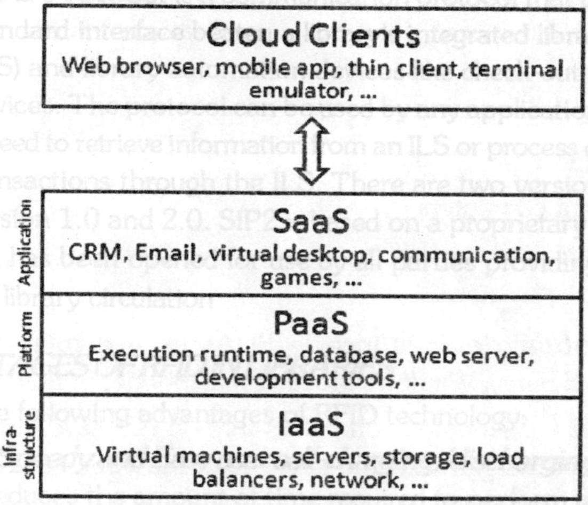

Fig. 2. Showing types of cloud computing

3. Infrastructure as a Service (IaaS)

This type of cloud computing is also sometimes referred to as HaaS or Hardware as a Service and it involves both storage services and computing power. Amazon's Web Services, one of the major players in this area, offers two main products including the Elastic Compute Cloud (EC2), which provides computing resources, and Simple Storage Service (S3) for data storage.

Companies are using Amazon's Web Services to host or backup their websites, for content delivery, to run high performance computing simulations, to host media collections, and much more. Most of these cloud services are available on a pay-per-usage basis, differing from the SaaS subscription model, enabling customers to scale up or down depending on their need at any given time and only pay for what they've used.

CLOUD COMPONENTS

In a simple, topological sense, a cloud computing solution is made up of several elements clients, the datacenter, and distributed servers.

Each element has a purpose and plays a specific role in delivering a functional cloud based application, We are discussing here in detail.

1. Internet
2. Datacenter
3. Client computers
4. Distributed servers

Clients

- ***Mobile devices*** include PDAs or smartphones, like a Blackberry, Windows Mobile Smartphone, or an iPhone.
- ***Thin***- Clients are computers that do not have internal hard drives, but rather let the server do all the work, but then display the information.
- ***Thick*** - This type of client is a regular computer, using a web browser like Firefox or Internet Explorer to connect to the cloud. Thin clients are becoming an increasingly popular solution, because of their price and effect on the environment. Some benefits to using thin clients include
- ***Lower hardware costs***-Thin clients are cheaper than thick clients because they do not contain as much hardware. They also last longer before they need to be upgraded or become obsolete.
- ***Lower IT costs*** - Thin clients are managed at the server and there are fewer points of failure.
- ***Security***- Since the processing takes place on the server and there is no hard drive, there's less chance of malware invading the device. Also, since thin clients don't work without a server, there's less chance of them being physically stolen.
- ***Data security*** - Since data is stored on the server, there's less chance for data to be lost if the client computer crashes or is stolen.
- ***Less power consumption*** - Thin clients consume less power than thick clients. This means you'll pay less to power them,

and you'll also pay less to air-condition the office.

- ***Ease of repair or replacement*** - If a thin client dies, it's easy to replace. The box is simply swapped out and the user's desktop returns exactly as it was before the failure.
- ***Less noise*** - Without a spinning hard drive, less heat is generated and quieter fans can be used on the thin client.

Datacenter

The datacenter is the collection of servers where the application to which you subscribe is housed. It could be a large room in the basement of your building or a room full of servers on the other side of the world that you access via the Internet. A growing trend in the IT world is virtualizing servers. That is, software can be installed allowing multiple instances of virtual servers to be used. In this way, you can have half a dozen virtual servers running on one physical server.

The number of virtual servers that can exist on a physical server depends on the size and speed of the physical server and what applications will be running on the virtual server. Clients are, in a cloud computing architecture, the exact same things that they are in a plain, old, everyday local area network (LAN). They are, typically, the computers that just sit on your desk. But they might also be laptops, tablet computers, mobile phones, or PDAs—all big drivers for cloud computing because of their mobility. Anyway, clients are the devices that the end users interact with to manage their information on the cloud. Clients generally fall into three categories:

DISTRIBUTED SERVERS

The servers don't all have to be housed in the same location. Often, servers are in geographically disparate locations. But to you, the cloud subscriber, these servers act as if they're humming away right next to each other. This gives the service provider more flexibility in options and security. For instance, Amazon has their cloud solution in servers all over the world. If something were to happen at one site, causing a failure, the service would still be accessed through another site. Also, if the cloud needs more hardware, they need not throw more servers in the safe room—they can add them at another site and simply make it part of the cloud.

INTRANETS AND THE CLOUD

While your operation is not big as Amazon S3 cloud computing, we can use the same sorts of principles within your organization to develop your IT infrastructure. By setting up thin clients to run applications and services on a local server, rather than on their desktops, you ease the costs of deployment and maintenance, as well as reducing power costs. Some organizations use cloud computing to deliver their corporate intranet. Intranets are customarily used within an organization and are not accessible publicly. That is, a web server is maintained in-house and company information is maintained on it that others within the organization can access. However, now intranets are being maintained on the cloud. To access the company's private, in-house information, users are having to log on to the intranet by going to a secure public web site.

CHALLENGES OF CLOUD COMPUTING

Providing Support for both Service Users and Service Providers7:

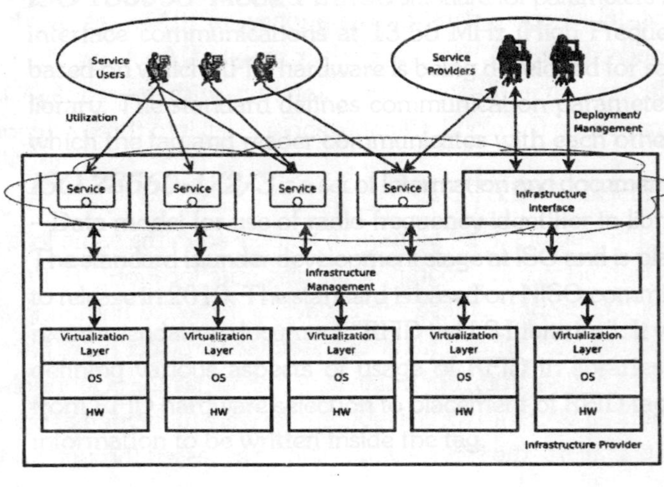

CHALLENGES OF CLOUD COMPUTING:

1. Service Providers: Development Services, or Build and Test Services,
   a. Software Engineering Methodologies and tools
   b. How to manage clouds for Application Lifecycle Management
   c. The Cloud manager can limit projects to certain clouds, control costs, manage security, or supplement resources during peak use
2. Service Users: easily usable clouds, hiding the deployment details from the user using virtualization,
3. Security and privacy are the biggest concerns.
4. Cost accounting data , and usage tracking for Multiple Clouds

CHALLENGES OF CLOUD COMPUTING

Examples of Current Support for IaaS

1. Apache Hadoop : A Java software framework that supports data-intensive distributed applications and enables applications to work with thousands of nodes and large amounts of data. http://hadoop.apache.org/

2. Nimbus is an open-source toolkit that, once installed on a cluster, provides an infrastructure as a Service cloud to its client via WSRF-based or Amazon EC2 WSDL web service APIs. http://www.nimbusproject.org/

CHALLENGES OF CLOUD COMPUTING

Examples of Current Support for PaaS and IaaS

1. Sun Cloud is an on-demand Cloud computing service operated by Sun Microsystems. The Sun Cloud Compute Utility provides access to a substantial computing resource over the Internet for US$1 per CPU-hour.
2. The Rackspace Cloud is a web application hosting/cloud platform provider ("Cloud Sites") that bills on a utility

computing basis. It has branched out into cloud storage ("Cloud Files") and cloud infrastructure ("Cloud Servers"), http://www.rackspacecloud.com/

3. Kaavo provides solutions for deploying and managing on-demand applications and workloads in the cloud. http://www.kaavo.com/home

ISSUES

1. Privacy : The cloud model has been criticised by privacy advocates for the greater ease in which the companies hosting the cloud services control, thus, can monitor at will, lawfully or unlawfully, the communication and data stored between the user and the host company. Instances such as the secret NSA program, working with AT&T, and Verizon, which recorded over 10 million phone calls between American citizens, causes uncertainty among privacy advocates, and the greater powers it gives to telecommunication companies to monitor user activity. Using a cloud service provider (CSP) can complicate privacy of data because of the extent to which virtualization for cloud processing (virtual machines) and cloud storage are used to implement cloud service. The point is that CSP operations, customer or tenant data may not remain on the same system, or in the same data center or even within the same provider's cloud. This can lead to legal concerns over jurisdiction.

Postage and delivery services company, Pitney Bowes launched Volly, a cloud-based, digital mailbox service to leverage its communication management assets. They also faced the technical challenge of providing strong data security and privacy. However, they were able to address the same concern by applying customized, application-level security, including encryption.

2. Compliance : In order to obtain compliance with regulations including FISMA, HIPAA, and SOX in the United States, the Data Protection Directive in the EU and the credit card industry's PCI DSS, users may have to adopt *community* or *hybrid* deployment modes that are typically more expensive and may offer restricted benefits. This is how Google is able to "manage and meet additional government policy requirements beyond FISMA" and Rackspace Cloud or QubeSpace are able to claim PCI compliance.

3. Legal : As with other changes in the landscape of computing, certain legal issues arise with cloud computing, including trademark infringement, security concerns and sharing of propriety data resources. The Electronic Frontier Foundation has criticized the United States government for considering during the Megaupload seizure process that people lose property rights by storing data on a cloud computing service.

4. Open Source : Open-source software has provided the foundation for many cloud computing implementations, prominent examples being the Hadoop framework and VMware's Cloud Foundry. In November 2007, the Free Software Foundation released the Affero General Public License, a version of GPLv3 intended to close a perceived legal loophole associated with free software designed to be run over a network.

5. Security : As cloud computing is achieving increased popularity, concerns are being voiced about the security issues introduced through adoption of this new model. The effectiveness and efficiency of traditional protection mechanisms are being reconsidered as the characteristics of this innovative deployment model can differ widely from those of traditional architectures. An alternative perspective on the topic of cloud security is that this is but another, although quite broad, case of "applied security" and that similar security principles that apply in shared multi-user mainframe security models apply with cloud security.

The relative security of cloud computing services is a contentious issue that may be delaying its adoption. Physical control of the Private Cloud equipment is more secure than having the equipment off site and under someone else's control. Physical control and the ability to visually inspect the data links and access ports is required in order to ensure data links are not compromised. Issues barring the adoption of cloud computing are due in large part to the private and public sectors' unease surrounding the external management of security-based services. It is the very nature of cloud computing-based services, private or public, that promote external management of provided services. This delivers great incentive to cloud computing service providers to prioritize building and maintaining strong management of secure services. Security issues have been categorised into sensitive data access, data segregation, privacy, bug exploitation, recovery, accountability, malicious insiders, management console security, account control, and multi-tenancy issues. Solutions to various cloud security issues vary, from cryptography, particularly public key infrastructure (PKI), to use of multiple cloud providers, standardisation of APIs, and improving virtual machine support and legal support.

Cloud computing offers many benefits, but it also is vulnerable to threats. As the uses of cloud computing increase, it is highly likely that more criminals will try to find new ways to exploit vulnerabilities in the system. There are many underlying challenges and risks in cloud computing that increase the threat of data being compromised. To help mitigate the threat, cloud computing stakeholders should invest heavily in risk assessment to ensure that the system encrypts to protect data; establishes trusted foundation to secure the platform and infrastructure; and builds higher assurance into auditing to strengthen compliance. Security concerns must be addressed in order to establish trust in cloud computing technology.

6. Sustainability : Although cloud computing is often assumed to be a form of "green computing", there is no published study to substantiate this assumption. citing the servers affects the environmental effects of cloud computing. In areas where climate favors natural cooling and renewable electricity is readily available, the environmental effects will be more moderate. (The same holds true for "traditional" data centers.) Thus countries with favorable conditions, such as Finland, Sweden and Switzerland, are trying to attract cloud computing data centers. Energy efficiency in cloud computing can result from energy-aware scheduling and server consolidation. However, in the case of distributed clouds over data centers with different source of energies including renewable source of energies, a small compromise on energy consumption reduction could result in high carbon footprint reduction.

7. Abuse : As with privately purchased hardware, customers can purchase the services of cloud computing for nefarious purposes. This includes password cracking and launching attacks using the purchased services. In 2009, a banking trojan illegally used the popular Amazon service as a command and control channel that issued software updates and malicious instructions to PCs that were infected by the malware.

8. IT governance : The introduction of cloud computing requires an appropriate IT governance model to ensure a secured computing environment and to comply with all relevant organizational information technology policies. As such, organizations need a set of capabilities that are essential when effectively implementing and managing cloud services, including demand management, relationship management, data security management, application lifecycle management, risk and compliance management.

ADVANTAGES OF CLOUD COMPUTING

Some of the major advantages are given bellow,

Lower-cost computers for users : This point is one of the financial advantages of cloud computing. There is no need to purchase powerful and expensive equipment to use cloud computing since all the processing is not at your local computer but in the cloud. Since the application runs in the cloud, not on the desktop PC, that desktop PC does not need the processing power or hard disk space demanded by traditional desktop software.

Better performance : Due to the fact that no programs or files are loaded on the local PC, users will not experience delays when switching on/off their computers and also the internal network will be much faster since no internal traffic will occur.

Less IT infrastructure costs : The IT department of large organizations could experience decreasing on the expenses in regards with infrastructure with the adoption of the cloud computing technology. Instead of investing in larger numbers of more powerful servers, the IT staff can use the computing power of the cloud to supplement or replace internal computing resources.

Less maintenance costs : Maintenance costs also will be reduced using cloud computing since both hardware and software maintenance for organizations of all sizes will be much less. For example, fewer servers are necessary in the organization which means that maintenance costs are immediately lowered. As to software maintenance, there is no software on the organization's computers for the IT staff to maintain.

Lower software costs : Using cloud computing there is no need to purchase software packages for each computer in the organization, only those employees actually using an application need access to that application in the cloud.

Automatic software updates : All the software's need update and the great thing with cloud computing is that you do not have to worry for any updates and also your organization will not have any additional expenses when a new upgrade or update is necessary.

Increased computing power : When using cloud computing, you can use the cloud computing power since you are no longer limited to what a single desktop computer can do.

Unlimited storage capacity : The cloud offers virtually limitless storage capacity but at any time you can expand your storage capacity with a small additional charge on your monthly fee.

Increased data safety : There is no point to worry for disk failures or a disaster at your office. All the data is stored in the cloud.

Anywhere access to your documents : When you are in the cloud, there is no need to take your documents with you. Instead, you can access your actual PC from anywhere that there is Internet access available.

Latest version availability : One more thing in relation with documents is that when you edit one document at the office and then you go somewhere else and open it, the latest version will be displayed since as I already aforementioned all the work is done centrally in the cloud.

Use your computer from anywhere : This is one of the biggest advantages of cloud computing. Basically, when you use this technology, you are not limited to work on a single PC. You just use your "cloud PC" from anywhere and any PC and your existing applications and documents follow you through the cloud. Move to a portable device, and your applications and documents are still available.

DISADVANTAGES

Internet connection is required : It is impossible to work if your Internet connection is down. Since you are using Internet to connect to your "cloud PC", if there is no Internet connection simply you cannot connect.

Low-speed connections are not recommended : This is not a very important disadvantage since everybody today has at least 1 Mbps connection at work and at home. However, it is important to mention that cloud computing cannot work with slow Internet connections such as dial-up since web-based applications often require a lot of bandwidth to download, as do large documents.

Sometimes is slow : Also, with fast connections, sometimes you might experience delays since web-based applications can sometimes be slower than accessing a similar software program on your desktop PC. The reasons for that are because of the demanding upload and download bandwidth that web applications need.

Stored data might not be secure : Data is stored "in the cloud". However, where exactly is the cloud and is it really secure? These are questions arising for users that have confidential data.

Your data is 100% in the cloud : All the data that you had until now on your local PC, it is stored in the cloud. Theoretically, data stored in the cloud is safe since a cloud hosting company uses several ways of backup in order ensure that on any case the data will not be lost. However, if your data is missing (even one in a million), you have no physical or local backup of your data.

CONCLUSION

Cloud computing has recently emerged as a compelling paradigm for managing and delivering services over the Internet. The rise of cloud computing is rapidly changing the landscape of information technology, and ultimately turning the long-held promise of utility computing into a reality. However, despite the significant benefits offered by cloud computing, the current technologies are not matured enough to realize its full potential. Many key challenges in this domain, including automatic resource provisioning, power management and security management, are only starting to receive attention from the research community. Therefore, we believe there is still tremendous opportunity for library professionals to make groundbreaking contributions in this field, and bring significant impact to their development in the library services. As the development of cloud computing technology is still at an early stage, I hope this Chapter will provide a better understanding of the Issues and challenges of cloud computing.

REFERENCES

1. Paul Young (1994) Assistant Director, directorate for computer and information science and engineering. National Science Foundation NSF Announces Awards for Digital library Research. NSF PR 94-52, Washington, D.C: NSF.
2. Michael Miller. Cloud computing: Web-based Applications That Change the Way You Work and Collaborate Online [M].Que Publishing, 2008 .
3. Reddy Raghunatha T, Digital Era: Utilize of Cloud Computer Technology in Digital libraries. International Joural of Digital Libraries Services, 2012
4. Ammar, Henny H. Cloud Computing: Benifits and Challenges.The 3rd Palestinian International Conference on Computer and Information Technology PICCIT 2010, , 2012-12-05.
5. Suresh Chandra Padhy et al / VSRD Technical & Non-Technical Journal Vol. 3 (3), 2012.
6. Kroski, E. (2009). Library Cloud Atlas: A Guide to Cloud Computing and Storage Stacking the Tech. Retrived at 2012-12-05 from Library Journal.com: http://www.libraryjournal.com/article/CA6695772.html
7. Mitchell, E. D. (2010). Using Cloud Services for Library IT Infrastructure. Retrieved 2012-12-05, from code4lib Journal: http://journal.code4lib.org/

articles/2510.

8. Google App Engine. http://code.google.com/appengine.
9. Li Yongxian, Luan Xulun, Li Sensen(2009). Libraries Meeting Cloud computing Technology Era Academic Library and Information Tribune.
10. Yang Mingfang, Yuan Xilin(2009). Digital Libraries under the Cloud Computing Environment [J]. Library Development.
11. Huang Fuyan(2008). Research on the Development of Library Information Service Models in the Information Culture Environment, OJ. Xiangtan University.
12. Sultan, N. (2010). "Cloud Computing for Education: A New Dawn?," International Journal of Information Management, 30, 109–116.
13. Cauley, Leslie (2006). "NSA has massive database of Americans' phone calls". USATODAY.com. http://www.usatoday.com/news/washington/2006-05-10-nsa_x.htm. Retrieved 2012-12-05
14. Winkler, Vic (2011). Securing the Cloud: Cloud Computer Security Techniques and Tactics. Waltham, MA USA: Elsevier. p. 60. http://www.elsevier.com/wps/find/bookdescription.cws_home/723529/description#description.
15. "FISMA compliance for federal cloud computing on the horizon in 2010". SearchCompliance.com.http://searchcompliance.techtarget.com/news/article/0,289142,sid195_gci1377298,00.html. Retrieved 2012-12-05.
16. 6. Srikantaiah S et al (2008) Energy aware consolidation for cloud computing. In: Proc of HotPower.
17. Urgaonkar B et al (2005) Dynamic provisioning of multi-tier Internet applications. In: Proc of ICAC.
18. Valancius V, Laoutaris N et al (2009) Greening the Internet with nano data centers. In: Proc of CoNext.

3

Application of Cutting Edge Technologies in an Academic Cataloging Department : Linking Classroom with Practice

Dr. Sasekea Harris

ABSTRACT

The connection between classroom learning and practice is not always a seamless activity. This chapter provides LIS students with a description of emerging technologies applied in the cataloging department in an academic environment. In this regard LIS students are poised to establish the connection between what was taught in cataloging classes with what is practiced in an academic cataloging department which uses emerging technologies to fulfill its functions. In this way, the chapter is valuable as it makes a contribution to the learning of cataloguing technologies and to demystifying the complex

interweaving between cataloguing classroom activities and library cataloguing practice.

INTRODUCTION

Practice has an important role to play in contextualizing and clarifying what is taught within a classroom setting. Too often students do not readily and independently make the connection between library classroom activities and library practice. "Findings suggest that employers cannot rely solely on cataloging courses to prepare promising students for successful careers within the community of catalogers" (Hall-Ellis, 2008, p. 327). Similarly, Mugridge's (2008, p. 76) survey of newly graduated cataloguers reveal one of the things they would have done differently is to get some form of hands-on practice through fieldwork or other options. This underlines the need for applied practice to bridge the gap between classroom and the library work environment. This chapter suggests the best way to do this is to provide opportunities that underscore the nexus between classroom activities and library practice. This is an initiative underscored by Hosein and Bowen-Chang (2011, p. 752) who note greater collaboration between library schools and libraries can provide the practicum to bridge the training gap between the MLS students and the new cataloguers. In Jamaican library schools students do not get the opportunity to daily utilize the emerging cataloguing technologies in their classroom activities. To make up for this, each year, cataloguing lecturers, from the Department of Library & Information Studies (DLIS) at the University of the West Indies (UWI) Mona Campus as well as the Mico University College et al, make arrangements for their students to visit the UWI Mona, Main Library, Cataloguing Section in order to help students see how their classroom learning activities translate into real life cataloguing working activities. This chapter provides a documentation of this translation and connection. In this regard it begins with an overview of the UWI Mona, Main Library, Cataloguing Section with the objective of establishing a contextual framework. A description of the emerging technologies applied is presented and examples of how these are used to fulfill the responsibilities of the cataloguing section follow. By establishing the connection between classroom activities and library practice, this chapter can be regarded as making an incremental contribution to the teaching and learning of cataloguing, its emergent technologies and its application within an academic context.

UWI MONA, MAIN LIBRARY, CATALOGUING SECTION

The Cataloguing Section is one of several departments within the Main Library. The section comprises nine cataloguing staff (3 librarians, 5 paraprofessionals & 1 attendant). Cataloguing is centralized: the section provides the cataloguing for all the libraries comprising the UWI Mona library system and performs a number of activities, namely:

- Original cataloguing
- Copy cataloguing
- Add-to cataloguing
- Metadata creation for West Indian photographs and other images
- Bibliographic searching of local & global catalogs
- Importing & exporting of records
- Retrospective conversion
- Post-cataloguing material preparation for the shelves and the bindery
- Database maintenance
- Card catalogue & shelf list maintenance
- Authority records creation for the Funnel Group Project

The section uses the Library of Congress classification system and its related products to catalogue materials in a variety of formats, namely: monographs, serials, CD-ROMS, DVDs, audiocassettes, manuscripts, maps and electronic resources. Cataloguing is automated; accordingly, the section uses a number of emerging technological products such as: Machine-Readable Cataloging (MARC) Bibliographic Standards, Aleph Integrated System, Online Computer

Library Centre's (OCLC) Connexion Client, CATCD Authority Files and CONTENTdm.

CONNECTING CLASSROOM LEARNING WITH PRACTICE

In your cataloguing class you learnt the catalog is one of four tools used to achieve bibliographic control and that there are two types: card catalog and Online Public Access Catalog (OPAC). The card catalog is a listing of the holdings of a library done on handwritten or typed or printed cards. Therefore, for every item in the library, there is a card representing this item; this card describes the item, for example, it gives the author, the title, the subject and the place of publication. These cards are filed in long narrow drawers in specially designed cabinets. You would have also learnt the OPAC is the card catalog in machine readable format. Consequently, instead of cards in drawers you now have bibliographic records in machine-readable format. As such, for each item in the library there is a bibliographic record available on the computer representing each item. Also, instead of accessing these by going into the drawers in the filing cabinet, you access these by going to a computer terminal or workstation.

However in order to achieve this search at a computer terminal certain processes must first be completed. The information that would have been typed on card catalogues must be transferred to the computer in order to produce an automated catalog. But the information written or typed on catalog cards cannot simply be typed into a computer to produce an automated catalog (Furrie 2003 p.3). The computer needs a means of interpreting the information on a cataloging card in order to produce an automated catalog. The MARC format provides this means. The MARC format is a description of bibliographic items in a digital form so that the computer will be able to read it.

In providing bibliographic description in cataloguing classes, you would have learnt a number of fields, for example: author, title statement, edition and subject. With MARC, these fields are referred to as tags

For example:

- Author, in digital form is described as........................100
- Title Statement, in digital form is described as 245
- Edition, in digital form is described as 250
- Subject, in digital form is described as 650

Therefore 100, 245, 250, 650 are called tags. MARC Bibliographic Standard facilitates the creation and dissemination of computerized cataloging from one library to another and between countries (Furrie, 2003, p. 4). Widespread use of the MARC standard has helped libraries to: avoid duplication of effort, acquire predictable and reliable cataloging data, share bibliographic resources, make use of commercially available library automation systems, and ensure bibliographic data will be compatible when one automation system is replaced by another (Furrie, 2003, p. 4). The following figure, Figure 1 shows an image of the abridged version of the manual for MARC Bibliographic Standard.

Fig. 1. MARC Bibliographic Standard
Source: (Cataloguing Distribution Service, 2013)

MARC provides the rules for describing bibliographic items in digital form. MARC however, is merely a standard; as such, it cannot be used by itself to facilitate an online catalogue search. In this regard the cataloguing section makes use of a number of emerging technological products to create entries for the catalog, namely: ALEPH Integrated System, OCLC Connection Client, CATCD Authority files and CONTENTdm. This chapter will describe the use of Aleph and Connexion Client in performing the functions of copy and original cataloguing.

CATALOGUING TECHNOLOGIES: ALEPH & CONNEXION CLIENT

The UWI cataloguing department purchased an integrated library system known as Aleph. This technological product combines a number of library functions on one platform. For example, it integrates acquisitions, circulations as well as monograph & serials cataloguing on one platform. It therefore has a module for each of these library functions. There is a module for: acquisitions, circulations, monograph cataloguing and serials cataloguing. It also provides two views: one for staff and one for users. The staff view is used as follows:

Acquisitions: acquisitions staff can place, track and arrive orders.

Cataloguing (Monograph & Serials): allows cataloguing staff to enter the bibliographic description of an item into the computer; import and export bibliographic records; edit bibliographic records; link an item in hand to a record on the system so that the user can view information about an item such as its exact location and its availability. Additionally, this module allows the section to search its own catalog (Aleph advanced search component). It also allows the section to search and import bibliographic records from the catalogue of selected libraries (Aleph multi-base component).

Circulation: allows circulation staff to loan and return library items.

CONNEXION CLIENT (CC)

CC is a cutting edge cataloguing technological product provided by OCLC. It has a number of components, notably: WorldCAT, Authority files and a Labelling program. CC allows the section to create new bibliographic records for items for the UWI library and it allows the section to share these records with other OCLC member libraries through WorldCAT. In this regard member libraries can view and import bibliographic records created by the section. Likewise, the section can view and import bibliographic records created by other member libraries. The section also uses CC's authority files, which provides authority records for subject names and authors. This minimizes the need to use the printed volumes of Library of Congress Subject Headings and the need to purchase updated volumes of same as CC provides current names. The labeling program allows the section to print date due and spine labels directly from displayed bibliographic records.

USING CATALOGING TECHNOLOGIES TO DEVELOP ENTRIES FOR THE CATALOGUE

In your cataloguing class you would have learnt there are two ways to develop entries for a catalogue: copy cataloguing and original cataloguing. Copy cataloguing as you would have learnt is the searching of a bibliographic database (for example OCLC's Connexion Client) or the catalogue of another library (for example Library of Congress) for a pre-existing bibliographic record to match the item in hand; importing that record into your integrated library system (for example Aleph); editing the record to enhance the quality (for example providing added subject headings) and to meet your library's cataloguing standards; adding holdings to the record (for example the location of the item) and linking the record to the item in hand. The following paragraphs provide an example of these processes in the cataloging section at UWI.

1. The librarian searches for the bibliographic record using Aleph advanced search option (Aleph Gui). This is done because acquisitions may have imported the record to facilitate creating

an order for the purchase of the item. The following figure, Figure 2, shows an example of this search.

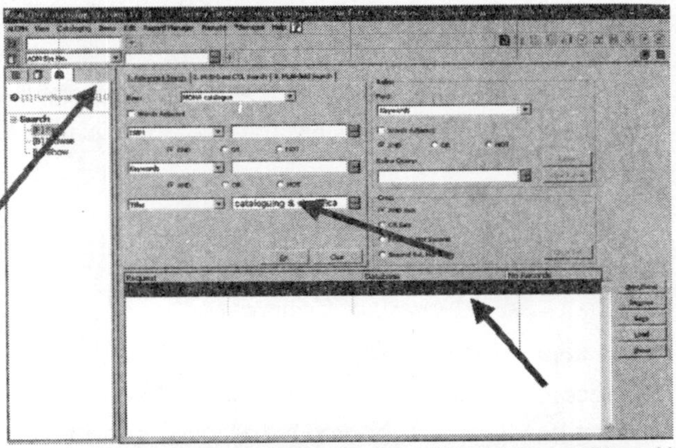

Fig. 2. Searching for a Record in Aleph Gui (Aleph Advanced Search)

2. If the record is found in Aleph Gui the librarian will edit the record to improve the quality of the record, and to reflect the library's cataloguing standards, for example adding the tag 049, which tells the physical location of the item, for example, BWMM would indicate the item is held in the Main Library at UWI Mona.

3. If the record is not found, the librarian searches Aleph multi-base also known as Z39. The following figure, Figure 3, shows an example of this search.

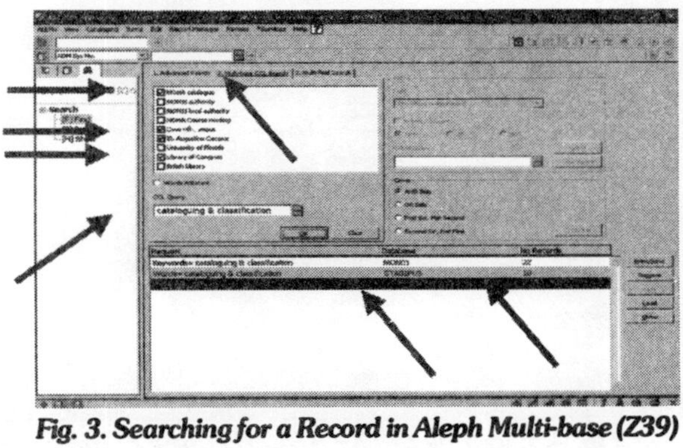

Fig. 3. Searching for a Record in Aleph Multi-base (Z39)

Note the multi-base search option searches not only the UWI Mona Campus catalogue but also the catalogues of UWI Cave Hill Campus, UWI St. Augustine Campus and the Library of Congress. One could also check the box beside the British Library to include a search of the British Library catalogue. Also note the search reveals the record is available at the following:

MON01............UWI Mona

STA01PUB.......UWI St. Augustine

LOC................Library of Congress

4. If the item is found in Aleph (Multi-base) the librarian imports the record and edits same. With regards to editing, all name / subject headings are checked in the CC authority files. All call numbers are checked in Aleph Gui (Advanced) to ensure they have not been used, and where used, the justification exists for re-use (for example, 2nd or 3rd edition of the same work). The following figure, Figure 4, shows an example of a successful search in Aleph for a record.

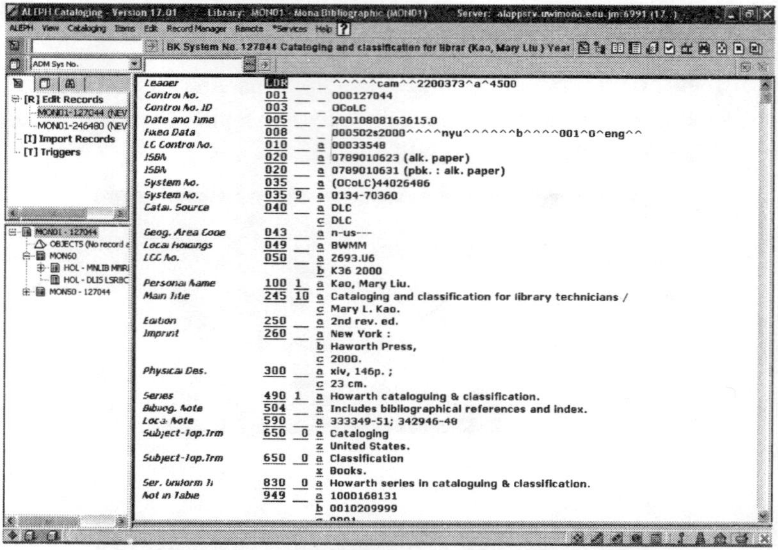

Fig. 4. Example of Z39 Record Found & Imported

5. The librarian then passes the item in hand to a clerical.
6. The clerical brings up the edited record in order to:
   a. Create holdings, so that the user can see the location of the item. The following figure, Figure 5, shows this.

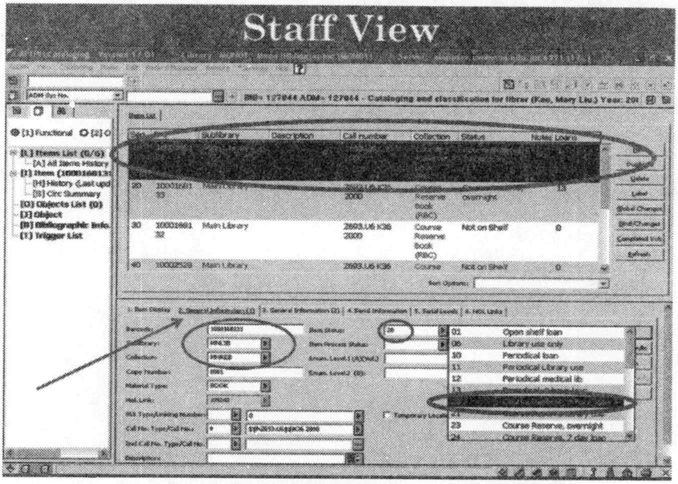

Fig. 5. Creating Holdings Information

   b. Link the barcode on the item to the record on the system so that the user will be able to view the record from the OPAC. The following figure, Figure 6, shows this.

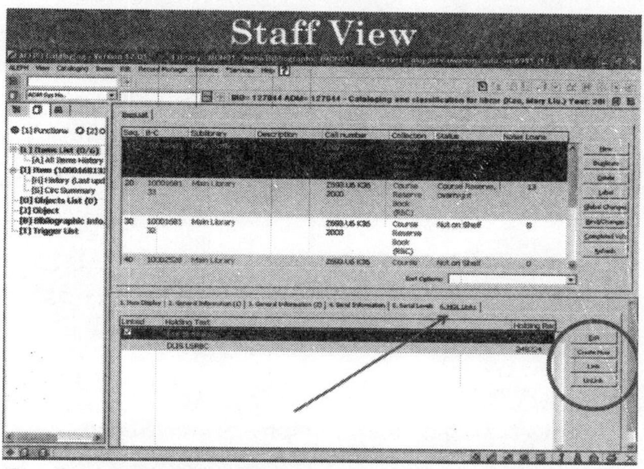

Fig. 6. Linking Item in Hand to the Record on the System

c. The staff then prints the date due and spine labels.

7. The following figures, 7 and 8, show what the users would see in the OPAC as a result of these aforementioned steps.

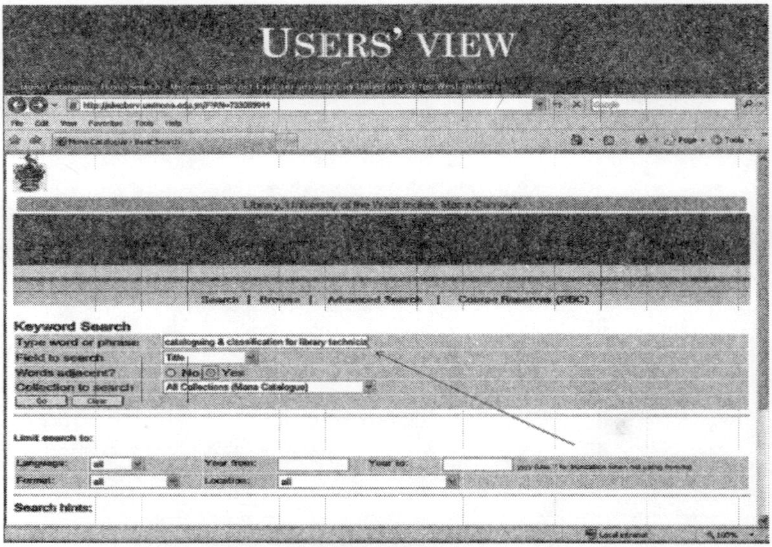

Fig. 7. Users' View of Aleph's Search Page

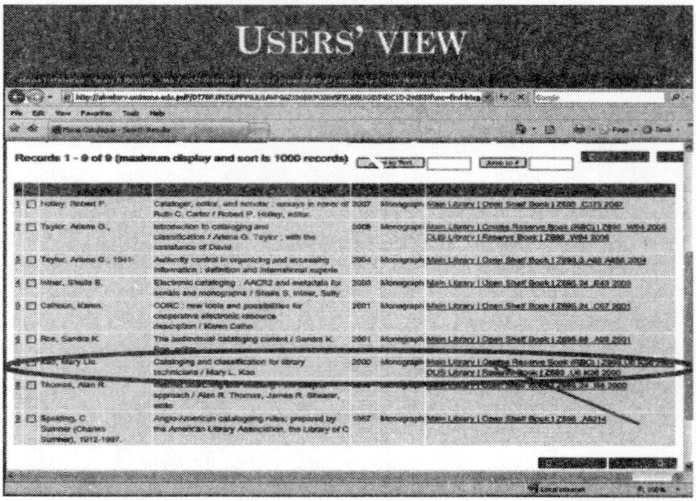

Fig. 8. Users' View of Aleph's Search Results Page

8. If the item was not found in Aleph (Advanced) or Aleph (Multi-base), a search would be done in CC. If found, the record would have been imported and edited. The following figure, Figure 9, shows CC's search page.

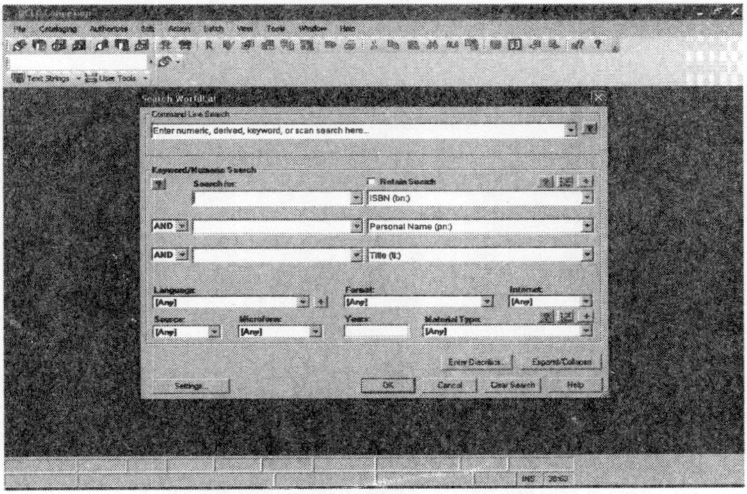

Fig. 9. Connexion Client Search Page

The following figure, Figure 10, shows an example of a record found in CC.

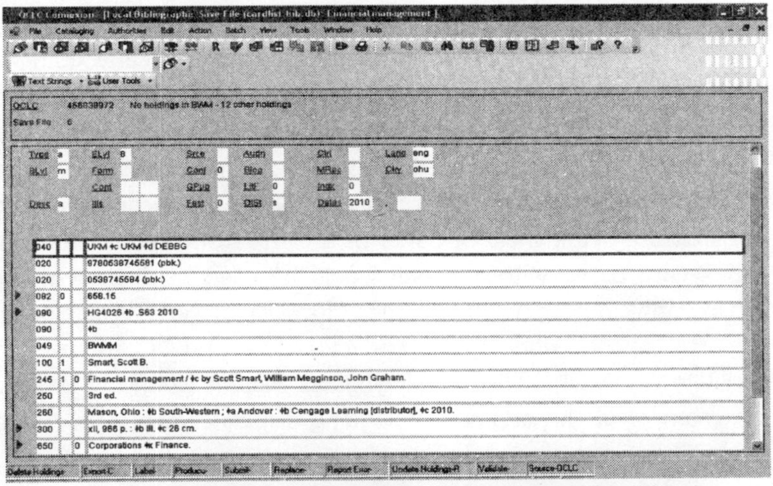

Fig. 10. Example of a Record Found in Connexion Client

Further, if the record was found in CC, the CC labeling program component would have been used to generate date due and spine labels. The following figure, Figure 11, provides an example in this regard.

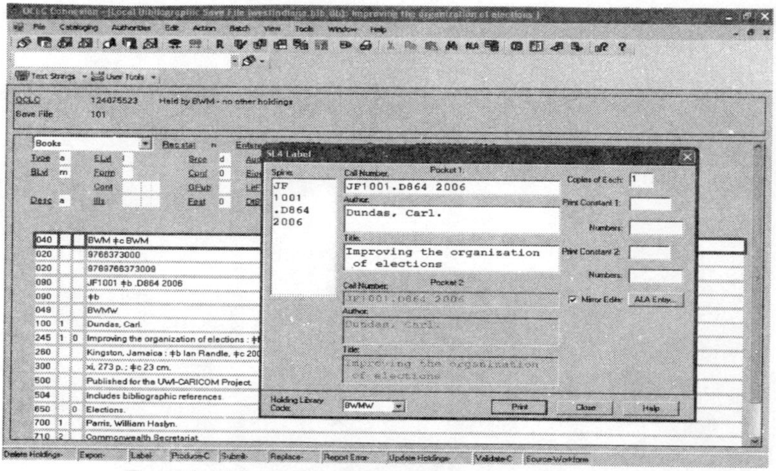

Fig. 11. Using CC to Create Date Due & Spine Labels for a Bibliographic Record

9. The record would then be exported (sent) to Aleph. The record needs to be exported to Aleph because it is Aleph's circulation module which facilitates the OPAC search.

You would have learnt in library class original cataloguing is the creation of a bibliographic record for an item which has no known or available pre-existing bibliographic record to the cataloger; it is therefore the creation of a bibliographic record which will serve as a model for other libraries to import or copy. In the Jamaican cataloging classroom a blank sheet of paper or a blank work form or a blank index card along with a pencil would be used to document the bibliographic description for an item. However, in the UWI cataloging department the technological products, Aleph and CC, are used to facilitate this activity. The following figures, Figures 12 and 13 provide an example of the original cataloguing display screen from Aleph and CC respectively.

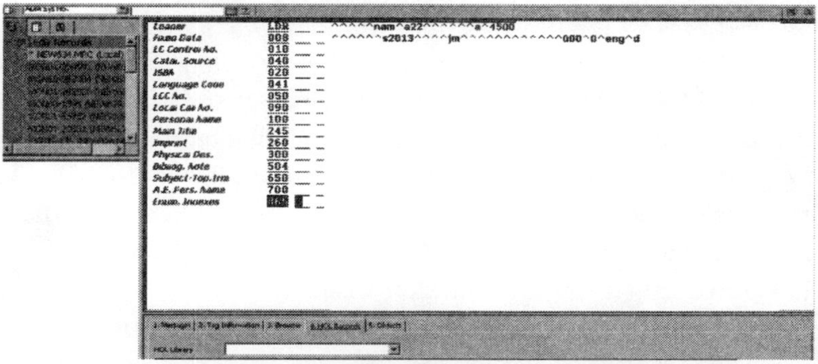

Fig. 12. Aleph New Bibliographic Record Creation Page

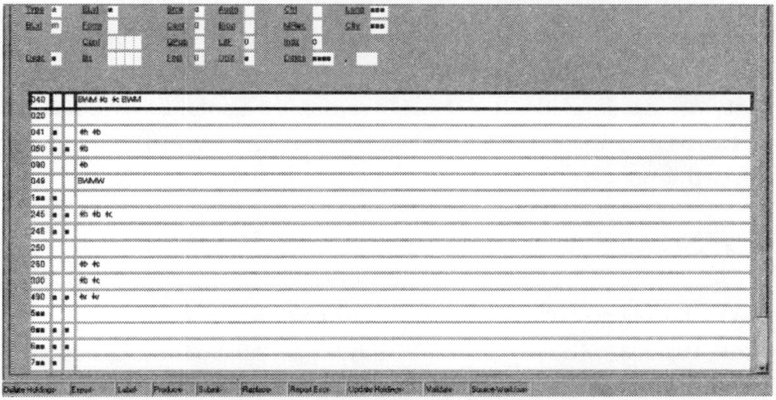

Fig. 13. CC New Bibliographic Record Creation Page

1. Using the relevant cataloguing rules and tools the librarian populates the respective fields as per Figures 12 and 13 and then saves the new record created. If CC is used the record is exported to Aleph.
2. The item is then passed to a clerical who will bring up this newly created record on the system, add holdings information and link the record in hand to the record on the system.
3. The spine labels and date due labels are generated and the item is prepared for the shelf.

Like copy cataloguing, after the completion of the original cataloguing processes the user is able to search the OPAC for this record.

CONCLUSION

This chapter responds to the need for establishing a nexus between cataloguing classroom learning activities and actual practice. In this regard highlights of the UWI Mona, Main Library, Cataloguing Section and the technological products used on the job to fulfill the responsibilities of copy and original cataloguing are presented. Accordingly, the use of MARC Bibliographic Standards, Aleph Integrated System and Connexion Client to achieve the section's responsibilities are underscored. While the description of the technological products is useful to establishing the connection between classroom learning and library practice, this is not a substitute for the physical interaction with these cataloguing technological products, which is outside the scope of the pages of this chapter. Notwithstanding this, the chapter remains a useful descriptive link between the cataloguing classroom and the library cataloguing department.

REFERENCES

Cataloguing Distribution Service. (2013). MARC documentation from CDS. Retrieved from http://2008.myvote.org/www.loc.gov/cds/marcdoc.html

Furrie, B. (2003). *Understanding MARC bibliographic: Machine readable cataloguing* (7th ed.). Washington D.C.: Library of Congress.

Hall-Ellis, S.D. (2008), Cataloger competencies. . .what do employers require? *Cataloging & Classification Quarterly,* 46 (3), 305-330.

Hosein, Y. and Bowen-Chang, P. (2011). Training cataloguing professionals at the Universit of the West Indies, St Augustine: part 2. *Library Review,* 60 (9), 748-761.

Mugridge, R. (2008). Experiences of newly-graduated cataloging librarians. *Cataloging& Classification Quarterly,* 45 (3), 61-79.

4

RFID System : A Boon for The Modern Libraries

Gopal Vipra

ABSTRACT

RFID is the latest technology to be used in library for security and theft detection. Though this emerging technology is not new; in fact it is currently being used, in numerous applications throughout the world. RFID uses are fast increasing and librarians are looking at RFID to streamline services and inventory control of Libraries. RFID has become the system of choice for the library operation and services. The paper discusses, RFID components and applications in the library as well as benefits and limitations.

Key Words : RFID Technology, LMS, Automation, Transponder, UHF, Inventory, Library Security, Smart Cards.

1. INTRODUCTION

RFID (Radio Frequency Identification and Theft Detection) is an automatic Identification and data capture technology. RFID uses radio signals to exchange data between tag and read/ write device (commonly known as reader). It is the latest technology to be used in different libraries for security of their holding and theft detection. In

RFID technology tags consist of wireless chips and antenna that are housed in a label or other protective casing and attached to the books, journals and magazines to be identified. In modern times there are several methods of Identification but the most common method is to store serial number which will identify the object on a microchip which is attached to an antenna. Library users have antennas for sending and receiving signals, a processor for decoding tag information and may have additional software for more advance data processing. Antenna may be separate from the processor and connected by cable for additional placement and configuration flexibility than it communicates the Data on to computers that can make use of it RFID is a form of identification that is contact less and does not require line of sight. Thought RFID technology is very costly and also new to the libraries but quite suitable for management of libraries and to meet out present challenges coming in the way of Librarians.

2. RFID SYSTEM COMPONENTS

RFID Cards : One card is issued to every Staff Member and Students. who are members of the library.

USB based Readers / Writer: Card Personalization /Reading/ Updating.

RFID Smart Labels: These are affixed to books.

EM Book Strips: to be affixed to books.

Midrange Reader/ Writer: Used by Counter Asstt. At the Issue/ Return Counter.

Self Check: Automatic check in and check out.

Gate Antenna: Installed at the Exit to provide Anti-Theft detection feature.

Host System: a system where the data resides and Application runs.

Application Software: This processes the data & generates reports of the activities of the library.

Online Web Access : a web site which will give role defined access to user and hosts OPAC

Library RFID System

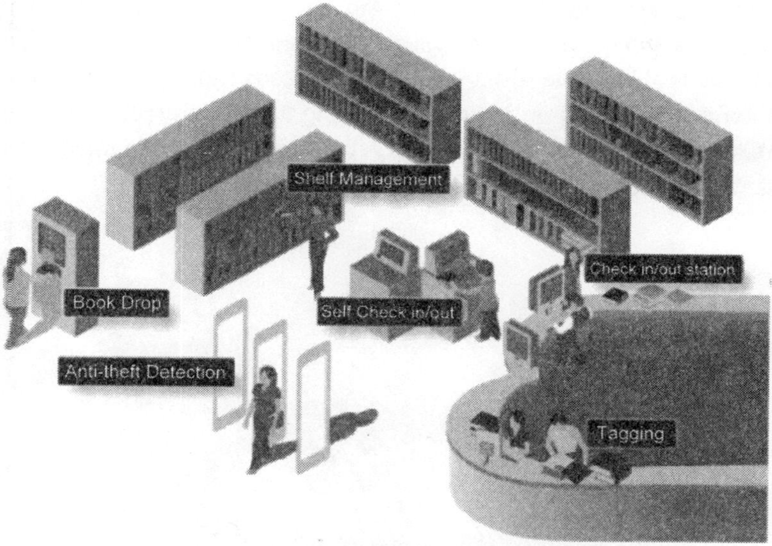

Library RFID System

3. RFID HARDWARE

(i) UHF Reader

HF Reader is link between RFID tags and the PC. HF Reader works on two ways, first read mode and second on write mode. In read mode HF Reader read information from tag and than sends the same to the PC (Read Mode) and in second mode it can read information from the PC and send to the RFID Tag (Write Mode). Adjustable active WiFi RFID Reader uses a built in omni directional antenna allowing it to identity transponder tagged item up to 100 meter in all directions. Library user can adjust the identification distance from five meter to hundred meters, which is quite enough for a modern library. For real time data retrieval WiFi Reader has dual operating modes which allow upload the data also.

As and when a tag passes through the Radio Frequency field the information stored on the chip in the tag will be interpreted by the reader and sent to the server that which in turn, communicates with the integrated library system when the RFID System is interfaced with it. To manage library function tags of the RFID are placed inside the book, which are covered with a property sticker. Antenna of the HF adjustable active RFID WiFi Reader passes through the field the information stored on the chip in the tag will be interpreted by the reader and sent to the server, which will communicate to integrated library system when the RFID System is interfaced with it.

UHF Reader

(ii) Adjustable Active RFID WiFi Reader

Adjustable Active WiFi RFID Reader - Specifications

Direction	Omni-directional, standard whip antenna
Range	0 to 100 m adjustable
Frequency	2.4 GHz to 2.5 GHz ISM
RF Output Power	0 dBm
Sensitivity	-90 dBm
Power	50 mA, 9 V
Modulation	GFSK
Mode	Direct Mode and Buffering Mode. In direct mode, readers upload messages to the host system in real time. In buffering mode, readers receive and save messages, which upload only when requested by the host system.
Buff Capacity	800 latest messages
Data Rate	1 Mbps
Interface	802.11b
Dimension	126 x 104 x 28mm

Adjustable Active WiFi RFID Reader - Operating Specifications:

Operating Temperature	-40 C to 80 C
Operating Humidity	95% Non-condensing

Multi-Detection: Yes

(iii) RFID ID Card

RFID ID Card is to be issued to each and every member of the library. It may be used as a regular ID Card as well as card is used to protect personal information of the member or to deliver secure transaction. No matter library users check out materials bar coded, magnetic strips or RFID. These are alternative, high quality library cards and their key tags that represent exceptional value. This may be combined with one or more key tags

Details to be Filled in ID Cards

Name of the Students : Naveen Mahawar

Fathers Name : Shri Madan Lal

Date of Birth : 25-01-1987

Name of the Institute : Rajasthan Technical University, Kota

Enrollment No.: 09EUCMExx001

Roll No.: 09/345

Session : 2009-10

Branch : Mechanical Engineering

E-Mail ID :naveen.mahawar1@gmail.com

Mobile No/ Emergency Contact No. : 9852626596

Permanent Address. : House No. 5 Gumanpura KOta

Our Web Site:

Message:

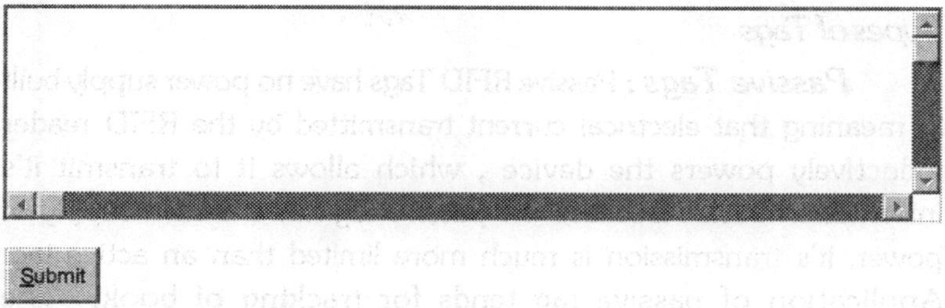

(iv) RFID Tags

Many Libraries are using Radio Frequency (RF) Chip technology to automatically identify the books. RFID (Radio Frequency Identification & Detection System) tag technology is being used in application that identifies or tracks the books. For this, RFID tags are being used to identify books. RFID tag is heart of the system. Tag can be fixed inside a book cover. Tags can be fixed on CDs and Videos directly. RFID Tags include a chip that typically stores a static number (ID) and antenna that enables the chip to transmit the stored number to the reader when a tag comes with in range of RF reader. The tag is powered by the reader's RF field and transmits its ID to the reader. Any reader using the RF signals can get the RFID tag to communicate it's contents. The details with RF Tags can be easily read form distance of several centimeters to several meters to allow easy tracking of books. Tags having characteristic of read/write are quite suitable for the libraries, because library can change or add information, if needed in future.

For Selecting RFID Tag for the library always following characteristics of the Tag be keep in mind.

- RFID tags should be of low cost, high volume manufacturing to minimize the cost.
- RFID tags should be readable by any compatible reader.
- Data storage of the RFID tag should be comparable to the bar code.

- Read Range of the RFID tags should suitable to the RFID system.

Types of Tags

Passive Tags : Passive RFID Tags have no power supply built in meaning that electrical current transmitted by the RFID reader inductively powers the device , which allows it to transmit it's information back . Because the passive tag has a limited supply of power, it's transmission is much more limited than an active tag. Application of passive tag tends for tracking of books. The communication between the reader and tag is achieved with magnetic couplery between the two antennas.

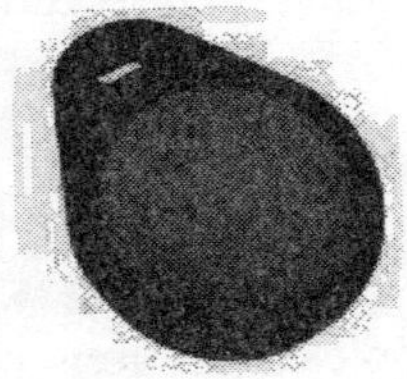

Passive Tags

Technical Specifications – 860 to 960 MHz Passive RFID Tag

Read Range	Up to 35 m
On Metal or Balanced	Balanced
Size	210 mm X 110 mm X 20.8 mm – 8.26 in X 4.33 in X 0.82 in
Weight (g)	300
Encasement	ABS (standard) or Polycarbonate (option)
Frequency Range (MHz)	860 to 960 (Global)
IC Type (chip)	Alien Higgs 3
Memory (bits)	512
Operating Temperature	ABS: -40°C to 85°C PC: -40°C to 120°C
Storage Temperature	ABS: -40°C to 85°C

	PC: -40 C to 120 C
IP rating	IP68
Shock and Vibration	MIL STD 810-F
	BS EN 60068-2
Attachment	Manual (standard)
	Foam adhesive (option)

Active Tag : An active tag usually performs a specialized task and has an on board power source, usually a battery. It does not require induction to provide current, as it is true of the passive tags. The active tag can be designed with a variety of specialized electronics including microprocessor, different type of sensors, or I/O device depending on the target function of the tag, this information can be processed and stored for immediate or later retrieval by the reader.

Active Tag

Active RFID tags, also called transponder because tag contain a transmitter that is always on and powered by a battery about size of a coin. Active tags are ideal in environment with electromagnetic interference since they broadcast the singles.

Specifications - Active RFID Tags

Performance

Read rate	Up to 100 tags/s (Identification Code only)Up to 35 tags/s @ 128 bit data reading
Max. response time	< 150 ms (single tag)
Multiple tag handling	Up to 2,000 tags in the read zone

Communication	
Read/Write range	Up to 100 m (300 feet) @ free air
Operating Frequency	868 MHz (EC) or 915 MHz (NA) ISM Band
Data rate (download to tag)	115.2 kbits/s
Date rate (upload to reader)	115.2 kbits/s
Maximum transmission power	0.75 mW ERP
Standards/ Certification	EN 300 220 (EC); FCC Part 15 (US);Industry Canada
Electrical	
Power source	Lithium battery (not replaceable)
Expected battery life	> 6 Years @ 600 times 128 bit readings/day
Battery monitoring	Yes
Temperature logging (option)	
Number of samples	13,312
Interval	User definable in intervals from 1 to 255 minutes
Accuracy	± 0.5 C (1 F) over a range of –40 C to 85 C(–40 F to 185ºF)
Resolution	0.25 C (0.5 F)
Data	
Data retention	>10 years without power
Write cycles	100,000 writes to a tag
Memory size	7,855 bytes user definable for one group of tags and 32,431 bytes user definable for another group
Identification code	48 bit fixed ID
Environmental	
Operating temperature	–40 C to 85 C (–40 ºF to 185 ºF)

Shock	50 G, 3 times DIN IEC 68-2-27Multiple drops to concrete from 1 m (3 ft)
Vibration	3 G, 20 sine wave cycles, 5 Hz to 150 Hz, DIN IEC 68-2-65 G, noise 5 Hz to 1000 Hz, 30 minutes DIN IEC 68-2-64

Physical (Industrial Housing)

Dimensions	131 mm x 28 mm x 21 mm(5.2 in. x 1.1 in. x 0.85 in.)
Enclosure	Plastic (ASA / Luran® S)
Weight	50 g (1.75 ounces)
Enclosure rating	IP 65

Semi active or semi passive tag : These tags also have an on board battery. The battery in this case is only used to operate the chip. Like the passive tag, it uses the energy in the electromagnetic field of wake up the chip and to transmit the data to the reader.

Semi active or semi passive tag

(v) Gate Antenna

The function of gate antenna in a RFID System for a library is to prevent theft. Gate antenna works on principal of electromagnetic with tattle tapes/tags. The gate antenna produces radio signals to activate the tag which is fixed inside a book's cover. And read and write data to it.

Gate antennas are required to be installed at the exit of the library. The function of gate antenna is to read the security setting which is stored in RFID tag and tattle tapes. Gate antenna decides whether the book/journals, CDs or any item should be permitted to be taken out of the library. If books/journals, CDs or any item of the library have not been properly checked out alarm of gate antenna will sound to alert library staff.

Gate antenna can be built in to door frame to receive the data of tag which is affixed at the back side of the book, when the book is passing through the door.

RFID Security Gates

Technical Specifications

- Network voltage: (110 V 60 Hz), (230 V, 50 Hz) 10 Amp.
- Consumption: d"1.5 Amp when reading (340 mA instandby)
- RFID frequency: 13.56 MHz
- Standard: 18000-3 and 15693 tags

- Security methods: Either AFI or EAS. AFI-value adjustable
- Alarm: Red light and buzzer in each panel. Adjustable volume and alarm length

Dimensions

- Width: 380 mm
- Height: 1.630 mm
- Thickness: 20 mm (100 mm at base)
- Distance between panels: 80 – 95 cm (depending on installation environment)

Installation option

- Bolted to floor with buried cables
- Bolted to floor with cable canal between panels
- Loose on base plate with carpet

(vi) Server

The server is the heart of the comprehensive RFID System, which processes the data, generates reports of all activities of the library. It is the communication gateway among the various components. It receives the information from one or more of the readers and exchanges information with the circulation database. Its software includes the SIP1 & SIP2 (Session initial protocol), APIs (Application Programming Interface) NICP (National Circulation Interchange Protocol) or SLMP necessary to interface it with the integrated library software, but no library vendor has got fully implemented NCIP approved NISO (Koppel, 2004). The server typically includes a transaction database so that report can be produced.

Server

(vii) Hand Held Reader

In RFID system it will help in reading the cards/titles when on move. Hand held reader can work with the local WiFi network to take care of mobile issue and return of books. It can be carried/ moved along the book on the shelves without touching them.

Following requirement will be covered.

If the system utilizes a personal data terminal, all other applications can be written for the each inventory wand.

A. The books misplaced by the user or staff can be searched.

B. Requested book can be searched individually.

C. It can screen the complete book collection on the shelves for inventory control.

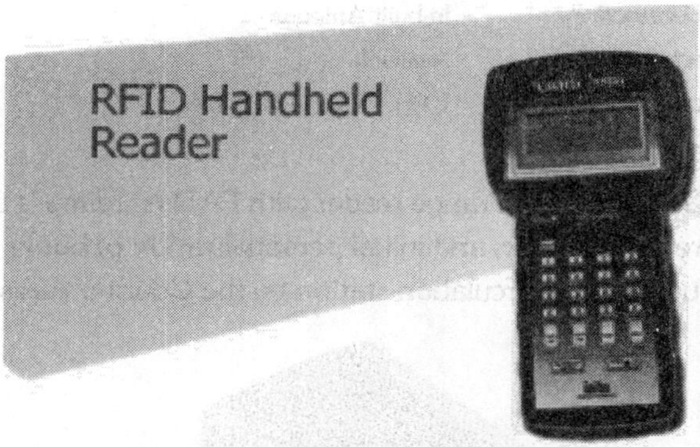

Some Key Features & Benefits	***Application Area***
High sensitivity	Short range UHF inventory
Enterprise-class management and monitoring	Validation access control
Frequency Supported:865-867 MHz, 869 MHz, 915 MHz, 950 MHz.	Tag data monitoring and storing
Reads multiple tags with a single scan	
Built-in Antenna	
Data storage capability	
Max. working range: 1.5m reading and 1m writing range	
Software control flexibility	
Field-upgrade capability	

Specification of Hand held RFID Reader	
AIR-Interface Protocols	EPC C1G1/ C1G2 and ISO 18000-6B/6C
Tag Supported	Alien, STMicro, Fujitsu, NXP, Rafsec, Atmel, Avery Dennison, TI, Hitachi, Impinj, Omron, Caen RFID
Frequency	865-867 MHz, 869 MHz, 915 MHz, 950 MHz
Working Range	Ideal range: 1m writing and 1.5m Reading range
Anti Collision Performance	Supported
Software Support	USB Flash Drive (Optional)

Host Interface Connectivity	In-built Antenna
Firmware Upgradation	Available
Regulation Supported	ETSI, FCC, India (TRAI)

(viii) MID Range Reader

In RFID system a mid range reader with PAD Antenna is used for issue and return of books and initial personalization of books and journals. It is used at the circulation station by the Counter Assistant

MID Range Reader

Specification of MID Range Reader

Product:	8dbi mid-range UHF integrative reader with WIFI
Work frequency:	860~960MHz(customizable)
Work mode:	FHSS or Fixed frequency
Tag protocol:	ISO18000-6B,EPC CLASS1 G2 standards
Antenna gain:	8dbi circularly polarized
Data Interface:	RS232,RS485,Wiegand,WIFI,etc.
Dimension:	255mm*255mm*34mm
GW:	1.5KGS

BOOKS ISSUANCE PROCESS (SELF ISSUANCE KIOSK)

- Members with a valid RFID ID Card enter the Library and searches for a book with the help of UHF reader/Hand Held Reader. He/ She can locate a book and bring it over to the automated self issuance kiosk for getting it issued.
- Books to be issued are placed over a PAD Antenna which is

connected to a PC based software application through a mid range reader.

- On valid identification of the ID Cards books are issued to the member and corresponding entries are made in database. On issue of book also anti theft system is turned off for the corresponding book.

Books Issuance Process

Book Return Process (Auto Deposit Box)

- Member with a valid RFID ID Card approaches an auto deposit box with the books to be returned.
- Books to be returned are deposited on the drop box which has an inbuilt pad antenna connected to it,
- Books returned are processed in the database and are available for further use by other members.

Book Return Process (Self Return Process)

- Member with a valid RFID ID Card approaches at self return kiosk with the book to be return.
- Books to be returned are placed over a PAD antenna which is connected to a PC based software application through a mid range reader.

- On valid identification of the books entries are made in the database and the books are available for future use.

Book Return Process

THEFT DETECTION SYSTEM

Anti Theft Gate placed at the EXIT of the library are activated in case the user forgets to make an issuance entry at the issuance kiosk. In case the entry is made at the issuance kiosk the anti theft feature is turned off for that transaction

BARRIERS TO RFID ADOPTION

As per law of physics and authorities of regulatory of RFID there are certainly two principal barriers to global implementations for low powerful tags. RFID system can be global implementations for low powerful tags, RFID system can be put under saying "high speed, high frequency, high capabilities, high cost" still applies. With some exceptions barriers of RFID system can be grouped in to two types.

- Low cost but capable passive tag system.
- High cost specified tag for operation at high speed and long distance.

BENEFITS OF RFID SYSTEM

- Faster seaming of the data stored on the RFID Tag.
- The RFID Cards can be used for multiple applications like library management, Access control of library literature\ holding, Activities of staff also.
- A longer lifecycle than a bar code.
- RFID is quite suitable and helpful for the centralized repository.
- Superior detection rate.
- Simple and easy way to self checking for books loan and returns.
- To improve the efficiency of junior staff experience to senior staff leads to run the system.
- Automated returns of books that speeds up sorting of books and re-shelving for the next library user to access.
- It allows sending automated e-mails and letters generation for the library managers.
- RFID system is highly scalable and modular system design with scope for customization.
- It increases asset utilization.
- RFID is helpful for better system access control.
- RFID system ensures minimum hassles for student and staff and so improves students and staff satisfaction.
- Since all the processes follow an online scheme of things all the reports are available at anytime anywhere basis.
- RFID also ensures there is no manual intervention required from the library staff for the entire process.
- Identity validation in this system is accurate.
- RFID consist of multilayered security.
- All activities are browser based; hence the system can be search from any where.
- RFID minimize use of paper. (Enviro friendly System)
- It is highly efficient dot net and SQL server based system

- Use of RFID in libraries ensures identity validation is accurate and secures transactions, and possibilities of duplicate transactions are nil.

LIMITATIONS OF RFID SYSTEM

- Removal of exposed tags (transponder) from the books by the users, it keeps out of RFID system to the book, journal and CDs.
- High cost of tags (transponder) is also major problem.
- User's privacy concerns.
- Collision of tags and reader creates hurdles with RFID.
- Gate antenna sensor (Reader) problem, if a tag is removed from the book or journal.
- The cost of RFID system is very high. It is very difficult for the small libraries to purchase RFID for them.
- If the book is bound after the application of tag, it will reduce the capacity to read the radio signals transmitted by the reader. It will be time consuming also.
- Non availability of parts of RFID in India.
- Library professional should be highly technical professional to work with RFID Systems.
- RFID tags (transponder) are not flexible enough, if the library wish to insert them in the spine of the book.
- Knowledge about the RFID system is must for the library users, without which it is not easy to avail services.
- The tags used by library RFID vendor are not compatible even when they confirm to the same standard because the current standard only seek electronic compatibility between tag & readers.

CONCLUSION

RFID is a promising technology that can revolutionize. The way we lead in our libraries, however this become a reality in libraries certain security issues like book protection and theft detection should be ensured. There is ample scope in the field of RFID to improve and innovate to allow RFID technology to be incorporated in to the libraries. The area of security of RFID solutions is becoming more and more important because of increasing use of such systems. The need to analyze plan, coordinate test and development of RFID technology is crucial for a successful integration in the libraries.

It has been observed that RFID technology is not yet widely installed/ used in the libraries. Although RFID systems are tracking books of the library. It is quite helpful to library staff and it speeds up check in /check out of books and inventories. RFID frees staff to do more user's service tasks.

There is a hesitation in adoption of RFID technology because of so many features of the technology are not well understood by the users and staff of the libraries. Although developments in RFID technology continue to extend it's faster processing. RFID technology is increasing popularity among libraries as the early adopters of this technology have shown that it makes good economic sense for libraries.

It is unanimously accepted the RFID technology is costly but some limitations are also there. As far as my opinion RFID technology is accurate, cost saving and minimize the manpower. For example no need of manpower in circulation section for issue and deposit of books and there are certain chances to reduce manpower in other sections of the library in near future if we calculate the salary, DA,

Medical allowance, LTC, Bonus, etc and compare the amount with expenditure involved in RFID the RFID Technology will be definitely cheaper. I urge librarians to go ahead with the development of advance technology for yours libraries.

REFERENCES

1. An Overview of RFID (2003). Library Technology Reports39,(6),7-17.
2. Want R.(2004).RFID: A key to automating everything. Scientific American.290(1), 56-66 pp.

3. Kern, C and Geiges, L.(2000). Radio frequency identification in security applications – function and use in modern library systems PISEC – conference on security applications, Lisbon, Portugal 3-4 April 2000 San Francisco Public Library Technology and Privacy Advisory Committee (2005) Radio Frequency Identification and the San Francisco Public Library Summary Report October,2005.76p.

4. BossRichard W. (2003) RFID Technology for Libraries . Library Rechnology Reports,39 (6),6-58.

5. Erwin Emmet and Kern Christian (2005). Radio Frequency Identification in Libraries Aplis 18 (1), March 2005.20-28pp

6. Harvey Lehpamer : RFID Design Principals 2 Ed.(2012) 42 – 48., ARTECH HOUSE London

7. Yan Zhang . Laurence and T. Yang . Jiming Chen, : RFID and Sensor Networks (2010). CRC Press T&F Group Landon

8. Boss, Richard(2004). RFID Technology in Libraries. ALA Technical Notes prepared on 14 May 2004 located at http://www.ala.org/ala/pla/plapubs/technotes/rfidtechnology.cfm

9. Ward, D.M. (2004) March: RFID system. Computer in Libraries,19-24

10. Kern, C (1999) RFID technology : recent development and future requirements Proceedings of the European conference on circuit theory and design ECCTD99, 30.08.-02.09.1999 Stresa, Itly 1999 1 pp 25-28,

11. Finkenzeller, K. (2003). RFID Handbook Fundamentals and Applications in contact less smart cards and identification 2nd ed. NY, Wiley & Sons 2003

12. Albert Lozano – Nieto : RFID Design Fundamentals and Applications (2011) CRC Press T&F Group Landon

5

Library 2.0 Technologies and its Applications: Role of Librarians and Information Professionals

Mukesh Mangal

ABSTRACT

The paper highlights the importance of Library 2.0 technologies, and role of Library Professionals in the acquisition of information and knowledge for development. The paper shows that despite the rapid diffusion of Library 2.0 in modern context. Library 2.0 encompasses a range of new and contemporary technological tools and techniques that are used for evolving collaborative environment required for Library 2.0.These tools and techniques can broadly be grouped into five categories, i.e.1) Content Delivery: RSS Feed, HTML Feeds, Streaming Media, Podcasting, Vodcasting and SMS Enquiry Services; 2) Synchronous Communication: Instant Massaging(IM); 3) Collaborative Service Platforms: Social Networks, Tagging, Social Bookmarking Services and YouTube; 4)

Collaborative Publishing tools: Blogs and Wikis; 5) Hybrid Applications, Programs and Tools: Mashups, Ajax (Asynchronous Java Script and XML), Library Tool Bars and Application Programming Interface (API). These tools and techniques are useful for libraries in proving new services and making existing services available in new and interesting ways. Applications of Web 2.0 technologies in libraries will result in a meaningful and substantive change in libraries, its collection, services and methods of delivery of services. The library's collection will change, becoming more interactive and fully accessible. The library's services will change, focusing more on the facilitation of information transfer and information literacy rather than proving controlled access to it. The implications of these revolutionary technologies are enormous and are discussed in the paper.

In the changed scenario of web technology and scholarly communications, university libraries manage the research output, organizational knowledge and information resources that support R & D activities can broadly be divided into three categories, i.e. 1) Library Websites; 2) Library Blogs; 3) Institutional Repositories also discussed in the paper.

Keywords: Library 2.0, Blogs, Social Networking, Library 2.0, Web 2.0, Digital Library.

INTRODUCTION

We are living in exciting and challenging information industry era. As the information professionals, we take seriously our responsibility to deliver services including disseminating information, providing forums to create and share new knowledge, enabling collaboration, and connecting scientists and students. Library 2.0 technologies are enabling us to take such services to a new level and make them more interactive and participatory for our users.

Library 2.0 is the' application of interactive, collaborative, and multimedia web-based technologies to web-based library services and collections' and suggests this definition be adopted by the library science community.

Library 2.0 is a term that provides focus to a number of ongoing conversations around the changing ways that libraries should make themselves and their services visible to end users and to one another.

Tagging, Blogs, Wikis and RSS Feeds are changing the traditional library functions of indexing, cataloguing and information dissemination. Libraries today utilize Wikis and RSS Feeds to deliver library news and catalogue updates: they also solicit patron's feedback and participation in the form of Blog comments and the ability to alter existing information.

Library 2.0 is a concept of a very different library service, geared towards the needs and expectations of today's library users.

Jadon and Rajput listed the advantages of library 2.0 as:

(a) Individual access converts to community access.

(b) Open access to information will be automatic.

(c) No physical information required, track able information events will take their place.

(d) No research project will be initiated without an informatics associate on the team.

(e) Copyright will no longer exit because it will be replaced by clickable licenses among communities.

The challenges of Library 2.0 in Indian libraries are:

(a) Financial crunch

(b) Lack of ICT infrastructure

(c) Lack of training and orientation program

(d) Technical illiteracy in library personnel's and users

Thus Library 2.0 (interpolated from Web 2.0) as a buzzword used to describe all sorts of activities that constitute a major transition by modern libraries in their outlook, services, resources, etc,. To reach out to non-users and potential users, than a pertinent question in librarianship, particularly in the context of less and least developed countries, would be.

LIBRARY 2.0 AND ITS DEVELOPMENT

The term "Library 2.0" was coined by ***Michael Casey*** on his blog LibraryCrunch as a direct spin-off of the terms Business 2.0 and Web 2.0. Casey suggested that libraries are at a crossroads where many of the elements of Web 2.0 have applicable value with in the library community, both in technology-driven services and in non-technology services. According to him, Library 2.0 is all about library users-keeping those we have while actively seeking those who do not currently use our services. It is about embracing those ideas and technologies that can assist libraries in delivering services to these groups, and it is about participation-involving users in service creation and evolution. In addition to Casey, other blogging librarians have begun conceptually exploring what Library 2.0 might mean, and because of this discussion with very wide parameters, there is some controversy over the definition and relative importance of the term. The nature of this controversy Lawson (2006), Peek (2005), and Tebbutt (2006) explore and begin to adequately rectify, and Crawford (2006) provides a very through account of the ambiguity and confusion surrounding the term, partially suggesting that there is nothing inherently novel about the idea. There is simply no need to use the term Library in these environments. It is a much more useful theory if it is focused on web-services, much as Abrams (2005) has defined it. Users interact with and create resources with one another and with librarians. In some ways, Maness (2006) stated that it is a virtual reality for libraries, a Web manifestation of the library as place. A Library's presence on the Web in Library 2.0 includes the presence of that library's constituency and utilizes the same applications and technologies as its community, a concept Habib (2006) recognizes in a very useful model for Library 2.0 in regards to academic libraries.

Amazon, Google, ebay, Skype and other initiatives of the Information Revolution do not threaten the progressive library. Rather, they create whole new opportunities for the professionals to engage with an empowered, interested and skilled set of audiences. Library 2.0 is a concept of a very different library services, geared towards the needs and expectations of today's library users. In this vision the library makes information available wherever and whenever the user requires it, and seeks to ensure that barriers to use and reuse are removed.

The four conceptual underpinnings to Library 2.0 are (Maness, 2006):

(i) It provides a multi-media experience

(j) It is socially rich

(k) It is user-centered

(l) It is communally innovative

Jack M. Maness defines Library 2.0 as "The application of interactive, collaborative, and multi-media web-based technologies to web-based library services and collections."

Library services, in Library 2.0, are constantly updated and re-evaluated to best serve library users. Proponents of this concept expect that ultimately the Library 2.0 model for service will replace traditional, one-directional service offering that have characterized libraries for centuries.

Transformation from Library 1.0 to Library 2.0

Collection (print or electronic) in libraries is catalogued and classified and made accessible through Library OPAC to users to explore. Users are given open access to these resources within libraries, they are also allowed to borrow these resources to be returned for someone else to use. In Library 2.0, however, the content and information can come from the patrons also. Although, traditional libraries maintain manuscripts and unpublished works by local authors and researchers, but it did not have a way to provide a platform to their users to publish their own ideas, through, and experiences. With availability of technological solutions, libraries are now adopting tools and technique to collaborate with an aim to preserve its collective knowledge and experience. The librarians and libraries should recognize the fact that Internet and search engines are now the main source of information for users. Besides, Library 2.0 also recognizes that human beings do not seek and utilize information as individuals, but as communities.

Library 2.0 is virtual reality of the library, a place where one can not only search for books and journals, but interact with a community, a librarian, and share knowledge and understanding with them. Library 1.0 moved collections and services into the online environment, and Library 2.0 will move the full suite of library services into this electronic medium.

Web 1.0 began as a platform for business and organizations to broadcast information to the people. Web 2.0 evolved into a dynamic, interactive and collaborative platform that facilities exchange of information and knowledge amongst users. In other words, Web 2.0 facilitates users to express their views and publish them online through services like blogs and wikis.

Tools and Techniques

Library 2.0 is independent of technology given the fact that every library activity built with active participation and feedback of its user community qualifies to the concept of Library 2.0. Availability of technologies gives libraries the ability to offer improved, customer-driven services to their users.

Library 2.0 environments can broadly be grouped into five categories as below:

(1) Content Delivery

(a) RSS Feeds

RSS (Really Simple Syndication) is a method for delivering regularly changing or updated Web content. Many blogs and Internet publishers syndicate their content as an RSS feed to allow people to subscribe to it easily. The RSS feed includes full or summarized text along with metadata related to authorship, publishing date, etc.

(b) HTML Feeds

The HTML codes can be placed onto the web sites and the resulting HTML feed can be customized to compliment the page. HTML feeds allows quicker access information to visiting users.

(c) Streaming Media

The streaming of video and audio media is an important application that existed before Web 1.0 and finds its application in Web 2.0 too. With availability of computer and network infrastructure to support multimedia streaming, library instruction delivered online began incorporating more interactive, media-rich facets.

(d) Podcasting

The Podcasting name comes from the activity of broadcasting and listening to the file on an Apple iPod player, and was used in an article in The Guardia newspaper as a synonym for rather clumsy 'audioblogging'

Usage of Podcasts in library is:

(1) Speeches by visiting authors

(2) Recordings of book reviews for all ages

(3) Audio training sessions and leased databases

(4) Podcast tour about the library services and about the usage of the library.

(5) Children's story times and book club promotions

(e) Vodcasting

The Vodcasting stands for 'video-on-demand'. While postcasting is used for delivering audio files, vodcasting is used for delivering video content.

(f) SMS Enquiry Service

The SMS (Short Message Service) in a library allow patrons to use their mobile phones to SMS their inquiries to the library.

(2) Synchronous Communication

(a) Instant Massaging (IM)

Software used in libraries for 'live reference services' are usually much more robust than the simplistic IM applications. Libraries are already offering live reference service using Ims 24x7x365 in a collaborative fashion.

(3) Collaborative Service Platforms

(a) Social Networks

Social networks are relatively new kinds of virtual communities that are structured to delineate and build on relationships that members have with each other by virtue of their being part of that community. They are perhaps the most promising and embracing technology which enable massaging, blogging, streamlining media, tagging, etc.

Some of the more popular social network websites include: Facebook (http://facebook.com), Myspace (http://www.myspace.com), Linkedin (www.linkedin.com), Friendster (http://www.Friendster.com), etc. LibraryThing (http://wwwlibrarything.com) is a library social network site and a place for members to register the books they have read, will read, or are in the process of reading. It promotes social interactions, book recommendations, self-classifications and monitoring of new books.

(b) Tagging

Tags are usually chosen informally and personally by author/creator or by its consumer/viewers/community. Tags are typically used for resources such as computer files, web pages, digital images, and Internet bookmarks. In Library 2.0, users could tag the library's collection and thereby participate in the cataloguing process. The best thing about tagging is that everyone is allowed to categorize the information the way they want. The University of Huddersfield, West Yorkshire, UK, for example, has introduced Library 2.0 features into their library catalogue.

(c) Social Bookmarking Services

In a social bookmarking system, users can save links to web pages that they want to remember and/or share with other users. These bookmarks can be made public, or saved privately or shared only with specified people or groups of people. The authorized people can usually view these bookmarks chronologically, by category or tags, or via a search engine.

itList, Blinklist, Clip2, HotLinks, ClickMarks, Simpy, BlueDot, Diigo, etc. are some of the popular bookmarking services. Libraries can make use of social bookmarking sites using RSS feeds for subject disciplines or in areas of specialization relevant to them.

(d) YouTube

YouTube allows users to upload, tag, and watch, rate, review, view, and blog, video footage and even create play lists. It can be used as a publishing tool for marketing of library.

(4) Collaborative Publishing tools

(a) Blogs

The term blog was coined by ***Jorn Brger*** in 1997 and refers to a simple webpage consisting of brief paragraphs of opinion, information, personal diary entries or links, called posts, arranged chronologically way of publishing to the web, obviating the need for dedicated web-publishing software, and replacing it with a combination of web-forms for inputting information and templates for displaying it.

Use of blogs in LIS applications are:

(1) Serve as a platform where the users can file their concerns, queries and suggestions regarding the services and activities of the library.

(2) As collection development, where the users request the resources.

(3) As another form of publication.

(4) As discussion forum.

(5) Marketing of the information as well as the library.

(b) Wikis

Wikis is a type of website that allows and encourages visitors to add, edit, change and hopefully improve on the existing content with the use of collaborative editing the wikis take the ethos of the open-sources software movement with its realization of the benefits of the collaboration resource management and development.

Wikis uses in libraries are:

(1) Reference resources wiki can be built for frequently asked questions.

(2) Social interaction and discussion among the librarians and users.

(3) For creating subject guides, subject gateways, etc.

(4) It can also be used by the users to share information and

enhance the content.

(5) Hybrid Applications, Programs and Tools

(a) Mashups

Mashups are web applications that combine data from more than one source into a single integrated tool. They are aggregations of content from different online sources to create a new service. Many people are experimenting with mashups using Amazon, eBay, Flickr, Google, Microsoft, yahoo, and YouTube APIs, which has led to the creation of the mashups editor.

(b) Ajax (Asynchronous Java Script and XML)

Ajax is a cross-platform technique usable on many different operating systems, computer architectures, and web browsers as it is based on open standards such as JavaScript and the Document Object Model (DOM). There are free and open sources implementations of suitable frameworks and libraries.

(c) Library Tool Bars

Toolbars are used in common applications such as Microsoft Word, and as add-ons for web browsers such as Internet Explorer and Mozilla Firefox. The INFLIBNET Centre has developed its tool bar to show-off its e-resources, databases, products and services.

(d) Application programming Interface (API)

API utilizes the syntax and elements of the programming language to make the API convenient to use in this particular context. Language-independent APIs are written in a way that they can be called from several programming languages. This is a desired feature for a service style API which is not bound to a particular process or system and is available as a remote procedure call. Example of API is Windows API, Scopus API that enables a user to select Scopus data elements to your own mashups.

Role of Librarians

Librarians over the time have employed evaluated and researched better means of preserving and scholarly content. Library professionals always try to be in tune with the technological developments and are ready to harness them in order to provide better and faster services to its clientele.

In the changed scenario of web technology and scholarly communications, university libraries manage the research output, organizational knowledge and information resources that support R & D activities by way of the following means.

(1) Library Websites

Many University libraries syndicate their users about the new additions, new services and products, etc. Websites is the public face of an institution through which it communicates. Like-wise, homepages of the library websites are the junctions through which university libraries impart a good percentage of its users. RSS feeds are the most widely used Library 2.0 tool in the library websites by which the subscribers are notified of the latest additions to the websites.

(2) Library Blogs

Library blogs act as an effective means of collecting user suggestions and feedbacks. It helps the libraries to self-evaluate its services and products. Libraries can maintain multiple blogs for different purposes. Developing and maintaining a separate blog for scholarly communication may receive a warm acceptance from the academics. Library blogs provide space for interaction by the users. Library 2.0 tools like facebook, Twitter, Flickr, YouTube, etc. can be incorporated in the blogs. Many academic libraries maintain library blogs (The Duke University Libraries maintain library blogs for different categories like 'Data & GIS' 'Scholarly communications @Duke', etc.).

(3) Institutional Repositories

Institutional repositories play a greater role in resources mobilization within and outside the universities. IRs promote self-archiving of scholarly literature and web 2.0 environment facilitate the users to add comment and review the content thereby the scholars can evaluate their work and understand what others think about it. This is beneficial in the sense that the scholars will become more conscious about the quality of their work. IRs are an important source of scholarly literature. Open access initiative and IRs have changed the way academics get access to scholarly literature. Institutional repositories play a greater role in resource mobilization within and outside the universities.

CONCLUSION

As we are moving into the information society, access to and use of information and knowledge has become indispensable for societal development. Applications of Library 2.0 technologies in libraries will result in a meaningful and substantive change in libraries, its collection, services and methods of delivery of services. The library's collection will change, becoming more interactive and fully accessible. The library's services will change, focusing more on the facilitation of information transfer and information literacy rather than providing controlled access to it. Library 2.0 tools offer an opportunity to taking research and advancing practices in the application of technology to enable the advancement of knowledge on unparalleled scale and at unprecedented rates. Nonetheless, library schools in general, have not kept pace with these changes – they have been slow to react and updated their curriculum.

Library 2.0 encompasses a range of new and not-so new technologies tools and techniques used for evolving Library 2.0 environment. Implementation of some of these tools and techniques are likely to improve reputation and standing of libraries in the community. These new services and ongoing changes are likely to make libraries more interesting, more relevant and better acceptable place.

University libraries being the channels and managers of scholarly literature, cannot keep its face away from such changes in the web environment. Incorporating Library 2.0 tools with its various online services, the university academia can receive better, timely and interactive environment for scholarly communication. Library 2.0 also promotes collaborative research, which in turn is an unavoidable academic activity in universities. To make this effectively and efficiently, policies with vision are to be framed by the universities.

REFERENCES

Mangala, Hirwade (2010). Library and Web 2.0. *Information Age*, 4(3).

Mangala, Hirwade (2010). Editorial. *Information Age*, 4(3), 3-4.

Anderson, P. (2007). All that glisters is not gold: Web 2.0 and the librarian. *Journal of Librarianship and Information Science*, 39(4), 195-198.

Sudhier, K.S. (2011). Developments in Web 2.0: Challenges for LIS Professionals. In Dineshan Koovakkai and T.M. Vasudevan (Ed.), *Library 2.0 and Information Management*, (pp. 59-75). New Delhi: Atlantic Publishers.

Beena, C., Archana, S.N. and Jayasree, V. (2011). Managing Scholarly Communication in the Web 2.0 Environment: The Role of University Libraries. In Dineshan Koovakkai and T.M. Vasudevan (Ed.), *Library 2.0 and Information Management*, (pp.82-89). New Delhi: Atlantic Publishers.

Stephens, Michael (2009). Libraries and the Read/Write Web. In Rachel Singer Gordon (Ed.). *Information Tomorrow: Reflections on Technology and the Future of Public and Academic Libraries.* (pp. 97-112). New Delhi: Ess Ess Publications.

Levine, Jenny (2009). Library 2.0. In Rachel Singer Gordon (Ed.). *Information Tomorrow: Reflections on Technology and the Future of Public and Academic Libraries.* (pp. 145-158). New Delhi: Ess Ess Publications.

Tilwani, T.D. and Agrawal, Anil (2011). Web 2.0 and Libraries: An Overview. In M.S. Rana, D.C. Ojha and N.K. Swain (Ed.). *Benchmarks in ICT Applications in LIS Practices: Essays in Honour of Dr P.K. Gupta.* (pp. 208-216). Jodhpur: Scientific Publishers.

Pareek, A.K. (2011). Web 2.0 and Library 2.0: A New Avenue for Library Services. In M.S. Rana, D.C. Ojha and N.K. Swain (Ed.). *Benchmarks in ICT Applications in LIS Practices: Essays in Honour of Dr P.K. Gupta.* (pp. 340-346). Jodhpur: Scientific Publishers.

Rana, Madan Singh and Gupta, Sobhagyawati (2011). Faculty-Librarian Relationship: A Collaborative Partnership in Achieving the Vision of 21ST Century Academic Libraries. In M.S. Rana, D.C. Ojha and N.K. Swain (Ed.). *Benchmarks in ICT Applications in LIS Practices: Essays in Honour of Dr P.K. Gupta.* (pp. 314-323). Jodhpur: Scientific Publishers.

Rana, M.S. and Gupta, Sobhagyawati (2011): Web 2.0 based Information Services in Libraries: Creating Collaborative and Interactive Learning Environment for Users, presented and published (Abstract) in International Conference on 'Web Based Learning and Library Management' jointly organized by Uttam Devi Moham Lal College of Engineering and Jaipur Engineering College and Research Centre, Jaipur, January 30-31, 2011.

Arora, Jagdish (2009). Library 2.0: Innovative Technologies for Building Libraries of Tomorrow. In Sanjay Kataria, B.S. Nigam and Rama Kant Shukla (Ed.).

Emerging Trends and Technologies in Libraries and Information Services. (pp.19-30). New Delhi: KDB Publications.

Thanuskodi, S. (2012). Library 2.0 Applications as Information Awareness Tools for Arts and Science College Librarians in Coimbatore City. In Dillip K Swain (Ed.). *Electronic Age Librarianship.* (pp. 148-162). New Delhi: Ane Books.

Kamba, Manir Abdullahi (2012). Information Development: Social Networking and Library 2.0 in Nigeria. In Dillip K Swain (Ed.). *Electronic Age Librarianship.* (pp. 122-135). New Delhi: Ane Books.

Casey, Michael (2005). Working Towards a Definition of Library 2.0. *LibraryCrunch.*

Casey, Michael (2006). "*LibraryCrunch:bringing you a library 2.0 perspective*", available at: http://www.librarycrunch.com/ (accessed 18 January, 2010).

Habib, M. (2006). Conceptual model for academic library 2.0. *Michael Habib's weblog on library and informationscience.* Available at: http://mchbib.blogspot.com/2006/06/conceptual-model-for-academic-library.html (accessed 10 June, 2006).

O'Reilly,Tim(2005).Whatisweb2.0?.availableat:http://www.oreillynet.com/pub/aoreilly/tim/news/2005/09/30/what-is-web-20.html#mememap (accessed 18 may, 2006).

Lawson, S. (2006). Library 2.0: Rapid response to rapid change. *Colorado Libraries,* 32(2), 19-21.

Tebbutt, D. (2006). Is all the talk of web 2.0 just a lot of codswallop?. *Information World Review,* 221, 9.

Jadon, N.S., Jadon, Gopal Singh and Rajput,Prabhat Singh (2007). Library 2.0 and Web 2.0 emerging technologies: its application in libraries. In *Developing Library and Information resources and services in the internet era.* 53rd All India Library Conference Proceedings, Hyderabad, December 13-16, 2007, pp. 266-72.

6

Role of WiFi in Development of Public Library Services: A Study with Special Reference to Rajasthan

Dr. D. K. Shrivastava

ABSTRACT

The development of computer and non-computer connected devices has allowed for growth in the installation of technologies based on radio frequencies and microwaves which permit wireless connection between various computers and/or laptops. WiFi technology (Wireless Fidelity) offers the possibility of fast connections via radio frequencies without the use of cables or sockets. Bluetooth, WiFi, PDAs, WiMAX (broadband WiFi) are all technologies which permit voice and data communication without the use of cables. The paper discusses the WiFi Technology and its relevance to the Public

Libraries of Rajasthan and special reference to Govt. Divisional Public library Rajasthan. further it conclude with a remark to imbibe Wi-Fi Technology for wireless connectivity among national and international networks for transmission of information over the networks in an effective and efficient manner without loss of time irrespective of location to save the time of users in Public Libraries.

Key Words : WiFi technology, Bluetooth, PDAs (Personal Digital Assistance), WiMAX, IEEE, LAN.

INTRODUCTION

Public library presents an opportunity for enhancing the dignity of individual human being. It is a potent force and the future will be greatly influenced by its vitality, variety, quality and extent .Most of the Public libraries today have more than just books and printed reference materials for patron use. Granted, printed materials still comprise a great deal of information contained in today's libraries but more and more libraries are expanding the resources available to the patrons. Libraries are starting to embrace technology as a method of increasing the library experience and resources available to patrons and guests at the library location. Most libraries today use some form of an electronic cataloging system or an ILS system which integrates most all of the libraries functions into electronic form to perform such tasks as tracking books loaned out, where books are located in multi-library systems, patron information and library Card barcodes, overdue books and the fees and fines levied against the patrons account and a great deal more. In using an ILS system with the book catalog in electronic form library patrons are able to perform searches on the libraries book collection much faster than could be done using the old card catalog method. Not only are books (both fiction and non-fiction) available but now there are also different sources such as DVDs and Cassette Tape books, DVD movies, electronic books on-line and access to on-line databases and the Internet as well. Most all but the smallest libraries offer some form of Internet access, mostly as Public Access computers setup within the library location that patrons can use to access both internal information resources (databases and online card catalogs) as well as Internet resources for information and research. Some libraries choose to "filter" the content of websites patrons and guests can access for many different reasons, mostly due to the "type" of content contained in some "types" of websites and protecting younger library patrons from some of the forms of information on the Internet. We all know what I mean by "type" of content. Other libraries choose to not filter any content and leave it to the discretion of the patron and/or guest to do the right thing. I am not going into a debate over which is the best method here as that is not the reason for this article. I only bring it up as it is a "sticky" point in discussions on Internet access in libraries and other public locations.

CONCEPT OF WIFI TECHNOLOGY

Wi-Fi is trademark of the WiFi alliance formerly the wireless Ethernet computability alliance, the trade organization that tests and certifies equipment compliance with the 802.11x Standards.

Fig. 1. Wi-Fi Technology

WiFi is a wireless local area networking that connects the computers to one another or to the internet using radio links in an unlicensed part of the radio spectrum, 2.4 GHz. it replaces the cable that runs from a computer to a network socket in space and Culture the wall with an invisible radio link.

WiFi is a radio standard used for wireless computer networking that replaces costly coaxial cables with a band of microwave spectrum that would be possible to set up a series of receivers with overlapping ranges to provide a network that bypasses conventional telecoms networks and enables access to networks from mobile terminals. A worldwide group of visionary amateurs sees WiFi as the perfect way to break free from government regulation and the giant telecoms companies.

BENEFITS OF WIFI TECHNOLOGY

The benefits of WiFi could be

1. It uses an unlicensed bit of the broadcast spectrum, this means less regulatory controls in many countries;
2. it offers faster and cheaper net connections;
3. Allow for a more dynamic network to be grown and frees network devices for cables;
4. no enforced time limit to connect;
5. Spread out at a larger table in a quieter area of the building ;
6. many reliable and bug free WiFi products are on the market and competition amongst vendor has lowered process considerably since its inception, and
7. WiFi is flexible network and while connected on a WiFi network, it is possible to move about without breaking the network connection.

Precautions

However on the other hands, WiFi technology is cautioned with respect to the following –

1. the WiFi uses the 2.4 GHz spectrum, which is crowded with other devices, which may cause degradation in performance;
2. Power consumption is fairly high compared to other standards, making battery life and heat a concern,
3. a WiFi connection is less secure then a wired network,
4. Signal strength varies with in the library,
5. Users do not configure it properly. in addition, WiFi communally uses WEP (Wired Equivalent Privacy) protocol for connection,

which has been shown to be easily breakable even when properly configured and

6. These WiFi networks have limited range with home router using 802.11 b or 802.11g might have arranged of 150 ft (46 m) indoor and 300 ft (92 m) outdoors.

REASONS FOR ADOPTING TECHNOLOGIES IN PUBLIC LIBRARIES

Why would Public libraries want to offer Internet access to their patrons? One would think that Public libraries, repositories of information and reference materials, would use their limited funds to purchase more printed materials for patrons to use. Well – that is not as cost effective as providing a mix of local reference materials and access to the Internet. There is a tremendous amount of information on the Internet – something along the lines of over 9.4-Billion websites at current count! If you don't believe this just do a search on Google for the word "www", which is the first part of most website URL addresses. This number does NOT include any WebPages contained within the websites! Needless to say that is a pretty large number of website covering all sorts of information!

Fig. 1. On-line Reading Room facility by using WiFi Technology

The Internet, being a vast network of computers interconnected together world-wide, contains so much information that if you were to start looking at web pages you would never reach all of them in a life-time, probably not in three life-times! What better reason would a library have for offering access to the Internet! Think of all that information a patron would have access to and can search for using today's current search engines (Google being one such search engine). If you were to build a library large enough to contain all the information on the Internet you had better have very deep pockets! I suspect the library at Kota Division would not have been anywhere near big enough to contain all the information! Of course to access the Internet you need an Internet connection, a local network to connect the computers together with each other and to the Internet connection and computers for the patrons and guests to use. All of this hardware and connection to the Internet costs money but there are some Government programs, at least in the United States and I suspect other countries as well, that can help out with the costs and there are some private corporations that offer grant funding or hardware (The Bill Gates Foundation is one such entity). There are even some Internet providers out there who will offer free access for educational institutions. Most of the time libraries fall into the educational institution category.

WIFI HOTSPOT TECHNOLOGY AND VIRTUAL PUBLIC ACCESS COMPUTERS

If you have an Internet connection, either a cable modem connection, DSL connection or a T-1 circuit and you offer patrons access through Public Access computers you can increase the capabilities to allow more patrons access to the Internet through a method I like to refer to as "Virtual Public Access Computers". What I mean by "Virtual Public Access Computers" is just a way of describing a method where a patron or guest of the library can use their own laptop as a personal public access computer by way of WiFi Hotspot technology! At first glace some people will say that does not help in allowing the general patron population with access but stop and think about it for a moment. If a patron or guest has their own laptop with wireless capability then it is one less Public Access Computer required to allow them access to the libraries electronic resources and the Internet at large.

WiFi technology brings the ability to allow more patrons access at the same time than would be possible with just wired Public Access Computers. A WiFi system actually increases the ability to allow patrons and guests greater access to the libraries electronic resource that would otherwise not be available in a timely manner. Case in point – if a patron wants to do some research on the Internet at the library because there is some printed material contained within the library the patron or guest will have to wait until a Public Access computer is available for their use. If the library has WiFi capabilities and the patron has their own laptop with wireless capability they would not have to wait for a wired Public Access Computer to become available – they just open their laptop, turn it on and use the WiFi system as their access to the libraries electronic resources!

WiFi technology is a Win-Win situation for both the patrons and the library. The library gets more foot traffic and utilization which usually translates into budget increases to meet the patron demand and the patrons can use their own laptop or wireless PDA to access the libraries electronic resources. The existence of a WiFi connection also brings in a younger, technology savvy demographic group which may not normally frequent a library. Some of the younger generation tend to view a library as a "Quieter than Death" location and shy away not realizing the great wealth of information residing on the other side of the door! Another very good reason is that not only can a patron access the electronic resources offered by the library but can also store the information they find into their laptop for further use when not at the library! Most Public Access Computers are either configured so the patron has to print the material on a printer (at an additional cost) or store the information on limited space floppy disk or on thumb-drives if the technology is allowed at the library. Since the patron or guest is using their own computer they can save the results of searches and webpage content directly on their computer for later review or use in research or reports. This ability is very helpful for individuals attending higher education institutions and need to create reports and perform research for their field of endeavor. By having the ability to create a copy of the information on their laptop they are able to use the information where ever they may be working on their reports or research and have the information available for reference material to back up their presentations.

Fig. 2. Wi-Fi Reading Room of Public Library

The development of computer and non-computer connected devices has allowed for growth in the installation of technologies based on radio frequencies and microwaves which permit wireless connection between various computers and/or laptops. Wifi technology (Wireless Fidelity) offers the possibility of fast connections via radio frequencies without the use of cables or sockets. Bluetooth, wifi, PDAs, WiMAX (broadband Wifi) are all technologies which permit voice and data communication without the use of cables.

These technologies (wireless technologies) are replacing connection cables. Bluetooth wireless networks with a range of 100 meters, or WiFi systems with a longer range, allow us to be permanently connected. All these systems emit pulsating electromagnetic waves similar to those emitted by mobile phones.

The Spanish State adopts the specified international guideline of 5 GHz frequency for wireless systems (WiFi) connected to the fixed high-speed network. It designates a frequency of 14 GHz for possible connection to Internet from aero planes (American Airlines is one of the companies who have planned to incorporate this service in the third semester of this year) and it earmarks the frequency band of 2500 to 2690 megahertz for future developments in third-generation mobile phone systems, known as UMTS.

BROADBAND & PUBLIC LIBRARIES

Public libraries provide essential services to their communities through broadband Internet technologies. Broadband through public libraries enables millions of people to have access to E-government, employment, education, health and other Internet-enabled services and resources. Furthermore, public libraries offer broadband Internet connectivity at speeds that often exceed what is available at work or in the home, and public libraries offer a wide range of free computer and Internet use instruction that depend on broadband access. The 2011-2012 Public Library Funding & Technology Access survey1 found that: 6.9% of public libraries still have connectivity speeds lower than 1.5 Mbps 41.1% of public libraries report connection speeds are insufficient to meet patron needs some or all of the time 90.5% of public libraries offers wireless (Wi-Fi) Internet access

PUBLIC LIBRARIES DEPEND ON BROADBAND CONNECTIONS

Public libraries offer free access to computer workstations, broadband, and Wi-Fi. Connection speeds have increased gradually for public libraries, but many of today's applications (e.g., social networking, streaming video) demand greater bandwidth and higher connection speeds. The public library service context is one in which multiple public access computers, staff computers, and patron devices (i.e., laptops and handheld mobile devices) connected via the library's Wi-Fi are in continuous use as they access broadband-intensive services and resources, often using the same connection. It is likely the strain on public library broadband systems will continue to increase as patron's come to rely on new interactive, multimedia, and high-resolution applications and programs.

While slightly more than half (58.3%) of public libraries reported in 2010-2011 that their broadband connection meets patron needs, more libraries are expected to report insufficient connections in coming years unless funding to improve broadband infrastructure is increased. To successfully fulfill their critical role as important Internet access providers in their communities, public libraries need funding and infrastructure to support high-speed broadband Internet connections. Though libraries have steadily increased their bandwidth capacity over the years, the combination of an increase in the number of users and in the bandwidth requirements of the content – particularly the explosion of social media and user-generated content – has only increased bandwidth challenges. As more people rely on public libraries for Internet access, and as more of these people use a greater range of high bandwidth education, government, and entertainment content, the bandwidth capacity of libraries becomes an increasingly significant issue.

RISKS INVOLVE USING IN WIFI TECHNOLOGIES

WiFi is the abbreviation of Wireless Fidelity, a set of guidelines for wireless networks (networks in which communication between components takes place via electromagnetic waves); these adhere to technical specifications in compliance with protocol IEEE 802.11 or WI-FI; this is a standard communications protocol of the Institute of Electrical and Electronics Engineers IEEE. The IEEE is a global professional association which, among other things, establishes protocols and guidelines of operation for wireless communication systems. Wifi was created for use in local wireless networks of computers, or LAN (Local Area Network), in order to access the internet.

Wifi routers emit a maximum of 100mW, but despite this, they pose a risk to the school-age population when in proximity, in particular to the head, of children of pediatric age, when the brain and nervous system are still forming. Wifi technologies emit when information is transferred. However, connecting by cable gives a better connection and faster speed. Wifi should only be used as a last resort, when it is impossible to establish a connection via cable, and only when absolutely necessary. It should not be installed in children's bedrooms nor anywhere near the same. It's true that a wifi router emits a lower frequency (in the order of 100mW, compared with 2W which is emitted by a mobile phone) however, in many companies and educational institutions routers emit in close proximity to people, in particular to their head. People are exposed in a continuous and extensive manner in their workplaces, and in teaching centers during school hours.

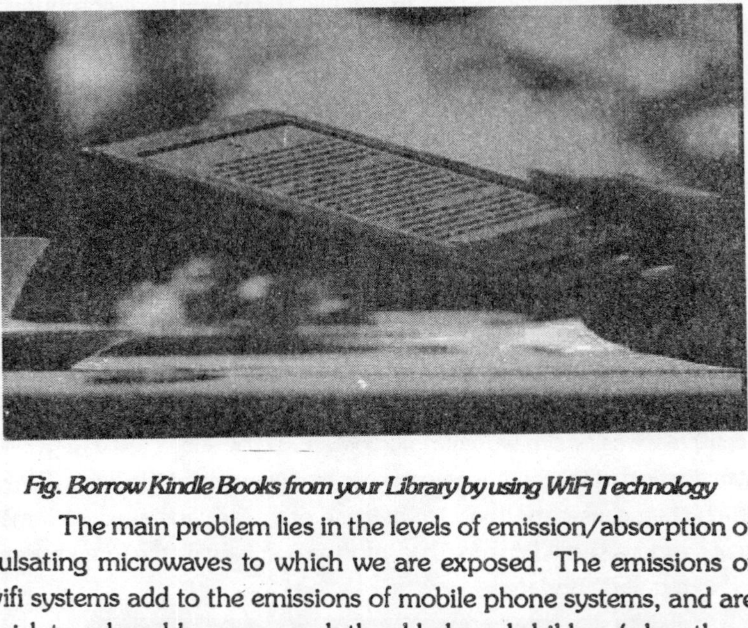

Fig. Borrow Kindle Books from your Library by using WiFi Technology

The main problem lies in the levels of emission/absorption of pulsating microwaves to which we are exposed. The emissions of wifi systems add to the emissions of mobile phone systems, and are a risk to vulnerable groups such the elderly and children (when these systems are installed in, for example, teaching centers); they also pose a threat to workers in companies where employees are continually exposed to these emissions. One of the emerging risks in the European workplace is electromagnetic waves, which pose physical risks identified as very dangerous in a recent report by the European Risk Observatory for the European Agency for Health and Safety at Work.

Media polemic about the use of wifi technologies began in the UK, after an investigation by the programme Panorama, on the state-owned channel BBC, revealed the dangers that this type of technology can pose for humans. The programme centered its theory on the fact that the emissions created by these radio electric waves are three times more powerful than those emitted by mobile phone devices, and that potential adverse effects would therefore be proportional to these. The British Department of Health and Safety wants to see an end to the debate between scientists and experts, and instead conduct a systematic study into whether emissions by wifi systems can adversely affect public health; given that in the UK the majority of computers in educational centre's are connected via wifi, this is obviously a source of worry for teachers and parents of students.

The International Commission for Electromagnetic Safety (ICEMS), in its international conference: Precautionary EMF Approach: rationale, legislation and implementation, in the city of Benevento, Italy, (22-24th February 2006) arrived at a series of conclusions, which they summarized in the "Benevento Resolution", in which they suggest: A promotion of alternatives to wireless systems of communication, for example: the use of fiber optic and coaxial cables. ICEMS proposes that all future urban wireless systems (for example WIFI, WIMAX, broadband systems which use cable or electrical wires or similar technologies) should be subjected to a public investigation of the potential exposure to electromagnetic fields (EMF) which they cause and that, in the case of already installed systems, local councils should ensure that information is available to everyone and is regularly updated.

Fig. Internet users in Public libraries

The University of Lake head, in Ontario, Canada, has eliminated wifi connections from places where internet connection via optic fiber is not possible. Fred Gilbert, President of the University, is cautious about using such technology, saying "We don't know what impact the use of electromagnetic waves can have on people". He based this measure on recent studies which show a correlation between cancer cases in animals and humans and these types of electromagnetic fields.

IMPACT OF WIFI ON PUBLIC LIBRARIES AND COMMUNITY CENTER

As every body knows that the public libraries are the local centre of information, making all kinds of Knowledge and information readability available to its users. So it's very clear that Public libraries has wide range of library clientele or readers like: Doctors, Professors, Engineers, Farmer, Children's, Housewife's, Neo-literates etc. but now almost readers become tetchy savvy and people come to the library withy their own computer hardware . This is not surprising and demonstrates the impact of ICT on the society. a modern laptop is at once an online information retrieval device, a research tool, a DVD Player, a music Player, a personal finance ledger, a writing tablet, a games machine and many more things decide .it is only natural that people want s to bring in their on Laptops and record the results of their research or experiences in Library. Currently this is only possible offline, which is fine if you only wish to record results gleaned from hard copy resources. With a WiFi hot spot in a place , a library will be also able to offer execs to online resources held locally such as CD-ROM databases or on the internet on a individual own Laptop.

In the Rajasthan at present all the public Libraries are governed by Department of Language and Library, Govt of Rajasthan Jaipur. Right now there are Seven Division Libraries, 33 District Libraries, 9 Departmental Panchayat Samiti libraries, 228 Panchayat Samiti Libraries run under Supervision of Schools and their Librarians and total libraries in Rajasthan is 278 and 39 Kids libraries run parallel by Some of Libraries.

Table : Overview of Total Public Library in Rajasthan

S.No.	Kinds of Public Library	Kinds of Public Library
1	State Central Library	01
2	Divisional Libraries	07
3	District Libraries	33
4	Panchayat Samiti Library Departmental	09
5	Panchayat Samiti Library Run under Schools	228
6	Kids Libraries	39

Almost Libraries are providing the traditional library services accepting the Government Divisional Library Kota.Intially Government Divisional Library Kota has taken the Initiative to establish the hot spot area or e-resource centre for the local community of Kota where people simply turn on their own wireless-enabled laptops or personal digital assistants(PDAs),pay fee online and then start to surf online. The Key point is that these people do not have physically "Plug in" their computer to a network. The network signals is broadcast by WiFi Technology

CONCLUSIONS

In the Rajasthan, almost all Public Libraries excepting Panchayat Samiti Libraries are having Broadband connections and telephone but only few libraries are using WiFi facilities and among of them only Divisional Library of Kota is Providing WiFi facility to the Library clientele or readers while 90% libraries of England have WiFi and Broadband facility to readers. The facts is that Kota is Known as" Knowledge Hub" or Coaching City of India, so almost More then one lacks Students come to the Kota to take Coaching and amongst them few are tacky savvy and having their own laptop and Tablet and smart phone and entertain the local library for using e-journals , e-books, e-News, e-content on freely basis by the help of WiFi but it is strongly recommended that Develop the Resources and Manpower to provide online services by the Public libraries but it can be possible by The Librarian who is having vast Knowledge of Computer Science and information and Communication technology.

Finally, WiFi is a very useful among the readers to acquire knowledge without paying any fee and its improving readers strength of public libraries. So adopt WiFi and relax the readers.

REFERENCES

AA. VV: Benevento Resolution 2006. Electromagnetic Biology and Medicine, Volume 25, Issue 4 2006. pp. 197-200.

Bertot, J.C., & McClure, C.R. (2007). Assessing sufficiency and quality of bandwidth for public libraries. Information Technology and Libraries, 26(1): 14-22.

Bertot, J.C., McDermott, A., Lincoln, R., Real, B., & Peterson, K. (2012). 2011-2012 Public Library Funding & Technology Access Survey: Survey Findings & Report. College Park, MD: Information Policy & Access Center, University of Maryland College Park.

Bouras, C., Giannaka, E., & Tsiatsos, T. (2009). Identifying best practices for supporting broadband growth: Methodology and analysis. Journal of Network and Computer Applications, 32(4), 795-807.

Carl Blackman, USA, Martin Blank, USA, Michael Kundi, Austria, Cindy Sage, USA, et alii: BioInitiative Report: A Rationale for a Biologically-based Public Exposure Standard for Electromagnetic Fields (ELF and RF).Release Date: August 31, 2007. pp. 610-612

Francesco Boella, Francesco Mozzo, Francesco Panin, Livio Giuliani: Perspectives in risk management in Italy: the impact of WiMax and Wifi (PP presentation) Foundations of bioelectromagnetics: towards a new rationale for risk assessment and management. 6th ICEMS Workshop, December 17, 2007, Venice, Italy.

Jange, Suresh & Sheikar, Amruth (2005). "WiFi technology: visible infrastructure for networking" Libraries, Information Literacy and Lifelong Learning.: Conference Proceedings of 51st ILA Confernce, Kurukshetra, 16-18 Dec.2005.pp.29-33

Mandel, L. H., Bishop, B. W., McClure, C. R., Bertot, J. C., & Jaeger, P. T. (2010). Broadband for public libraries: Importance, issues, and research needs. Government Information Quarterly, 27(3), 280-291.

Pastore, E., & Henderson, E. (2009). Data note: Libraries use broadband Internet service to serve high need communities. Washington, D.C.: Institute of Museum and Library Services.

7

Overview of Radio Frequency Identification (RFID) Technology in Indian Libraries

Dipendra Singh Sajwan

ABSTRACT

The libraries are growing day by day and it is necessary for large libraries to implement such facilities which save their time and also user friendly. RFID is one of the best technology associated with the maintenance and security aspects and streamlines workflow in the area of self service, book returns shelf management and inventory. This chapter addresses many issues associated with RFID technology in the libraries.

INTRODUCTION

Radio Frequency Identification (RFID) is a next generation of Auto Identification and Data Collection technology which helps to automate business processes in an Open environment with security. It is a generic term that is used to describe a system that transmits the identity (in the form of a unique serial number) of an object or person wirelessly, using radio waves. This automation can provide accurate and timely information without any human intervention.

RFID is not only a single technology, today there are hundreds of different RFID products in the market. RFID tags are used for automated toll-taking for cars, RFID chips are used to track animals on farms or identify lost pets and RFID used in DVD's to prevent movie piracy etc. In the context of the library, RFID is used for book identification, for self check-out, check-in, for sorting, conveying of library books and also for thief detection. The aim of using RFID technology is to increase the efficiency, reduce data entry errors, save time and spare staff to perform more value added functions.

According to the Harrod's Librarians glossary and reference book "RFID an alternative to the barcode that uses tiny microchips in tags to hold and transmit detailed data about the item tagged"

WHAT IS RFID

The RF in RFID stands for "radio frequency" and "ID" means "identifier." It was first developed during World War II but it has had to wait fifty years before it has been able to deliver on its original promise. The advent of tiny integrated circuits ("chips") allowed solution designers to add intelligence to the movement of goods through the supply chain and when a chip and an aerial were attached to a sticky label the RFID "Tag" was born. The whole device (microchip and antenna) is packaged as a paper-thin adhesive label which may come in a variety of shapes and sizes appropriate to the labeling of books, videos, DVDs and CDs etc. This RFID tag can be applied to library resources in various ways to improve both stock management and security.

RFID machinery (staff workstations, self-service units, security gates, stock management devices) interrogate the tags by radio – in a similar way (but at a different frequency) to the way in which PC wireless networks operate. This equipment may simply read the tag to identify the item, or it may add or change data on the tag attached to the item. This equipment can also read the security element which may be in the tag and this can be used to trigger an alarm when the item is moved near to a sensor such as security gates in a library.

RFID V/S BARCODES

Many libraries installed barcode systems where a barcode is placed in each book and the LMS (Library Management System) uniquely identifies the book by reading the barcode, using a barcode scanner. This technology has enabled self service and self return to operate successfully for many years, functions which have since come to be synonymous with RFID technology. RFID tags and barcodes both carry information about products. However, there are following important differences between these two technologies:

1. Barcode readers require a direct line of sight to the printed barcode where as RFID readers do not require a direct line of sight to RFID tags.
2. RFID tags can be read at much greater distances and RFID reader can pull information from a tag at distances up to 300 feet. The range to read a barcode is much less, typically no more than fifteen feet.
3. RFID readers can interrogate, or read forty or more tags per second are possible. Reading barcodes is much more time-consuming, due to the fact that a direct line of sight is required, if the items are not properly oriented to the reader it may take seconds to read an individual tag. Barcode readers usually take a half-second or more to successfully complete a read.
4. Line of sight is required for barcodes thus the printed barcode must be exposed on the outside of the product, where it is subject to greater wear and tear where as RFID tags are typically more rugged, since the electronic components are better protected in a plastic cover. RFID tags can also be implanted within the product itself, guaranteeing greater ruggedness and reusability.

5. Barcodes have no read/write capability, thus you cannot add to the information written on a printed barcode. RFID tags, however, can be read/write devices. RFID reader can communicate with the tag, and alter as much of the information as the tag design will allow.
6. RFID tags are typically more expensive than barcodes, in some cases, much more so.

COMPONENTS OF AN RFID SYSTEM

A comprehensive RFID system has four components:

1. RFID tags that are electronically programmed with unique information
2. Readers or sensors to query the tags
3. Antenna
4. Server on which the software that interfaces with the integrated library software is loaded.

RFID Tags : The heart of the system is the RFID tag, which can be fixed inside a book's back cover or directly onto CDs and videos. It is also known as a transponder, the tag consists of an antenna and silicon programmable chip encapsulated in glass or plastic. The tags contain a very small amount of information with a capacity of at least 64 bits. Tags can be active, passive or semi-active.

An active tag contains some type of power source on the tag, whereas the passive tags rely on the radio signal sent by the reader for power. Most RFID applications today utilize passive tags because they are so much cheaper to manufacture.

Semi-active tags are not yet commercially available but will use a battery to run the microchip's circuitry but not to communicate with the reader. Semi-active tags rely on capacitive coupling and carbon ink for the antennas rather than the traditional inductive coupling and silver or aluminum antenna used in passive tags.

Readers or sensors : An RFID reader consists of a transmitter, receiver, antenna and a decoder. They communicate with RFID tags, identify them and receive data stored on the tag.

Antenna : The antenna produces radio signals to activate the tag and read and write data to it. Antennas are the channels between the tag and the reader, which controls the system's data acquisitions and communication.

Server : It is a link between Reader and Library automation system. In other words, it is the communication gateway among the various component. It receives the information from one or more of the readers and exchanges information with the circulation database.

RFID APPLICATION IN LIBRARIES

Librarians are always known as early adopters of technology, as seen in case of Computer and later in case of Bar-codes. Later on standards like MARC and OCLC becoming popular among libraries for sharing bibliographic information with other libraries. In last decade there is various library automation software's being emerging in the libraries for automated the library services. The next wave to automation in Library industry is RFID Technology. RFID plays vital role in redefining the library process to make everyone's job easier right from user's to library staff. RFID provides a platform to automate most of the process performed by the library staff. Library staff whose job is meant to be helping user's, use library resources at the fullest, is always busy handling the books. RFID helps to automate this process and provides them an opportunity to better utilize their time in serving users. There are some following RFID applications which help today's libraries to increase efficiency and reduce cost.

1. ***Staff Station :*** The RFID staff Station is an elegant desktop station that enables librarians to quickly and efficiently process the check-out or check-in of loaned items. When a stack of tagged items is placed over a station, they are immediately identified and processed in a single operation.
2. ***Facilitating self-check :*** Self-check, or checking out your own books, is much easier with RFID technology because the book does not have to be positioned or angled under a barcode scanner, but can be simply moved within range of an RFID

reader. Self-check saves money directly, by reducing labor costs for circulation (check-out) activities, and indirectly, by reducing opportunities for repetitive stress injuries. Furthermore, self-check is inherently more private than requiring another human to handle and inspect the items you wish to check out of the library.

3. ***Sorting Station :*** When combined with book return stations, sorting units provide an effective way to automatically sort the items that have been returned to the library. The automated sorting unit is a fully integrated conveyor system which sorts returned RFID enabled items into any number of designated return bins at a rate approaching 40 items per minute.
4. ***Sensor Gates :*** The sensor gates are two or more Theft Detection Pedestals which are independent of each other and also have overlapping protection zones providing additional security. Any item that has not been checked-out either by staff station or self check-out station will be detected as it goes past these pedestals. RFID Sensor Gates feature the most modern detection algorithm that constantly detects any unauthorized item removal.
5. ***Automated Sliding Doors :*** The Automated Sliding Doors are used in combination with the Sensor Gates. When an unauthorized item removal is detected at the sensor gates, the sliding doors close automatically to stop the person from moving out with the books. It has a facility of adjusting holding time, opening time and closing time.
6. ***Shelf management system :*** The wireless Shelf Management System streamlines inventory processes and makes locating and ordering items on the shelf an easy and fast task for librarians. Representing the leading edge in wireless RFID reader technology.
7. ***Tag Programming Station :*** A programming station is used to link the programmable code on the tag affixed to a volume to the existing bar code used for identifying it. This operation is

very short and easy to perform. It has options to lease or buy, to use in the stacks or in the back office.

8. ***RFID printer :*** RFID printer is used to print the labels with an individual barcode, library logo, etc. When the print is applied, it simultaneously programs the data in to the chip. After this process, the RFID label is taken from the printer and applied to the book.
9. ***External Book Return/Drop Box Station :*** Libraries can offer a distinct service that is very useful for users, such as the ability to return books when the library is closed. An external book return is a machine with a slot with a chip RFID reader integrated into the wall. It works the same way as the self checkout station. The user identifies himself/herself (if required by the library), and then puts the book(s) in to the slot. Upon completing the return, the user will receive a receipt showing how many and which books were returned. Since they have already been checked in, they can go directly back onto the shelves. These units can also be used with sorter and conveyor systems.

RFID STANDARDS USED IN INDIAN LIBRARIES

1. ***ISO 180003- Mode 1*** is a ISO standard for parameters for air interface communications at 13.56 MHz (High Frequency), based on which RFID hardware is being developed for sage in library. The standard defines communication parameters on which the tag and reader communicates with each other.
2. ***ISO 28560-1/2/3*** is a set of Information and documentation – Data model for use of radio frequency identifier in libraries. The standard is under development stage at ISO and is planned to release in 2010. The standard is based on NISO committee's recommendation document "RFID in U.S Libraries". It will be defining various aspects of usage of RFID in libraries right from RFID hardware selection to placement of RFID tags and information to be written inside the tag.

3. ***SIP2 Protocol*** is a communication protocol that provides a standard interface beaten a library's integrated library system (ILS) and library automation devices like check-out , check in devices. The protocol can be used by any application that has a need to retrieve information from an ILS or process circulation transactions through the ILS. There are two versions of SIP, version 1.0 and 2.0. SIP2 is based on a proprietary protocol, but has been opened for use by all parties providing systems for library circulation

ADVANTAGES OF RFID IN LIBRARIES

The following advantages of RFID technology:

1. Speedy and Easy user self-charging/discharging : The use of RFID reduces the amount of time required to perform circulation operations. This technology helps Liberians eliminate valuable staff time spent scanning barcodes while checking out and checking in borrowed items. For the users, RFID speeds up the borrowing and return procedures and save the time needed for circulation operations.

2. Reliability : the readers are highly reliable. Several vendors of RFID library systems claim an almost 100 percent detection rate using RFID tags. Some RFID systems have an interface between the exit sensors and the circulation software to identify the items moving out of the library. Where a library user to eave the library and not be caught, the library would at least know what had been stolen. If the user card also has an RFID tag, the library will also be able to determine who removed the items without properly charging them.

Other RFID systems encode the circulation status on the RFID tag. This is done by designating a bit as the "thief" bit and turning it off at time of charge and on at time of discharge. If the material that has not been properly charged is taken past the exit gate sensors, an immediate alarm is triggered. Another option is to use both the "thief" bit and the online interface to an automated library system, the first to signal an immediate alarm and the second to identify what has been taken out.

3. High-speed inventorying : A unique advantage of RFID systems is their ability to scan books on the shelves without tipping them out or removing them. A hand-held inventory reader can be moved rapidly across a shelf of books to read all of the unique identification information. Operations such as managing material on the shelves, identifying missing items and taking stocks regularly will be feasible.

4. Automated material handling : Another advantage of RFID technology is automated materials handling. This includes conveyor and sorting systems that can move library materials and sort them by category into separate bins or into separate carts. This significantly reduces the amount of staff time required to ready materials for re-shelving.

5. Tag life : RFID tags last longer than barcodes because the technology does not require line of sight. Most RFID vendors clam a minimum of 100,000 transactions before a tag may need to be replaced. The security is combined into a single tag.

DISADVANTAGES OF RFID IN LIBRARIES

The following are the disadvantages of RFID technology:

1. RFID systems can be easily disrupted : Since RFID systems make use of the electromagnetic spectrum (like Wi-Fi networks or cell phones), they are relatively easy to jam using energy at the right frequency. Although, this would only be an inconvenience for consumers in stores (longer waits at the checkout), it could be disastrous in other environments where RFID is increasingly used, like hospitals or in the military in the field. Also, active RFID tags can be repeatedly interrogated to wear the battery down, disrupting the system.

2. RFID Reader Collision : Reader collision occurs when the signals from two or more readers overlap. The tag is unable to respond to simultaneous queries. Systems must be carefully set up to avoid this problem, many systems use an anti-collision protocol. Anti-collision protocols enable the tags to take turns in transmitting to a reader.

3. RFID Tag Collision : Tag collision occurs when many tags are present in a small area; but since the read time is very fast, it is easier for vendors to develop systems that ensure that tags respond one at a time.

4. The contents of an RFID tag can be read after the item leaves the supply chain : An RFID tag cannot tell the difference between one reader and another. RFID scanners are very portable and it can read RFID tags from a few inches to a few yards. This allows anyone to see the contents of your purse or pocket as you walk down the street. Some tags can be turned off when the item has left the supply chain

5. RFID tags are difficult to remove : RFID tags are difficult for users/consumers to remove. Some RFID tags are very small (less than a half-millimeter square, and as thin as a sheet of paper) others may be hidden or embedded inside a product where users/consumers cannot see them. New technologies allow RFID tags to be "printed" right on a product and may not be removable at all

6. RFID tags can be read without your knowledge : Since the tags can be read without being swiped or obviously scanned, anyone with an RFID tag reader can read the tags embedded in your clothes and other consumer products without your knowledge.

7. RFID tags can be read greater distances with a high-gain antenna : For various reasons, RFID reader/tag systems are designed so that distance between the tag and the reader is kept to a minimum. However, a high-gain antenna can be used to read the tags from much further away, leading to privacy problems.

RFID IMPLEMENTATION IN LIBRARIES PHASE WISE PLANNING

RFID Implementation in Libraries Phase wise Planning for deployment of complete solution Overview:

1. Estimated timeline for tagging 4 Lakhs (four lac) items Procurement of Hardware : Sourcing of RFID hardware i.e. Readers, Tags & Antenna needs to be done before starting anything else.

Once the hardware specification and respective products are finalized specific read regions can be decided and implantation can be done.

2. Tagging books : Each and every book needs to be tagged. The process needs 2-3 people continuously sticking tags to specific area of the book as decided earlier from the findings during the pilot test.

3. Integrating Middleware : Integrating middleware with the present library software systems and testing the results for improvements and errors.

4. Performing Test Cases : Predefined set of test cases will be performed in scenario based format to check out unit level and system level performance for accuracy and greater throughput.

5. Training Staff : This part of the implementation will include training staff on various aspects of RFID Technology and the new system in place. There will a demo which will include all the process in the system.

6. Process Improvement : The errors and improvements found out from the test cases will be revisited to make system perform in better way.

PRACTICAL ISSUES IN SELECTION OF RFID FOR THE LIBRARY

While selecting RFID technology to the library there are some of the technical issues which should be keep in mind.

1. RFID hardware and software for library should be compatible with global protocols such as SIP2, NCIP, ISO 18000-3, ISO 15693, ISO 14443A & ISO 28560. Vendors should make hardware and software upgrades in future to conform to standards.
2. Special emphasis on staff training and local support.
3. RFID tags for library use should be passive, 13.56 MHz High Frequency tags should be used. The typical read range of tags for library applications should not be increased substantially beyond the present range of 8-20 inches for smaller tags in

future. Only tags including standardized EAS & AFI feature should be used in libraries.

4. The system will utilize ISO/IEC 18000-3 Mode 1 Tags programmed so that they should work for identification of items in other libraries.
5. Security implementations for RFID in libraries should not lock a compliant system into any one security possibility (EAS, AFI, Virtual deactivation), but rather leave security as a place for differentiation between vendors.

PRECAUTIONS TAKEN BY LIBRARY STAFF FOR EFFECTIVE IMPLEMENTATION OF RFID TECHNOLOGY

1. Only authorized personal should have access to the RFID system.
2. No personal information should be stored on the RFID tag.
3. Preferably no static information should be contained on the tag that can be read by unauthorized reader.
4. Decision making: An RFID system is an investment. There are the initial purchases like tags, readers, conversion stations and software. In this equipment easy to use for both staff and patrons? Will there be data migration issues? Is there anything in the library that might physically interface with RFID signals? What kind of data security is available? Does the system allow for expansion/upgrading? In the end, will implementation fulfill the needs as stated in the policy? Future support and maintenance must also be considered.
5. Collaboration: Consult the people who will be working with the RFID system on a daily basis. Involve them in decision making and in work flow planning. Do staffs understand that with RFID implementation they may be taking on new roles? Confer with the local labor union.
6. Training: Library staff must be trained to use the RFID equipment. Front line staff should be prepared to handle patron concerns about privacy.

RFID IN INDIAN LIBRARIES

Jayakar Library, University of Pune is the first library in the country to implement RFID technology with the initiative of Prof. A S Kolaskar, the vice Chancellor and Dr. S K Patil, Universtiy Librarian and his team executing this technology.

The consideration of implementing RFID Technology is across all major libraries in India, the following visionaries institute and university have already taken the early lead in implementing of RFID in their libraries.

Some of the libraries using RFID technology in India are

1. Jayakar Library, University of Pune, Maharashtra.
2. Dhanvantri Library, Jammu University, J & k.
3. Indian Institute of Technology, Chennai.
4. Indian Institute of Science, Bangalore, Karnataka.
5. Bank of Baroda, Mumbai.
6. IIM Indore.
7. Indian Institute of Technology, Kharagpur.
8. IIM Khozikode, Kerala.
9. Indira Gandhi Center For Atomic Research (IGCAR, Kalpakkam)
10. Panjab University, Chandigarh.
11. Lolvely Professional University, Phagwara, Kapurthala, Punjab.
12. Punjab Engineering College, Deemed University, Chandigarh.
13. Dr. Tulsidas Library, Post Graduate Institute of Medical Research, Chandigarh.

CONCLUSION

RFID is the latest fast growing technology to be used in library for minimizing the theft of documents and as an access control systems. RFID based systems move beyond security to become tracking systems that combine security with more efficient tracking of materials throughout the library, including easier and faster charge and discharge, inventorying and materials handling. Since, RFID technology for the libraries in India is new and the future of Indian libraries depends on this technology, there is an urgent need to develop Indian libraries with RFID enabled technology to face global competition.

REFERENCES

1. BANSODE, S., and DESALE, S (2009) Implementation of RFID technology in University of Pune Library Program: *Electronic Library & Information Systems*, 43(2), 202-214.
2. PRYTHERCH, RAY (2005). *Harrod's librarian's glossary and reference book*. Ed.8. England: Ashgate.
3. SHIEN-CHIANG, Y. (2007). RFID implementation and benefits in libraries, *Electronic Library*, 25(1), 54-64.
4. *Electronic Frontier Foundation, RFID.* Available: http://www.eff.org/Privacy/Surveillance/ RFID/ (June 13, 2005)
5. BEDNARZ, A. (2003, November 3). Defense Department goes on offense with RFID. Network World Fusion. Retrieved August 4, 2004 from http://www.nwfusion.com/news/2003/1103forresterside.html
6. Berkeley Public Library. (n.d.). *Berkeley Public Library: Best practices for RFID technology*. Retrieved August 5, 2004 from http://berkeleypubliclibrary.org/BESTPRAC.pdf.
7. LANDT, J., CATLIN, B. (2001). Shrouds of time: *The history of RFID. Pittsburg, Pennsylvania*: AIM, Inc. Retrieved August 3, 2004 from http://www.aimglobal.org/technologies/rfid/resources/shrouds_of_time.pdf.
8. R. MOROZ (2004, July). *Understanding Radio Frequency Identification RFID (Passive RFID)*. Markham, Ontario: R. Moroz Ltd. Retrieved August 4, 2004 from http://www.rmoroz.com/rfid.html.
9. *U.S. Food and Drug Administration, Radiofrequency Identification Feasibility Studies and Pilot Programs for Drugs*; Guidance for FDA Staff and Industry. November, 2004. Available: http://www.fda.gov/oc/initiatives/counterfeit/RFID_cpg.html. (June 11, 2005)
10. BOSS. R. W. (2003). *RFID technology for libraries [Monograph]. Library Technology* Reports. November-December 2003.
11. SYED MD. SHAHID.(2005). Use of RFID Technology in Libraries. Library Philosophy and Practice,8(1), 9.
12. BOSS. R. W. PLA Tech Notes (May 14, 2004) *RFID Technology for libraries.* Retrieved from www.ala.org/ala/pla/plapubs/technotes/rfidtechnology.htm

13. MOLNAR, D., WAGNER, D. A. (June 2004). *Privacy and security in library RFID: Issues, practices and architectures.* Retrieved from www.cs.berkeley.edu~dmolnar/library.

14. SARMA, E. S. WEIS, S. A., ENGELS, D.W. (November 2002). White paper: RFID systems, security & privacy implications. Cambridge, MA: Massachusetts Institute of Technology, AUTO-ID Center.

15. ALA Library Fact Sheet Number 25 — *RFID: A Brief Bibliography* http://www.ala.org/ala/alalibrary/libraryfactsheet/alalibraryfactsheet25.htm

16. WARD, DIANE MARIE. "*Helping you Buy: RFID.*" Computers in Libraries 24:3

17. Intelligent RFID Library Installation (A Colchester Library Case Study)

18. http://www.niso.org/publications/rp/RP-6-2008.pdf

19. http://libraryrfid.typepad.com/libraryrfid/2004/04/new_email_list.html

20. www.rfidwizard.com

8

Overview of Virtual Learning Environment and Virtual Libraries

Dr. Parveen Kumar

ABSTRACT

This study provides an overview of a Virtual Library Environment. It discusses characteristics design and advantages of a Virtual Library and its environment. It also enumerates the key issues of Virtual Libraries. The Virtual Library provides access to tools such as databases, electronic journals, alerting services, online reference tools, and quality-selected web resources that improve the quality of teaching and research. Adaptivity in virtual learning environment has become a prominent research topic during the past decades and has led to a considerable number of web-based adaptive learning environments. The study also highlights the process of building a virtual library, collection development, acquisition and access of electronic resources in the virtual library, which are the basic skills required for the deployment and sustainability of the national virtual library.

Keywords: Virtual Library, Learning Environment, Virtual Learning

INTRODUCTION

The current technology revolution in society emerging from the development of Information and Communications Technologies is also transforming the learning paradigm. This technology facilitates communication and allows learners to access information in an open-ended way and to construct new knowledge representations in their minds, which is the basis for learning. Thus, learning will improve since the new technologies can help teachers to engage learners in active, constructive, intentional, authentic, and cooperative learning

Human beings learn the most that makes them the highest evolved form of life. No one can claim that learning is no more required at a particular stage of life. Differences in the infrastructure and other facilities at the place of learning create gaps and divides among individuals.

A number of institutions including the virtual institutions have started offering a wide range of courses on the web called web-based education tutorials or online courses or virtual courses. The web collects and creates knowledge resources from any place any time. Advancements in ICTs in the web era have enabled the LIS Schools to provide education by adopting maximum technologies in a Virtual Learning Environment (VLE). Modern library systems are also coming up to deliver their services in such an environment.

VIRTUAL LEARNING ENVIRONMENT

Virtual Learning (VL) takes place owing to developments in ICT. It removes all barriers in knowledge transfer and dissemination. The emergence of virtual library environment must be observed as a corollary to initiatives to unify the IT structures and to transform the learning process through innovative technology. A mix of sophisticated digital and Internet-based services and rapidly expanding global digital content have made possible a Virtual Learning Environment that delivers the capability to enhance the classroom experience or conduct learning apart from a physical campus. There are other initiatives taken in this direction by the Indian Institute of Technology (IIT), Consortium for Education Commission of the University Grants

Commission (UGC), National Council of Educational Research and Training (NCERT). They have developed interactive e-contents and some are also providing e-courses in the VLE.

ESSENTIAL COMPONENTS OF A VLE

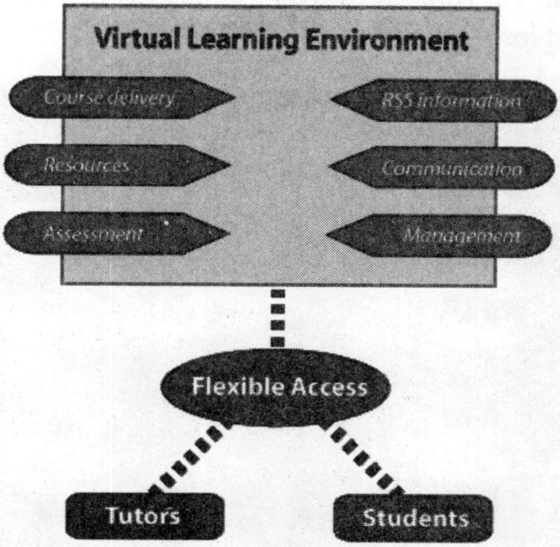

VIRTUAL LIBRARIES

There have been a lot of misconceptions about what a virtual library is: some consider the World Wide Web as a virtual library, while others consider the collection of URLs on a webpage a virtual library. A virtual library provides access to tools such as databases, electronic journals, alerting services, electronic reference, and quality-vetted e-resources.

Virtual Library is another kind of Digital Library which provides portal to information that is available electronically elsewhere. This is referred so to emphasize that the Library does not itself hold content. Virtual libraries are organized collections of digital information. It can offer resources from many sources and in many formats, including audio and video. Academic libraries can exist in two different spaces, a physical space and a virtual space. Each space enables different learning activities and serves different purposes for learning. Many libraries exist only in one space, whereas others maintain a hybrid space, both a physical and virtual space, in recognition of the distinct information uses and learning activities that can occur in each environment. All libraries, whether virtual or physical, create an environment for learning.

BUILDING A VIRTUAL LIBRARY

A virtual library collection is based on an established collection development and acquisition policy which takes into account the shift from owning information resources to licensing information and the aggregation of information in multi-disciplinary databases. The difficulty of evaluating and comparing electronic resources makes it necessary to have an electronic collections selection team.

The building blocks for a virtual library are its digital collections, which are not just a random assemblage of digital objects or uniform resource locators of free web- based resources (URLs). Building digital collections requires traditional library skills, in addition to information and web technology skills. The process of building a virtual library includes:

a. Digitization

Digitization involves the process of making non-digitally shaped materials available in digital format. The retrospective conversion of printed library cards into a machine-readable catalog represents one of the earliest digitization processes librarians have been involved with. Digital assets software such as DSpace, Eprints, Fedora, and Greenstone collect, index, and provide queries over a catalog of metadata records that are accessible locally and remotely.

b. Acquisitions and Collection Development

Acquisition involves acquiring and securing ownership of electronic resources such as databases, e-books and journals through licence. Subscribed electronic resources are stored on a remote server hosted by the vendor and made accessible to a target community after authentication and authorization.

Digital collections of information resources engage selection and organization based on an explicit collection development policy that addresses the information needs of a particular community. Storage and retrieval of digital resources for a virtual library is exclusively dependent on computers and electronic-network systems, hence in selecting materials, basic information on the hardware and software needed to access the resources and existing technology within the library must be taken into consideration.

ENABLING TECHNOLOGY FOR VIRTUAL LIBRARY

Virtual library services and digital resources are delivered over the Internet which depends on network operating systems running on web server computers. The enabling technologies deployed in a virtual library are web-based technologies that include web design using Hypertext Markup Language (HTML), Extensible Markup Language (XML), cascading style sheets (CSS), PHP coding, and web scripting languages such as JavaScript. Virtual library applications depend on relational databases for organization, storage and retrieval of information. Relational database management systems are installed on the web server hosting the virtual library, some popular relational database management systems includes MySQL, Oracle, PostgreSQL, and Microsoft SQL server.

Virtual library web servers are specially configured to authenticate users as they access various areas of the virtual library and run many applications that are crucial to delivering of services and digital resources. Popular web servers used by most organizations are Apache server and Microsoft's Internet Information Server (IIS).

Storage of electronic resources is either on a local server maintained by the library or parent institution of the library or on a remote server hosted by the vendor. Limits of network bandwidth and slow transmission speeds may make the effective access to virtual library resources problematic for many users.

ADVANTAGES OF VIRTUAL LIBRARIES

1. Virtual libraries offer opportunities for learning that are not possible in their physical counterparts. Whereas physical libraries operate with designated hours, virtual libraries are available anytime and anywhere there is an Internet connection.
2. Virtual libraries provide immediate access to a range of resources not available in physical collections. Virtual libraries often contain more up-to-date information than physical collections.
3. Virtual libraries can empower the user and promote informal learning.
4. Well-designed virtual library collections are organized and managed to increase productivity and efficiency of the user.
5. Virtual libraries can be customized for particular schools, grades, and subjects. This variety of formats in presentation and navigation is quite different from that of a physical library. Thus, virtual libraries support specific communities of interest, thereby, creating global communities of learners.
6. Virtual libraries break down the physical barriers between users and information sources.

CONCERNS ABOUT VIRTUAL LIBRARIES

- Virtual libraries require connectivity. If there is no Internet connection, the virtual library is inaccessible.
- Connectivity, however, is not the only concern with the use of virtual libraries. Even if students have access to virtual libraries, they may not possess the skills to access and utilize the information effectively.
- Virtual libraries still require skilled professionals to organize, maintain, and help students reap the benefits of this virtual learning environment.
- Although some virtual libraries are lists of websites and require little Internet searching ability, others demand knowledge of Boolean logic and advanced searching skills to realize the potential of the database.

CHARACTERISTICS

The characteristic features of the web based VLE are:

- It facilitates self learning at the learner's convenient time and place.
- It facilitates faster and cheaper delivery of the material.
- It enables to update learning materials speedily.
- It has changed the traditional library system of cataloguing only book materials.
- Cataloguing of NBM (Non Book Materials) includes not only databases but also websites.
- Greater emphasis is on access and not on collection.

ISSUES

Changing the Learning Culture: Migrating to the electronic learning environment calls for a change in the attitude of learners. The learners need to be trained in handling of the new media.

Training of Teachers: Teachers need to upgrade their skills in developing and delivering the course content through networks.

Training programme in web page designing, multimedia courseware production, HTML document preparation, etc is essential.

Courseware/software Development: Web based learning does not refer to just putting the learning material on the network. The material should be relevant, interactive, user-friendly, and able to facilitate the self-learning process. Trained manpower is required with the knowledge and skills both in software development as well as in teaching.

Equal Access to Technology: It must be assured that learners have equal access to the material provided on the net, immaterial of where they live or placed.

Maintain interaction with clients: The Virtual Library needs to maintain a 'human presence' by balancing both telephone and e-mail contact. Using e-mail exclusively changes the users' service style that users are accustomed to and increases the likelihood of lengthy correspondence.

Continued Visibility: The Virtual Library has to maintain an everyday presence in the virtual environment by activities including: posting news items on the Intranet home page, writing feature articles for the newsletter etc. and inviting people into the library when they are traveling in the vicinity.

Policies and Agreements: Users are often unsure of the service boundaries in the virtual environment. Highly visible policies outlining the virtual library's role and service level agreements means both parties have clearly defined roles and responsibilities. The Virtual Library's service level agreements and policies detail the services provided by the library, clients' obligations, request turnaround times and borrowing privileges etc.

Subscription based materials: One of the challenges to providing access to subscribed material will be how to handle access to subscription-based databases and aggregator services for journals and textbooks. Many vendors restrict access to IP address and require authentication of institutionally affiliated computers or remote users to access subscribed resources. Authentication can include automatic login username and password, automatic login using IP address, library authentication, and the use of proxy server. A proxy server provides remote access to IP restricted resources. After the proxy server authenticates and authorizes the user, it retrieves the restricted resource using the server's IP address and sends it to the user who is browsing from an un-authenticated IP address.

CONCLUSION

Virtual libraries are facing big challenges in their efforts to build a foundation for sustainable, ongoing effort. Several Virtual Libraries have claimed the vital new areas in scholarly and educational information service by way of technological provisions. Virtual Libraries are the new vision of the Libraries of future. Attention toward key issues/ challenges must be required.

The mere presence of virtual libraries, however, does not cause learning to occur. It is how these libraries are utilized by students and teachers that will enable learning. Virtual libraries present a new paradigm for learning in school libraries. They have the ability to transform the relationship between learners and resources, facilitating both formal and informal learning. With careful design and the support of skilled information professionals, virtual libraries can provide powerful environment for student learning.

REFERENCES

- Gbaje, Ezra Shiloba (2007). Implementing a National Virtual Library for Higher Institutions in Nigeria. *LIBRES Library and Information Science Research Electronic Journal*, 17(2), 1-15.
- Gunn, Holly (2002). Virtual Libraries Supporting Student Learning. *School Libraries Worldwide*, 8(2), 27-37.
- http://en.wikipedia.org/wiki/Virtual_learning_environment
- Koganuramath, Muttayya (2007). Virtual Library: an overview. *5th International CALIBER -2007, Panjab University, Chandigarh*, 08-10 February, 2007, 535-542.
- Singh, Ibohal & Devi, Madhuri (2009). Virtual Learning Environment: Issues and Challenges before LIS Schools and Libraries. *Collaborative Seminar: INFLIBNET and CEC January 29-30, 2009*, 178-187.

9

A Conceptual Framework for Developing a More Effective and Flexible Learning Management System (LMS) for Capturing and Leveraging Organizational Memory to Promote Organizational Learning and Innovation

Shweta Pandey
Shri Ram Pandey

ABSTRACT

The realities of global competition and increased learner sophistication have focused organizational attention on the need to develop a "learning culture". However, while much has been written on the importance of evolving a learning culture less attention has been given to understanding in a practical way the characteristics of "learning organization" and the way organizations can improve their learning management system. This paper presents a conceptual framework to develop a conceptual framework and architecture for a flexible, self-paced, and collaborative learning system supported by principles of knowledge management.

BACKGROUND

Organizational learning is increasingly becoming popular among organizations which are interested in increasing competitive advantage, innovativeness, and effectiveness. Argyris and Schon, two of the early researchers in this field, defined organizational learning as "the detection and correction of error". Fiol and Lyles define learning as "the process of improving actions through better knowledge and understanding". Dodgson describes organizational learning as "the way firms build, supplement, and organize knowledge and routines around their activities and within their cultures and adapt and develop organizational efficiency by improving the use of the broad skills of their workforces".

Stata (1989) states that although learning takes time, once the process has started, it feeds on itself and organizational members get better in their work. Landry (1992) also states that organizational learning is essential for innovation. Brown and Duguid (1991) view learning as a bridge between work and innovation. These views are similar to the concept of innovating adhocracies by Miller (1986) and Mitzberg (1979).

Argyris and Schon (1978) describe three types of organizational learning: Single-loop learning (SLL), Double-loop learning (DLL) and Deutero-learning (DL). In SLL organizational learning occurs when errors are detected and corrected and firms carry on with their present policies and goals. DLL occurs when, in addition to detection and correction of errors, the organization is involved in the questioning and modification of existing norms, procedures, policies, and objectives. DL occurs when organizations learn how to carry out single-loop and double-loop learning. The first two forms of learning will not occur if the organizations are not aware that learning must occur. Awareness of ignorance motivates learning (Nevis et al., 1995). This means identifying the learning orientations or styles, and the processes and structures (facilitating factors) required to promote learning.

Another interpretation of organizational learning and knowledge is given by Huber (1991). He stated that organizational learning occurs when organizations undertake sense-making and information interpretation activities. Organizations create knowledge by making sense of new stimuli with which they are constantly being bombarded with. Furthermore, the knowledge created is transmitted through the application of knowledge. In this view the creation of knowledge is not a solitary process, but is a result of interaction with others. In order to deal with new stimuli individuals are constantly exposed to, sense has to be made of such stimuli. The sharing of such sense making and consequent knowledge creation is through the use and application of language. Collectively individuals within an organization negotiate a shared understanding of knowledge held within their community.

Weick (1995) sees sense making as the process through which people reduce the complexity of their environment to a level from which they can make sense. Continuing with the idea of sense making as a meaning creating activity, Dougherty *et al.* (2000) describes sense making as, " the process through which various information, insight, and ideas coalesce into something useful, or 'stick' together in a meaningful way". Choo (2000) views knowledge not only as an "object or artefact, but also the outcome of people working together, sharing experiences, and constructing meaning out of what they do". Knowledge in organizations evolves as a result of the sense making that occurs from new stimuli and information that is absorbed into the existing body of knowledge.

Organizational memory refers to the repository where knowledge is stored for future use. It is also called "corporate knowledge" or "corporate genetics" by Prahalad and Hamel (1994). Decision makers store and retrieve not only hard data or information but also "soft" information, that is, information with meaning. This soft or interpreted information can be in the form of tacit know-how, expertise, biases, experiences, lists of contacts, anecdotes, etc. Organizational memory plays a very critical role in organizational learning. Both the demonstratability and usability of learning depend on the effectiveness of the organization's memory. The major challenge for organizations exists in interpreting information and creating organizational memory that is easily accessible Technology facilitates organizational learning and knowledge sharing in a big way. The learning management system (LMS) is a tool that handles all aspects of the learning process. LMS is the infrastructure that delivers and manages instructional content, identifies and assesses individual and organizational learning or training goals, tracks the progress towards meeting those goals, and collects and presents data for supervising the learning process of an organization as a whole (Szabo & Flesher, 2002)

Other tools that enable knowledge sharing are 'blogs' and 'wikis'. Wikis are socially mediated tools that are rich in potential for communication, information sharing, and collaborative endeavors. Blogs and wikis (user-edited, collaborative websites) have provided a democratic, accessible community of users responsible for its own content, supported by an open model of knowledge creation and communication. By supporting users who want to shape and share their content, while allowing other users access to the tools and means to modify the original contents, blogs and wikis continue to grow in utility. The collaborative design of blogs (via the comments feature) and wikis (through the direct editing of content by users) allows a process of bottom up editing, where the expertise is not in the hands of a few, but rather emerges from the combined efforts of the many.

The integration of online learning in organizations has hitherto focused on providing learners with the concepts and skills necessary to use the centrally run learning management systems. This has been useful for making the technology transparent for the learners who have never had exposure in working in a web-based learning environment. Learners are excited at having the power to design and publish their own online content, and the ability to develop their own online learning activities without facing any technical constraints. However criticism of learning management systems from learners come when attempts are made to design learner-centred online activities that are collaborative, reflective, experiential, participatory and networked across a wider community of peers or experts.

With the rise in popularity of technologies such as blogs, wikis,

RSS and community-building tools, new opportunities have been created for communicating, sharing ideas and engaging in the learning process. It is time for the focus of online learning support in organizations to move towards providing learners with the choice to create their own learning networks. These environments would ideally go beyond the artificial construct of an individual unit of study that make up their programs, and ideally beyond the individual program.

2. METHODOLOGY

The basic idea of conceptualization focus on developing a framework for a learner- centred as opposed to a course- centered system. This has been sought to be achieved by bringing together technologies such as wikis, blogs, RSS into one place. Specifically, we have examined and study the basic framework features of various the open source learning management system eg Moodle, Blackwell, Desire2 learn etc. The detail framework is as follows:

- Communication Tool
- File Exchange
- Internal mail, online notes
- Chat, whiteboard
- Productivity Tools
- Bookmarks, calendar
- Searching Within course
- Orientation/ Help
- Students Involvement Tools
- Group Work
- Student Portfolio
- Activities
- Others
- Administrative tools
- Course Delivery Tools
- Content Development Tools

While exploring the idea of how an integrated LMS that includes a sense making process shared through narrative can be conceived of that includes the characteristics of both Moodle and MediaWiki. Moodle facilitate creation and building the learning platform whereas Media Wikis provides collaborative platform to share knowledge artifact.

3. CONCLUSION

The concept of organizational learning is increasing becoming popular. A learning management system is a tool that facilitates the learning process. However, this has tended to be more course- centric rather than learner centric.

3.1. Issues and shortcomings

In working with Moodle LMS and Media Wiki application, I came across several shortcomings. Below you will find overview most important issues:

i. The "Tree falling in the Forest" Trouble: so much content, so little time

ii. The "Functional Fallacy": structuring content after functions

iii. The "Post Partum" Phenomenon: post and forget

iv. The "Ignore the Ramblers" Idea: ignoring commentators

v. The "Measure what I do" Malaise: only what is measured can be improved

vi. The "Pontification" Problem: when people are too much involved

vii. The "Content Generation Divide" Dysfunctionality: more than words

3.2. Solutions and recommendations

To address these issues and shortcomings, we recommend:

i. Record "Learning" Activity: basic relevant data capture

ii. Extractors and Converters: beyond ASCII text

iii. Deep Versions: multiple drafts and traces

iv. Expires By: forced content expiration

v. Deeper User Profiles: a mix of observation and configuration

vi. Beyond Commenting: capturing all data streams around content

vii. "Tres Facet Auditorium": require reviewers to complete content

With the availability of new web based tools such as wikis and blogs, potential exists for the capabilities of such LMS to be augmented to provide for tools that facilitate the creation of more learner centered networks. This study focus on developing a conceptual framework for creation of such a flexible learning management system that can support central features of work practice such as narration, collaboration, and social construction.

REFERENCE

Argyris, C., & Schon, D.A. (1978). *Organizational learning: A theory of action perspective.* Reading, MA: Addison-Wesley.

Dodgson, M. (1993). Organizational learning: A review of some literatures. *Organization Studies,* 14/3: 375-394.

Huber, G.P. (1991). Organizational learning: The contributing processes and the literatures. *Organization Science,* 2/1:88-115.

Prahalad, C. K., & Hamel, G. (1994). *Competing for the future,* MA: Harvard Business School Press.

Patton, M.Q. (1990). *Qualitative Evaluation and Research Methods.* Newbury

Mason, R.M. (1993). Strategic information systems: Use of information technology in a learning organization. *Proceedings of the Twenty-Sixth Hawaii International Conference on System Sciences 93,* CA: IEEE Press, 840-849.

Nevis, E. C., DiBella, A. J., and Gould, J. M. (1995). Understanding Organizations as Learning Systems. *Sloan Management Review,* Winter: 73-85.

Stata, R. (1989). Organizational learning - The key to management innovation. *Sloan Management Review,* Spring: 63-74.

10

Evaluation of Selected Internet Resources on Marketing of Library Services

Dr. Anna Kaushik
Lakkho Singh

ABSTRACT

No doubt emergence of internet resources in manifold formats provides new way to catch interest information form the web but internet resources trustworthiness always a question for information seekers. Therefore it is very necessary to assess these internet resources prior to use for variant purposes. This study aims to evaluate selected internet resources on marketing of library services on the basis of specific criteria developed for each identified category of internet resources available on internet. This study will able to serve a paradigm for evaluating quality of different kind of internet resources available on web on various subjects.

Keywords : Internet resources, evaluation, marketing of library services

INTRODUCTION

There are several types of Internet resources on marketing of library services available on Internet which becomes main sources of information to catch information for various purposes. But information available on internet may not have guaranty of the trustworthiness. On the other hand evaluation of internet always helpful to discovered strength, weakness and rating etc of the internet resources. There are many studies that have dealt with evaluation of Internet resources but evaluation parameters vary greatly as per the types and nature of internet resources for an example evaluation for a blog will be not same to criteria for evaluation of a database or other internet resources.

Some studies dealt with evaluation of Internet resources which include Smith (1997), Middleton et.al. (1999), Fritch and Cromwell (2001), Bauer and Scharl (2000) and Austria (2007), these studies were identified different parameters for evaluating the various types of Internet resources. Based on these studies and as per requirement of the present study, the criteria developed for evaluating of the different resources are given in Table 1.

For this study, key internet resources on area of marketing of library services available in each category viz. website, blog, training/ tutorial, e-book, e-publisher, bibliography, open archives, list serve , database and podcast were selected and evaluation of selected internet resources on marketing of library services was conducted during September1, 2010 to September 30, 2010.

Table 1 : Evaluation criteria for Internet resources

Internet resource category	*Criteria of evaluation*
Websites	Authority, Purpose, Objectivity/ Bias, Scope, Intended audience, Currency, Navigation, Layout, any special features
Blogs	Authority, Purpose, Subject focus, Intended audience, Currency, Navigation/ format, Scope, Lay out, any special features.
Bibliographies	Authority, Purpose, Subject focus, Coverage period, Arrangement, Scope, Objectivities/ bias, Number of pages, Format

E- books	Authority/ publishing body, Purpose, Intended audience, Subject focus, Year of publication, Format, Navigation/ ease of use
Newsletters	Authority/publishing body ,Purpose, Focusing area Free or paid, Scope, format ,Online from
Online training packages/ modules	Authority, Purpose, Targeted audience, Currency, Course content/ structure, Course design, navigation, Personal interaction, FAQ facility, Feedback provision.
Tool kits	Authority, Purpose, Targeted audience, Currency, Feedback provision, FAQ facility, Feedback provision
Podcasts	Authority, Purpose, Intended audience, objectivity, Currency, scope, format.
Reports	Authority, Purpose, Intended audience, objectivity, Currency, scope, format.
Databases	Authority, Purpose, Intended audience, objectivity, Currency, scope, format.
Institutional Repositories	Authority, Purpose, Intended audience, objectivity, Currency, scope, format.
List servs	Authority, Purpose, Intended audience, objectivity, Currency, scope, format.

DESCRIPTION OF EVALUATION CRITERIA

Authority: It is main criteria which lead users to tell that which source is true or false and credit of development of resources.

Purpose: The basic aim of the resources for what a resource was created.

Scope: It deals with the how depth information is covered and from its time span.

Objectivity: This point associated with biasness, advertisement etc.

Indented audience : Targeted people for whom a resource is developed.

Currency: This criteria deals with issues such as on which date a web resource was created and updated.

Format: In which format such as html, pdf, ppt etc. a resource has.

Feedback provision: This section tells about opinion of people who are connected with a programme or activity.

Subject focus: In which subject a resource basically concern.

Navigation: To use the resources without any difficulty.

Layout: How a resource looks and appeared.

Special features: This criteria connected with the issues of addition facilities such as web 2.0 application and other provisions provided within the resource.

EVALUATION OF WEBSITES

Websites are main source of information on Internet. Websites contain web pages including a home page. These were divided the websites into three sections viz. individual web sites, associations' websites and publishers' websites according to their publishing/ responsible body.

Individual website means a website is created by individual basis concern to explore his/her interest and works in a particular area by which one has attached with. In marketing of library area, following websites have been identified and their evaluation is done on the basis of preselected criteria:

Table 2 : Individual websites

Individual websites	*URL*
Marketing information and library services	http://dis.shef.ac.uk/sheila/marketing/default.htm
Marketing our libraries : On and off the Internet	http://www.librarysupportstaff.com/marketinglibs.html
Library and Information Services Marketing	http://clips.lis.illinois.edu/2003_09.html

The evaluation of the three websites done the parameters of authority, purpose, scope, objectivity, currency, intended audience, navigation, layout and special features is given in Table 3.

Table 3 : Evaluation of individual websites

Name of Website	Authority	Purpose	Scope	Objectivity	Currency	Intended audience	Navigation	Layout	Special features
Marketing Information and library services	Sheila Webber	To promote marketing concept s in real situation	Wide range of printed and electronic resource published form 1997 to 2001	No	5 August 2001	LIS professionals	Easy	Good	No
Marketing our libraries: On and off the Internet	Mary Niederlander	Not clear	Wide range of printed & electronic resource published form 1993 to 2005	No	May 31 2005	LIS professionals	Easy	Good	Yes, Advanced search facility, visitor counter
Library and Information Services Marketing	*Marianne Steadley and Chuk Gray*	Not given	Wide range of printed and electronic resource published form 1997 to 2003	No	Not given	Not given	Easy	Good	Not provided

When we evaluate the above website from different angle especially by authority criteria, it is discovered that only one authority namely Sheila Webber who created a individual website, was fully associated with marketing library services area being a member of marketing section and published good volume of literature. But, nowadays, she is shifted to information literacy area.

Form the three website's sections point of view, Marketing Information and library services website divided in to 10 sections, marketing our libraries: on and off the Internet websites, got 14 sections and Library and Information Services Marketing had 10 sections. Every section of each website provides various links to access the resources on marketing library and information area.

Of course, navigation feature is available in all three selected websites, but when we look at the logical arrangement of the resources listed on the subject, it was found that "Marketing Information and library services" website resources are more arranged in logical order in comparison of other two websites' resources. Though, the maximum volume of resources on subject are covered by only website namely "Marketing our Libraries: On and off" but its resources were found unorganized and "Library and Information Services Marketing" contains ten resources on each section.

It is interesting to note that no one website found update which is the most essential criteria to evaluate Internet resources.

The coverage period of the three websites are viz. "Marketing Information and library services, Marketing our libraries: On and off the Internet and Library and Information Services Marketing" from 1997 to 2001, 1993 to 2005 and 1997 to 2003 respectively.

EVALUATION OF ASSOCIATION WEBSITES

There are various associations which have special interest to develop and promote the activities in particular area through their websites for which these have been developed special section under their websites' banner, are categorized as associations' website shown in Table 4.

Table 4 : Associations' websites

Associations' websites	*URL*
ALA-Public Relation Association	http://www.ala.org/ala/mgrps/divs/llama/llamacommittees/publicrelationsb/publicrelations.cfm
(The International Federation of Library Associations and Institutions)	http://www.ifla.org/VII/s34/index.htm
(CILIP) Chartered Institute of Library and Information Professionals	http://www.cilip.org.uk/specialinterestgroups/bysubject/publicitypr/

The evaluation of the Associations' websites based on authority, purpose, scope, objectivity, currency, intended audience, navigation, layout and special features is shown in Table 5.

If we look the geographic coverage of above three associations then found that CILIP and ALA association belong to national level whereas IFLA is a international association which contains various resources such as projects, marketing awards, Newsletter, conference paper in different languages and emailing addresses. Other two associations are not providing large volume of resources in comparison to IFLA association marketing section. The currency criterion is met only by IFLA. But special feature criteria especially search facility is provided by all three websites. Navigation and layout part are found strong in all three websites.

EVALUATION OF PUBLISHERS' WEBSITES

In present era, various electronic publishers have emerged and they also have keen interest to developed promotional activities through their websites. The prominent publishers who have created literature for marketing library services are given in Table 6.

The evaluation of the publishers' website based on authority, purpose, scope, objectivity, currency, intended audience, navigation, layout and special features is shown in Table 7.

Table 5 : Evaluation of associations' website

Name of Website	Authority	Purpose	Scope	Objectivity	Currency	Intended audience	Navigation	Layout	Special features
Marketing @ your library by ALA	ALA	To promote the public relation among libraries	Not given	US focus	Not given	Not given	Easy	Good	Search facility
IFLA (The International Federation of Library Associations and Institutions)	IFLA	Not clear given	Various resources from 2000 to 2009	No	29 October 2008	Not given	Easy	Good	Search facility
(CILIP) Chartered Institute of Library and Information Professionals	CILIP	Not given	Not given	Uk focus	Not given	Not given	Easy	Good	Search facility, RSS, site map

Table 6 : Publishers' websites

Publishers' websites	*URL*
Emerald	http://i nfo.emeraldi nsight.com/librar ians/mar keting/index.htm
Elsevier	http://w ww.else vier.com/wps/fi nd/librar ianshome.librar ians

Emerald, a well known electronic publisher has produced a wide range of journals in library and information field rather than Elsevier. The main purpose of marketing our library section is to promote the library activities whereas Elsevier librarians' section has lack of above information. In authority point of view, Emerald library corner provides information about author who creates the material but Elsevier does not give such information its authority may be judge form publishing body. From scope criteria, Emerald provides its promotional material in series of 12 installments while Elsevier publisher mainly focuses on training and bibliography suits which contains in two sections. Both electronic publisher, Emerald and Elsevier contain special features such as free membership to access the entire series and twitter, delicious, RSS, You Tube respectively. The main criteria to assess the quality of website namely currency is not available in both websites.

EVALUATION OF ELECTRONIC BOOK

An electronic book is simple printed book which is available in electronic format. The electronic books identified our marketing library services are a given in Table 8.

The evaluation of e-books on the criteria of authority, purpose, intended audience, subject focus, year of publication, navigation, format, scope and number of pages is shown in Table 9.

Table 7 : Evaluation of publishers' websites

Name of Website	*Authority*	*Purpose*	*Scope*	*Objectivity*	*Currency*	*Intended audience*	*Navigation*	*Layout*	*Special features*
Emerald	Emerald (Lisa Ennis)	Promotion of libraries services	All literature divided in 12 Sections	Not present	Not given	LIS professionals	Easy to use	Good	Yes (member ship form)
Elsevier	Elsevier	Not given	Not given	Not provided	Not present	Not available	Easy	Good	Yes (RSS, Twister, video)

Table 8 : Name of the e- books

Name of E- Books	*URL*
Marketing the Small Library	http://www.skyways.org/KSL/development/marketingthesmalllibrary.pdf
Marketing Information Products and Services A Primer for Librarians and Information Professionals	http://www.idrc.ca/en/ev-9397-201-1-DO_TOPIC.html or http://www.idrc.ca/en/ev-9397-201-1-DO_TOPIC.html#begining
Guidelines for the Teaching of Marketing in the Training of Librarians, Document lists, and Archivists.	http://www.eric.ed.gov/PDFS/ED325127.pdf

In authority purpose, only two e-books namely "Marketing information products and services and Guidelines for the teaching of marketing in the training of librarians, documentalists and archives" are created by prominent authority in the field of marketing the library service, in which one book is edited by prominent authority and other e-books Guidelines for the Teaching of 'Marketing in the Training of Librarians, Document lists, and Archivists' was written by Rajean Savard. All three books got information regarding year of publication and all three books available freely in portable Document Format (PDF) while "Marketing information products and service :a primer for librarians and information professionals" e- book available freely in both PDF and HTML formats. As far as publishing body concern, The Local Library Division Kansas State Library for "Marketing the small library" and IDRD/ Tata McGraw- Hill for Library and information services are belong to national level but UNESCO for Guidelines for the Teaching of Marketing in the Training of Librarians, Documentalists, and Archivists" e- book connected with international level.

EVALUATION OF BIBLIOGRAPHIES

Bibliography may be systematic list of information sources such as books, journal articles and websites often arranged in alphabetical order for variant specific purposes/ subject.

Table 9 : Evaluation of e-books

Name of E-book	Authority	Purpose	Intended audience	Subject focus	Year of publication	Navigation	Format	Scope	No of Pages
Marketing the Small Library	The Local Library Division Kansas State Library	Apply marketing concepts in library	LIS profess-ional	Marketing library services	2002	Easy	PDF	5 chapters	70
Marketing Information Products and Services A Primer for Librarians and Information Professionals	AK Jain, Ashok Jambhekar, TRRP Rao, SS Rao	Marketing application in library	LIS profess-ionals	Marketing library services	1999	Easy	PDF and HTML	9 Chapters	480
Guidelines for the Teaching of Marketing in the Training of Librarians, Document lists, and Archivists	Rejean Savard/ UNESCO	Marketing training	Information professional, Teachers	Marketing and teachninh	1998	Easy	PDF	6 modules	121

Table 10 : Name of bibliographies

Name of bibliography	URL
Putting your library on the map	http://www.dowling.edu/library/papers/marje/BibMarketcon.doc
Will It Make My Teeth Whiter? Selling the Library without Selling Out	http://www.fearless-future.com/wordpress/wp-content/uploads/2007/04/bibliography.pdf.
Selected References on Marketing Special Libraries	http://web.archive.org/web/19991001064727/38.241.117.66/membership/irc/market.html
Marketing of Sci-Tech Resources : A mostly annotated bibliography	http://mysite.du.edu/~jokraus/sla-st/marketing.html

Table 10 provided a list of selected bibliography on marketing of library services.

Table 11 depicts that in respect to authority criteria most of bibliographies on marketing library service area compiled by individual basic while other two bibliographies namely "Selected References on Marketing Special Libraries and Marketing of Sci-Tech Resources : A mostly annotated bibliography" developed under the banner of Special Library Association (SLA) which is well known association in LIS profession. Purpose statement is given only by one bibliography titled "Library Marketing into the 21st Century: A selected annotated bibliography" whereas rest selected bibliographies have lack of such information. Arrangement of sources in selected bibliographies are found in alphabetical order while three bibliographies having arrangement style in source wise as well as alphabetical order. A bibliography "Library Marketing into the 21st Century: A selected annotated bibliography" comprises 14 pages in which introduction, articles, books/ manuals, audio recordings, videotapes, Internet resources, list serves/ Discussion lists and marketing planning software imbedded in 9 headings which are much more resources in comparison to other above selected bibliographies on the subject. Out of seven selected bibliographies, the four bibliographies appeared in Portable Document Format (pdf), two bibliographies having

Table 11 : Evaluation of bibliographies

Name of Bibliography	Authority	Purpose	Subject focus	Scope	Currency	Arrange-ment order	Number of pages	Format
Putting your library on the map	Deborah Formosa and Marjorie J. Fusco	Not provided	Library marketing	1993 to 2000	Not given	Alphabet ical	5 pages	DOC
Marketing of Sci-Tech Resources : A mostly annotated bibliography	Not given	Not given	Marketing concepts in Si and Tech. library	1991 to 2002	Not given	Alphabetical	Not given	HTML
Library Marketing into the 21st Century: A selected annotated bibliography	Patrick Meyer	Collect library marketing resources	Library marketing	1995 to 2004	Not given	Alphabetical and source wise	14 pages	PDF

Hypertext Markup Language (html) and one bibliography appeared in MS –Word (doc) format. In terms of number of items covered, "Putting your library on the map, Marketing Magic: Selected Bibliography and Sources, Will It Make My Teeth Whiter? Selling the Library without Selling Out, Bibliography – ELD Marketing/Outreach Session, Selected References on Marketing Special Libraries, Marketing of Sci-Tech Resources : A mostly annotated bibliography and Library Marketing into the 21st Century: A selected annotated bibliography" have 54,28,31,79 ,78,45 and 62 items respectively.

EVALUATION OF BLOGS

In present era, blogs has become a powerful tool of information communication and to get refection about blogger thoughts, ideas and options.

Reichardt and Harder (2005) described as "in very simple terms, a weblog, or blog, is a Web site resembling a personal journal that is updated with individual entries or postings" .The blogs identified on the subject of marketing library services given in Table 12 below.

Table 12 : Name of blogs

Name of blog	*URL*
Marketing-Mantra-for-Librarians	http://www.marketing-mantra-for-librarians.blogspot.com/
Illinois Libraries Matter	http://illinoislibrariesmatter.wordpress.com/ .
The 'M' Word- Marketing Libraries	http://themwordblog.blogspot.com/
Library Marketing Toolkit	http://nclibrarymarketing.blogspot.com/.
Bubble Room	http://www.libraryjournal.com/blog/820000682/post/890038889.html.
New Jersey Library Marketing News	http://nancydowd.wordpress.com/.

Evaluation of the blogs based on the criteria authority, purpose, scope/starting year, currency, intended audience, navigation, layout and special features is shown in Table 13.

Table 13 : Evaluation of blogs

Name of Blog	Authority	Purpose	Scope/ starting year	Currency	Intended audience	Navigation	Layout	Special features
Marketing-Mantra-for-Librarians	Dinesh Kr. Gupta	Not given	September, 2007	September	Not clear	Easy	Good	Yes, Social networking site, visitor location
Illinois Libraries Matter	The Marketing Committee of the Illinois Library Association	Not given	September, 2008	September 27, 2010	Not clear	Easy	Good	Yes, (Flickr)
The 'M' Word-Marketing Libraries	Kathy Dempsey, Tina Lackey and Nancy Dowd	Not given	June, 2006	September, 27, 2010	Not clear	Easy	Good	Yes, (visitor location)
Library Marketing Toolkit	Pam Jaskot	Not given	February, 2008	September 9, 2010	LIS staff	Easy	Good (Video corner)	Yes
Bubble Room	Alison Circle	Not given	July, 2004	September 27, 2010	Not clear	Easy	Good	Yes, (search facility)
New Jersey Library Marketing News	Not provided	Not given	February, 2008	September 1, 2010	Not provided	Easy	Good	Yes, blog serach, spam blocker, blog hits

It is clear from Table 13 that most of blogs created on individual basis especially persons who associated with library marketing activities. These blogs include Marketing mantra for librarian blog and The "M" word for marketing blogs are kwon as eminent authority in field of marketing library services while other blogs LIS professionals and association body namely" The Marketing Committee of the Illinois Library Association".

It is surprising to see that none blog had produced the purpose statement of the blog. Among these selected blogs, the oldest blogs identified namely "Bubble room" which posted its first entry on July, 2004 and newest discovered as blog" Illinois Libraries Matter" which first post found in the month of September, 2010.

Most of selected blog do not provide statement regarding intended audience, only one blog has clear indication towards intended audience. Navigation and layout criteria meet by each selected blog.

It is interesting to note that all selected blogs well equipped with the latest technology especially web 2.0 tools. Therefore, a special feature criterion is also meet by all of them.

EVALUATION OF TRAINING /TUTORIAL SITES

Training and tutorial sites on marketing library services are a few in number. Two sites could be located on training and tutorial shown in Table 14.

Table 14 : Name of training /tutorial sites

Name of trainings / tutorial	*URL*
Marketing the Library by Ohio Library	http://www.olc.org/marketing/index.html
ALA Washington Office Offers Free Online Advocacy Training by ALA	http://www.ala.org/ala/issuesadvocacy/advocacy/federallegislation/getinvolved/onlineadvocacy/index.cfm

The evaluation of training/tutorial sites based on authority, purpose, scope, objectivity, currency, intended audience, navigation, layout, feedback provision, special features is shown in Table 15.

Table 15 : Evaluation of trainings/ tutorials

Name of Training/ tutorials	Authority	Purpose	Scope	Objectivity	Currency	Intended audience	Navigation	Layout	Feedback provision	Special features
Marketing the Library by Ohio Library	Ohio Library Council	Not given	Not provided	Not available	Not given	Not given	Easy	Good	Not given	Yes (Whats new)
ALA Washington Office Offers Free Online Advocacy Training by ALA	American Librarian Association	Not given	Not provided	Not available	Not given	Not given	Easy	Good	Not given	Yes (search facility, webinars)

Both trainings provide an extensive range of resources including webinars, library 2.0 applications and podcasts on marketing library services area, developed under the banner of well known publishing body Ohio Library Council and American Library Association, denote its authority evidence. "Marketing the Library by Ohio Library" mainly focus on marketing applications should implementation to library services whilst "ALA Washington Office Offers Free Online Advocacy Training by ALA" principally covers advocacy aspects. It is surprise to see that both online training do not have purpose, scope, objectivity, currency and intended audience.

EVALUATION OF TOOL KITS

A set of reading material specially prepared for specific audiences and groups. The selected tool kits in the field of marketing library services depicted in Table 16.

Table 16 : Name of tool kits

Name of Tool kits	URL
Library marketing toolkit	http://www.proquest.com/en-US/utilities/toolkits/default.shtml
Introduction to marketing techniques by John Stanley Associates – library marketing tool kit	http://www.bobsbooks.com.au/catalog/pdf/LMTK%20Sample.pdf
Promoting you and your library by LexisNexis	http://www.lexisnexis.com/infopro/training/toolkits/default.asp .

The evaluation of toolkits based on the parameters authority, purpose, scope, objectivity, currency, intended audience, navigation, layout, format and special features is given in Table 17.

It can seen from the above table 17 that authority indicators associated with two well known database viz. Pro Quest and LexisNexis and one toolkits produced under the support of John Stanley Association."Promoting you and your library" tool kit produced by LexisNexis comprises a wide range resources under the different categories in comparison of other selected toolkits. The

Table 17 : Evaluation of toolkits

Name of Tool kit	Authority	Purpose	Scope	Objectivity	Currency	Intended audience	Navigation	Layout	Format	Special features
Library marketing toolkits	Pro-Quest	Library marketing	Not found	Not found	Not given	LIS profess-ional	Easy	Good	Html	Yes (search facility)
Introduction to marketing techniques by John Stanley Associates – library marketing tool kit	John Stanley Associates	Promotion of marketing techniques	Not found	Not found	Not given	LIS profess-ional	Easy	Good	Pdf	Not provided
Promoting you and your library	Lexis Nexis	Promotion LIS professional and libraries	Not found	Not found	Not given	LIS professi-onal	Easy	Good	html	Yes (search, news letter)

purpose of above three toolkits is to promote of library professional and libraries services through marketing techniques. It is surprised to note that all three selected toolkits do not meet scope, objectivity and currency criteria. Among three toolkits, two toolkits have html format and special features while one toolkit has pdf format but does not contain any special feature.

EVALUATION OF NEWSLETTERS

A brief regularly distributed publication contains news and current events, generally published through a particular organization or group on one specific topic called newsletter. The selected newsletters for evaluation are listed in Table 18.

Table 18 : Name of newsletters

Name of Newsletter	URL
Marketing Library services	http://www.infotoday.com/MLS/default.shtml
Marketing Treasure	http://www.chrisolson.com/marketingtreasures/mtresources.html
Media & PR	http://www.ssdesign.com/librarypr/

The evaluation of newsletter based on the parameters of authority, purpose, scope, objectivity, intended audience, navigation, layout and special features is give in Table 19.

Table 19 shows that two newsletters have authority and scope information while one newsletter has lack of such information. Purpose and intended audience criteria meet only by the one Newsletter namely "Marketing library services" which gives "ideas about the marketing the services to all types of libraries". It is interesting to see that above newsletter provide a free article full text in each issue of it. Currency criteria found in only one newsletter titled "Marketing Treasure". Navigation and layout criteria are equally found quite well and all three Newsletters meet got special feature criteria.

Table 19 : Evaluation of Newsletters

Name of newsletter	Authority	Purpose	Scope	Objectivity	Currency	Intended audience	Navigation	Layout	Special features
Marketing Library Services	Information Today, Inc (Editor Kathy Dempsey)	Ideas to marketing services	January/ February 1998 to September/ October 2010	Not given	Not given	LIS profess-ional	Easy	Good	Yes , Access to back vlume
Marketing Treasure	Chris Olson & Associates	Not given	Sept/Oct 1987 to July 25, 2006.	Not given	21-2-2005	Not provided	Easy	Good	Yes (index, archive, back issues)
Media & PR	Not provided	Not given	Not given	Not given	Not given	Not given	Easy	Good	Yes (article, toolbox)

EVALUATION OF MARKETING LIBRARY SERVICES WIKIPEDIA

Wikipedia is one of the most popular open source portal that pertaining the information on all most each topic. A wikipedia selected for evaluation given in Table 20.

Table 20 : Name of Wikipedia

Name of Wikipedia	URL
Library Success- marketing	http://www.libsuccess.org/index.php?title=Marketing

The evaluation of Wikipedia on the criteria of authority, purpose, scope, objectivity, currency, intended audience, navigation, layout and special features is shown in Table 21.

Wikipedia Library Success - marketing section provides access to some resources related to marketing library service field therein its contents bifurcate into five subheading such as success stories, marketing tips, marketing plans, blogs/ websites to watch and specific blog posts/ articles to checkout . *Meredith Farkas* is the authority of this Wikipedia who belong to LIS profession but exclusively marketing library service area. The main aim of this Wikipedia is to share the ideas among the library and information professionals. This Wikipedia also meets the criteria such as currency, intended audience, navigation, layout and special feature criteria.

EVALUATION OF REPORT/ HAND BOOK

A concise reference book providing specific information about a subject called as hand book. On other hand, report is a written document describing the findings of some individual or group on specific topic/ issue/ theme. The selected hand books and reports for the evaluation shown in Table 22.

Table 21 : Evaluation of wikipedia

Name of Wikipedia	Authority	Purpose	Scope	Objectivity	Currency	Intended audience	Navigation	Layout	Special features
Library Success marketing	Meredith Farkas	To share the ideas among LIS professionals	Not given	Not given	2 April 2010	LIS professional	Easy	Good	Yes (Search facility)

Table 22 : Name of hand books and reports

Name of report /hand book	URL
Promoting Special Library Services by SIA	http://w ww.libsci.sc.edu/bob/class/clis724/ SpecialLibrar iesHa ndbook/pr omoting.htm
Marketing for Public Libraries: report of a research project under the Public Library Research Programme (Hand book)	http://www.librarycouncil.ie/policies/documents/ Marketing%20project%20report%202008% 20final%20version.pdf

The evaluation of authority, purpose, scope, objectivity, currency, intended audience, navigation, layout, format and special features is given in Table 23.

It can see easily from Table 23 that both resources contain authority, currency, navigation, format and layout criteria. The basic aim of above report is to promote marketing techniques in public libraries through a project which started in 2004 and finished in 2008. The format of above report and hand book found as hypertext markup language (html) and format (pdf) respectively.

EVALUATION OF PODCASTS

An audio file on the Internet which got RSS feed called podcast. The discovered podcasts in the area of marketing library services listed in Table 24.

The evaluation of Podcasts based on authority, purpose, scope, objectivity, currency, intended audience, navigation, layout, format and length and size is given in Table 25.

Table 23 : Evaluation of hand books/ reports

Name of report/ handbook	Authority	Purpose	Scope	Objectivity	Currency	Intended audience	Navigation	Layout	Format	Special features
Promoting Special Library Services by SLA (Report)	Aimee Berry	Not given	Not provided	Not provided	April 21, 1999	Not given	Easy	Good	html	Not given
Marketing for Public Libraries: report of a research project under the Public Library Research Programme (Hand book)	Mayo County Library	Promote marketing techniques	2004 To 2008	Not given	2008	Public libraries	Easy	Good	PDF	Not given

Table 24 : Name of podcasts

Name of podcasts	*URL*
Understanding Todays Boomer Library Consumer	http://infopeople.org/training/webcasts/webcast_data/215/index.html
Guerrilla Marketing for Literacy	http://infopeople.org/training/webcasts/webcast_data/140/index.html

Table 25 displays that both podcasts (webcasts) meet authority criteria and both also podcasts produced by LIS professionals but the aim of both podcast found different. These podcast also got criteria such as currency, intended audience, navigation, layout size and format criteria. Understanding Today's Boomer Library Consumer and Guerrilla Marketing for Literacy got format of their files in Doc, pdf and doc, pdf, ppt formats respectively.

EVALUATION OF OPEN SOURCE ARCHIVES

The open source archives are open source portals hold various literatures on many fields and provide free access to all users. The selected open source archives in the field of marketing library services given in Table 26.

Two open sources archives have been identified which covers literature of library and information science area shown in Table 26.

From Table 27, it can be seen that both are open sources archives covering library and information science related aspects and available free to all users. While search made through "marketing" search term, DLIST produced 398 and E-LIS produced 143 results. The main purpose of the both archive to provide free information to all users but the coverage area of both archives found different as DLIST more focusing on information science subject whereas E-LIS much concerning with library and information science subject and target audiences also found same as per the coverage of the subject in each open source archive. Both open source archives provide their resources in portable digital format (pdf).

Table 25 : Evaluation of podcasts

Name of Podcast	Authority	Purpose	Scope	Objectivity	Currency	Intended audience	Navigation	Layout	Format	Length/size
Under-standing Today s Boomer Library Consumer	Matt Thornhill	To attract the customer	Not given	Not given	August 7, 2007	LIS profess-ional	Easy	Good	Doc, PDF	1.31 mb
Guerrilla Marketing for Literacy	Join Jose Cruz and Valerie Reinke	Literacy promotion	Not given	Not given	September 15, 2006	LIS profess-ional	Easy	Good	Doc, PPT, pdf	1.14mb

Table 26 : Name of open sources archives

Name of open source archives	URL
DLIST	http://dlist.sir.arizona.edu/arizona/handle/10150/105066
E-LIS	http://eprints.rclis.org/

Table 27 : Evaluation of open source archives

Name of open source archives	Authority	Purpose	Scope	Objectivity	Currency	Intended audience	Navigation	Layout	Format	Establishing year
DLIST	University of Arizona	To act as institutional repository in Information science	Information science and its related areas	Not given	Not given	Information science professionals	Easy	Good	PDF	2002
E-LIS	RCLIS, DoIS, AEPIC, and CILEA	To serve as a open source archive in LIS	Library and information science area	Febuary 21, 2010	September 15, 2006	LIS professional	Easy	Good	PDF	2003

EVALUATION OF DATABASES

The database is well known reference to fetch the scholar information through various journal and other source of information which covered by it. The database chosen for this study is listed in Table 28.

It is seen form Table 29 that the authority indicator is found that is world class popular publisher especially in management field. It purpose is to provide bibliographic information of scholar publication from various journals, newsletter covered under it pertain to library and information science area. The scope of this database is discovered wider as it covered 600 periodicals, plus books, research reports and proceedings in LIS field. It does not show the bias towards any corner and currency criteria also not found. LISTA also contains special features particularly in search and save facility, which provided by multi choice options. LISTA can be accessed freely.

EVALUATION OF LISTSERVE

Listserve basically is a mailing list of group of people who have common interest in particular field and activities through which any members of this group has platform to share the information and happening taking place in the particular area. The selected list of listserve is given in Table 30.

From Table 31, it can be seen that IFLA-L is powered by The International Federation of Library Associations and Institutions (IFLA) which is a well known authority in the field of library and information science at the international level. The IFLA- L purpose is to share the ideas, news and other updates among the subscribed users and targeted audiences, LIS professionals also clearly indicated. The scope of this listserve found wider as it provides about 70 mailing list in different areas of library and information science. It also meets the currency criteria that is September 27, 2010. IFLA- L is free to subscribe for any users.

Table 28 : Name of database

Name of database	URL
LISTA	http://w ww.libsucce ss.org/index.php?t itle=Marketing

Table 29 : Evaluation of database

Name of database	Authority	Purpose	Scope	Objectivity	Currency	Intended audience	Navigation	Layout	Special features
LISTA	EBSCO	To provide bibliographic information	Wide rage of about 600 periodicals LIS field	Not given	Not provided	LIS professional	Easy	Good	Yes (Search facility)

Table 30 : Name of listserve

Name of listserve	URL
IFLA-L	http://www.ifla.org/mailing-lists

Table 31 : Evaluation of listserve

Name of Wikipedia	Authority	Purpose	Scope	Objectivity	Currency	Intended audience	Navigation	Layout	Special features
Library Success-marketing	IFLA	To share the ideas among LIS professionals	Library related all subjects	Not given	September 27, 2010	LIS professional	Easy	Good	Yes (Search facility)

CONCLUSION

In this study, different Internet resources have been evaluated using different criteria developed for this purpose and found that maximum internet resources on the subject meet criteria such as authority, navigation, layout and other but not having criteria viz. purpose, objectivity and scope and large number of the Internet resources were not found up to date and suffers on the currency aspect. Thus, it is suggested that internet resources on marketing of library services should regularly update along with other trustworthy indicators in order to provide latest information to the users.

REFERENCES

1. Reichardt, R. and Harder, G. (2005). Weblogs: their use and application in science and technology libraries. *Science & Technology Libraries*, 25(3), 105-16 available at http://stlq.info/blogstl.pdf (accessed on May 10, 2009).
2. Smith, A.G. (1997). Testing the surf: criteria for evaluating Internet information resources. *Public-Access Computer System Review*,8(3),1-14.
3. Middleton, M. R. et.al. (1999). Internet site evaluation tool: students professional practice experience works towards the development of an Internet tool. *Education for Library and Information Services: Australia*, 16(2),15-17.
4. Fritch, J.W. and Cromwell, R.L (2001).Evaluating internet resources: identity, affiliation and cognitive authority in a networked world. *Journal of the American Society for Information and Technology*, 52(6),499-5
5. Bauer, C. and Scharl, A. (2000). Quantitive evaluation of Web site content and structure. *Internet Research*, 10 (1),31 - 44.
6. Austria, J.L.(2007). Developing evaluation criteria for podcasts. *Libri*,57(4),179-207.

11

Education Without Boundary in Digital Era; E-learning

Chandresh A. Shah

ABSTRACT

The cope with the rapid change of technology and to control the ephemeral rate of information generation, librarians along with their professional colleagues need to equip themselves as per the requirement of the electronic information society.

E-Learning is purely based on computer and communication technologies. The terminologies like computer based learning. It is the delivery of content via all electronic media through Internet, Intranet, Extranets television broadcast, CD-Rom documents, etc. E-learning poses lot of issues in the transformation of literature or knowledge from the conventional medium to ICT based format and web based services. The management system, user services and information literacy programs, learning environment -etc. of the libraries as well as users need to be totally changed to effectively address through E-Learning programmed.

Key Words: E-Learning, Digital libraries, on line learning

INTRODUCTION

E-learning is becoming an influential force in every faculty of education today. The development of Information and Communication technologies (ICT) has made remarkable changes not only in learning but in education at large including e-learning .The web is becoming a dominant technology where people have access to it (keegan,2002).E-learning means learning material hosted at one place can be accessed globally from may places. Great adaptability to the needs of the learner, more variety in learning experience, repeatability of the learning environment

WHAT IS E-LEARNING? (K.NATARAJAN-2010)

E-Learning is learning which takes place as a result of experiences and interaction in an internet environment. It is not restricted to a regular school day and can take place in a variety of locations including home, school and_community location e.g. libraries, cafes etc. e-learning refers to anything delivered, enabled, or mediated by electronic technology for the explicit purpose of learning. Basically, e-learning refers to use of information and communication Technology in education management. The letter 'e' in e-learning stands for "electronic" version of learning. The use of e-learning in academic activities is of two kinds namely online learning and offline learning, which are based on individual student and group of student based learning.

The similarly we can include the following term for the e-learning.

- Virtual learning
- Distributed learning
- Web-based learning
- Computer-based learning
- Online learning

The other part of the meaning of the e-learning is a term the covers many approaches. which have in common the use of ICT.E-learning is a technique of delivering educational content through Digital

Interactive Television ,Video-conferencing, audio-conference ,internet, intranet, www, Video-Audio tapes, CD/DVD Etc.

Finally, we can divide the E-learning in the two types,

- Synchronous E-Learning.
- Asynchronous E-Learning.

HISTORY OF E-LEARNING

The history of e-Learning can categorized in the following stages;

- Instructed-led Training Era (Pre -1983)
- Multimedia Era (1984-1993)
- First Wave E-Learning (1994-1999)
- Second Wave E-Learning (2000 Onwards)

OBJECTIVES OF E-LEARNING

- Distance education provided the base for E-learning's development.
- All students and teachers will have access to information technology in their classrooms, schools, communities, and homes
- All teachers will use technology effectively to help students achieve high academic standards.
- Research and evaluation will improve the next generation of technology applications for teaching and learning.
- Digital content and networked applications will transform teaching and learning.
- All students will have technology and information literacy skills.

CHARACTERISTICS OF E-LEARNING

The important characteristics E-Learning are given below;

- Immediacy
- Permanency

- Situating of instructional activities
- Accessibility
- Interactivity
- Adaptability

TECHNOLOGIES USED IN DELIVERING E-LEARNING

- Print (texts ,study, guides)
- Audio (Streamed, tapes)
- Video (streamed, video, cable T.V.)
- Data(Web pages, Online tests, Surveys and interactive tools)
- Asynchronous (E-mail. List serves, Web Forums, News groups)
- Synchronous (Chat, shares white boards, Teleconferencing video conferencing)

ADVANTAGES OF E-LEARNING

E-learning lessons are generally designed to guide students through information of help students perform in specific tasks. Information based e-learning content communicates information to the student. E-learning provides the following major advantages to the users.

- Reducing environmental impact
- Access to quality education
- Improved performance
- Increased access
- Convenience and flexibility to learners
- Affordable education
- Reducing overall cost
- Consistent Instruction

PRINCIPALS FOR ONLINE LEARNING

The following summary of principals for online learning and general design tips that help to engage learners in an online tutorial.

- Contiguity
- Multimedia
- Modality
- Redundancy
- Personalization

ISSUES AND CHALLENGES OF E-LEARNING IN DIGITAL ERA

Most of the libraries in India can be grouped under the Hybrid libraries category, wherein you have the conventional and electronic resources to meet the requirements of its users, communication and data transfer or interchange has become easy with the help of Internet and email attachments.

The issues of E-learning can be categorized as under.

- Copyright issues
- Psychological Issues
- Demography issues
- Sociological Issues
- Technological Issues
- Geographical Issues

CONCLUSION

E-learning allows for efficient transfer of knowledge in real time process, while at the same time empowering learner with the information technology awareness and skills crucial to succeed in the present Knowledge Revolution era.

E-learning is an important method of delivering Information Literacy Programmes and it is used by many library as well as institutions and information professionals as a way of supporting students on-campus and distance learning. E-learning offers the opportunity to different countries to work-together and to develop their own knowledge Society, through virtual communities.

REFERANCES

1. K.vanangamudi and K.Natarajan(2010);E-leaning; an experience, Pub; Agrobios ,jodhpur.
2. Keegan,D(2002)."The Future of learning;from e-learning to m-learning, information Analysis; Opinion papers.
3. Lehtinen,E.et al." Computer supported collaborative learning; A review "The J.H.G.I. Giesbers Reports on education,No.10.The Netherlands; University of Nijmegen.1999.
4. Open distance Learning quality Council (ODLDC),news letter.oct.2001.2nd july, 2012<http;//www.odlqc/in/20-c
5. Srivedi. T.R. "E-learning;A Review on the current Practices in higher edu.Insti." SALIS,9-11 Aug,2007;59-62.

12

The Digital Library: Myths, Concept and Structure

Dr Kanchan Kamila

ABSTRACT

Discusses the myths concerned with the term 'digital library' (DL), concept of DL in the true sense and structure of DL and concludes that advantages of DL will depend not only on topics traditionally dealt with by computer scientists, but also on superb engineering for human usability

Keywords : Digital Library, Myths, Structure, Resource Managers, Application Enablers

1. INTRODUCTION

Librarians and information professionals are going to progress into the 21st century then a clear and effective "digital library" model for library services and development will be increasingly important. An increasingly complex technological, social, legal, and economic environment defines many boundaries within which "digital library" services will evolve.

Librarians may discover that "libraries-without-walls" are actually only libraries with new walls – technologically bounded, legally restricted, and administratively hamstrung. The "digital library" may be equally impenetrable and as profoundly limiting to their patrons as the physical library which techno-pundits would suggest digital collections are intended to replace.

Exposing some myths about digital libraries sets the stage for a closer examination of the significant challenges to "digital library" development.

Myth 1: The Internet is the digital library.

The word "library" has been appropriated by many different groups to signify simply a collection of digital objects that people can access from their desktops – digital objects like electronic documents, and digitized pictures, sound, and video.

A global information network, of which the Internet is the seed, has the illusion of promising fingertip access to the world's information. A fairly spectacular example of what many people consider to be a digital library today is the World Wide Web. The Web is a gathering of thousands and thousands of documents. Many would call this huge collection of documents a "digital library" because they can read and use whatever they wish by accessing the Web, just as one can use technology to do banking in a "digital bank" or buy compact discs in a "digital record store".

But is this a "digital library"? In reality, the Internet and the World Wide Web are to libraries what a fleamarket is to the Library of Congress. For many common library requests, locating information on the Internet remains highly inefficient compared to traditional library sources, especially for unfamiliar users. Finding information is difficult, the quality of the information is quite variable, and reliable, professional assistance for the confused and lost is lacking.

Myth 2: The myth of a single digital library or one-window view of digital library collections.

Nicholas Negroponte, a guru of the digital cognoscenti, has called for the U.S. Congress to pass a "digital deposit" act to change the Library of Congress from a "depository" to a "retrievatory". His vision of the library is one where a "Library of Progress could be in the pockets of tomorrow's kids" and where citizens can get electronic access to a library without-walls where information is accessible anywhere and anytime. (Negroponte, 1995)

The challenges to this vision? Despite the utopianism of Negroponte's view, even modest moves towards increasing digital collections and services will be strongly affected by future copyright and licensing regimes, as well as prohibitive costs for digitization and support of technical infrastructure.

But more importantly, the digital future will be an unruly one composed of multiplicity of competing information providers. Libraries will be only one source of information. "Prime" information resources will probably be locked into proprietary collections – essentially "private digital libraries" which are accessible on a subscription or pay-per use basis. Developing interoperability standards for locating and retrieving information in this highly distributed and heterogeneous environment will be a considerable challenge in their own right.

Myth 3: Digital libraries will provide more equitable access, anywhere, any time.

A great deal of work must be done to turn this myth into reality. We can assume that a global computer network – the Internet or some descendant – will be the primary delivery mechanism for digital information. Equitable access is currently compromised by the fact that the Internet is not as ubiquitous as the computing press would have us believe. There are relatively few connections outside the more populated centers, the costs of access can remain high, and for the vast majority of the world's population in developing countries, having widespread Internet access may be the equivalent of walking on the moon.

Myth 4: Digital libraries will be cheaper than print libraries.

A common assumption among technology reporters about the costs of "digital libraries" is that digital is cheaper than paper. This contention is far from established in fact or in practice. Although many libraries project savings, especially when substitution strategies are used which replace selected serials titles with document delivery services, the cost/benefit analysis of making this switch remains unclear. In some cases, the switch to electronic serials may save the library money by offsetting the cost to users who must pick up the charge for document delivery.

Interplay between Commercial and Academic Activity

To understand what Digital Library (DL) technology is already available and what needs attention, it is helpful to remember that in this area commercial activity began more or less at the same time as academic activity. Commercial products already address some component classes identified later in the paper. The commercial presence is signaled by promotional material which claims:

> "DL offers the most advanced information management system available today. [It] is ... for large integrated collections of textual and image information and ... even an inexperienced researcher can use it effectively the first time.

"DL meets the growing need for document storage and retrieval through integration of optical storage, scanning and optical character recognition, powerful but inexpensive desktop computers efficiently networked, [etc.]. DL technology is currently being used by:

- Kiosk systems for public information
- Public utilities to manage regulatory correspondence
- Law firms for litigation support and ... knowledge systems
- Newspapers for electronic archives
- Engineers for their technical documentation
- Pharmaceutical firms to support approval testing
- Law enforcement agencies

- Publishers of scholarly journals for CD-ROM distribution
- Universities for full-text books, multi-media manuscripts, periodicals, and catalogs

"DL features include:

- Intelligent search and relevance-ranked retrieval
- Heuristic, expert search assistance
- Text, data, image, and video-clip support
- Hypertext and access to external collections
- Access via fill-in-the-blank forms and [other common paradigms]
- Printing, sorting, access control, session logging, and [other utility functions]
- Call interfaces for embedded reuse in other applications
- Portability across many operating systems.

2. *WHAT IS A DIGITAL LIBRARY?*

The NSF/ARPA/NASA *Digital Library Initiative, FY 1994* (Digital Library Initiative, 1994) states:

"Information sources accessed via the Internet are ingredients of a digital library. Today, the network connects some information sources that are a mixture of publicly available (with or without charge) information and private information shared by collaborators. They include reference volumes, books, journals, newspapers, national phone directories, sound and voice recordings, images, video clips, scientific data (raw data streams from instruments and processed information), and private information services such as stock market reports and private newsletters. These information sources, when connected electronically through a network, represent important components of an emerging, universally accessible, digital library."

DL workshop report (Fox, 1993) defines:

"A digital library is a distributed technology environment which dramatically reduces barriers to the creation, dissemination, manipulation, storage, integration, and reuse of information by individuals and groups."

A ***digital library*** is a machine readable representation of materials which might be found in a university library together with organizing information intended to help users find specific information. ***A digital library service*** is an assemblage of digital computing, storage, and communications machinery together with the software needed to reproduce, emulate, and extend the services provided by conventional libraries based on paper and other material means of collecting, storing, cataloguing, finding, and disseminating information. A full service digital library must accomplish all essential services of traditional libraries and also exploit digital storage, searching, and communication.

Public, private, professional, school, commercial, and other kinds of library emphasize different services, different kinds of information, and different service styles. While any digital library instance may thus offer only partial services, the technology suite from which library instances are assembled must permit assembly of a full service library. In addition, this suite must shield the user who wishes to draw on multiple libraries from inter-library differences which are irrelevant to him.

What distinguishes a conventional library from a heap of things to read is organization provided by someone other than the authors of the collected materials. For a small, private collection this could be shelf organization; for a large collection it is typically a descriptive catalogue (*descriptive information in 3"x5" catalogue card*) which is distinct from the collection, with at least one catalog record associated with each item held.

Not every database (*information collection or knowledge database*) is a library, but every library is a database. What distinguishes a library from an arbitrary database are certain data integrity and security rules that constitute an implicit contract between custodians and users.

Organization can also be provided by citations, whose analog in a digital system are hypermedia links. Usually embedded citations are provided only by document authors, whereas catalog records are provided by librarians or other agents.

A few circumstances and characteristics for which I expect Digital Libraries to emulate conventional libraries holding books, pictures, and other material objects communicate the flavour intended:

- users are usually elsewhere than the information they want, and often want to correlate items from several sources;
- whoever wants to use a library must show permission to do so;
- different patrons are permitted different actions and to see different parts of each collection;
- the catalogue and the collected items are used differently and not necessarily housed in the same place;
- to find specific information, each user must understand the catalogue structure;
- the catalogue may describe items in other libraries;
- documents contain cross references to other documents;
- documents are catalogued with text descriptors and also with conventional properties, such as author names;
- document identifiers are different from document names; a document may have several names, one for each context, e.g., "Tales of Hoffmann" in English, "Les contes d'Hoffmann" in French, and "Hoffmanns Erzählungen" in German;
- translations of a document may express essentially the same information, e.g., versions of classic literature in different languages;
- each stored item is valuable, often with part of its residual value owned by its authors or authors' assignees;
- part of the value provided by a library is the provenance information it holds for each item;
- items are put into libraries because, while each is thought

valuable for future reference, the specific individuals who will read it and the times when this will occur are not known.

3. STRUCTURE OF DIGITAL LIBRARY

A "complete" library service will contain many components from which each installation selects a subset and each user draws on an even smaller set. We need a distributed computing infrastructure and a framework for such components. Part of such a framework is provided by the concepts *resource manager* and *application enabler*, which are well known to architects of distributed computing services. Since they seem to be outside the experience of at least part of the digital library community we summarize them below. The concept of a resource manager will be seen to embrace notions from object-oriented computing and from client-server computing. A very similar notion has been implemented in such advanced information retrieval systems as CODER (Fox, 1987 and Fox and France, 1987). Given suitable operating system and communication services, all distributed computing services can be built as a set of application programs, application enablers, and resource managers, with only the resource managers directly invoking operating system and communication services.

Resource Managers and Application Enablers

A protected resource is the combination of a persistent data collection and a set of programs which define its semantics. To define the data semantics with absolute integrity, this program set must constitute the only access path to the data; it is called a *resource manager*. Services such as authentication, file subsystems, network directory services, database management systems, and digital library components can all be constructed as resource managers.

We have in mind a network of mutually supportive resource managers, each providing a relatively specialized service. Each resource manager distributes itself for remote applications and accesses any needed sibling acting as a user, i.e., using the sibling's client interface. Whether sibling service is local or remote is transparent; exploiting propinquity is regarded as a network optimization issue.

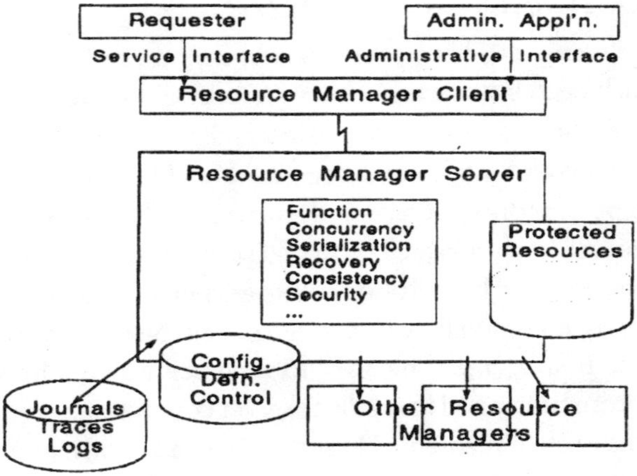

Fig. 1. Resources and resource management in a computing service network

Any encapsulated database can be contained in a set of resource managers; the storage subsystem of a digital library service is one example.

A resource manager is a service which combines state and processes and is accessible to multiple, concurrent clients (Figure 1). To qualify and be used as a resource manager, the program set and the data it manages (the protected resource) should satisfy the following criteria:

- The resource manager programs provide the only access path to the protected data, and therefore define and implement its semantics. (Practical systems always permit someone to bypass this proper access path, e.g., for data backup and recovery; alternative paths need to be protected by physical and administrative means if the data are to be safe.)
- Typically, the protected data are highly structured, possibly consisting of well- defined objects. Typically each protected resource consists of many such entities, called *items (object properties associated with object orientation).*

- The resource manager provides distributed access, doing so by having client and server portions connected by a private protocol. That the protocol is private distinguishes the resource manager approach from one based on open protocols, which must be standardized to be effective.
- To the extent consistent with achieving good performance and with practical aspects of software production and distribution, each resource manager avoids reproducing services that it can efficiently get from other resource managers. For instance, a library catalog manager could exploit a database manager, invoking it just as any other database manager client would.
- A resource manager often serves as an *access control enforcement function (AEF)* between a request initiator and a target, in the sense called for in international standards (International Organization for Standardization, 1988).
- As well as access control, a quality resource manager provides various data integrity protections, such as those called the ACID (Atomicity, Consistency, Integrity, Durability) properties (Gray and Reuter, 1993).

Thus each service instance encapsulates its own data within a cocoon – a form of object-oriented programming which is not necessarily bound to any particular programming language. There typically will be many instances of each kind of protected resource, with its associated resource manager defining the resource class, e.g., Network File Systems (NFS), DB2 databases, X.500 directories, X-windows services. Library content is a protected resource in the sense intended, and the library procedures defining access to the content constitute a resource manager. Resource managers are generic services.

Not all generic services need to provide network distribution or to hold data if they can do so indirectly by invoking resource managers. Services such as editors, filters, formatters, and other generic software constitute a class called *application enablers*. The purpose of such enablers is to make application programming easy and quick, or, optimally, avoidable entirely. Just as resource managers can be modularized by having each exploit other resource managers, application enablers can be cascaded. Figure 2 suggests how applications, application enablers, and resource managers can be layered to exploit layered open communications and to hide irrelevant operating system and machine differences.

What makes the modularization implicit in this model feasible today (it wasn't affordable until very recently) are the dramatic improvements in digital performance and costs already seen and yet to come. In addition, the *transport layer interface* depicted in the communication portion of Figure 2 allows the lower communication layers to choose efficient paths independently of how each resource manager calls communications (see Figure 1). For example, in one extant implementation (Gladney, 1993) the transport layer detects the occasions when the client and server happen to be in the same machine and uses local operating system services for inter-process communications; for the library application, the performance is close enough to what would be achieved by combining the client and server into a single program.

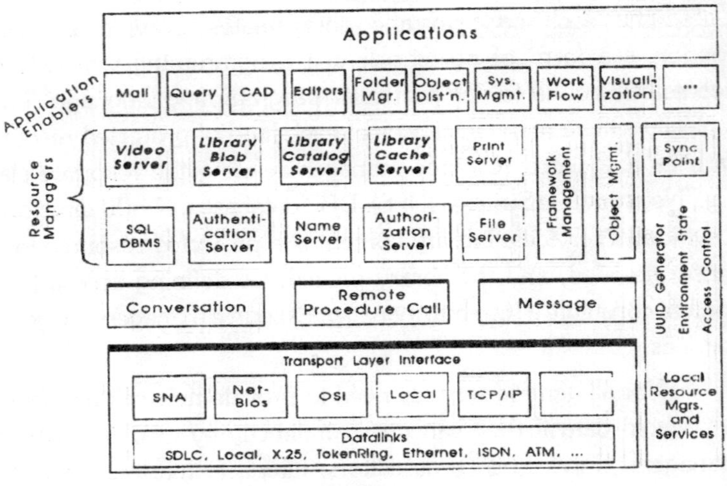

Fig. 2. Distributed data service software

Figure 2 displays Distributed data service software = operating system software + communications software + resource managers + application enablers: four digital library components are depicted with bold face.

Document Storage Subsystem and Document Servers

Document storage and access software can be realized in two layers above a base of file systems and database managers (See Figure 3). The lower one is a storage subsystem which stores and retrieves items to and from each library collection, updates and searches library catalog records, and limits who can manipulate which data – giving only services which are identical for all types of documents. Instances of the higher layer, which we call *document managers*, help applications or end users with their special kinds of documents and varied forms of presentation and manipulation.

The distinction between the document storage subsystem layer, which would be implemented as a set of resource managers, and document managers, which would be implemented as application enablers, deserves more careful articulation. Part of its reason is that we expect the storage subsystem layer to be difficult for most users to change or substitute, and document managers being made relatively accessible and malleable.

The storage subsystem limits its services to aspects which do not depend on the meaning or representation of items. With at most limited exceptions, items it delivers to requesting applications are faithful copies of items other applications stored (partial document access is commonly wanted, and sometimes transformations which improve presentation without adding information are valuable.). The storage subsystem manages data placement and replication, implements custodial responsibilities for data security, and hides irrelevant network and other environmental dependencies to the extent possible. It is convenient to think of its application programming interface in three parts: a query interface, intended primarily for identifying items of interest to a browser, should allow whatever inquiries do not violate item owners' confidentiality desires; a retrieval interface should deliver items with whatever timing and buffering is consistent with the data kind at hand and with the users responsiveness and cost objectives; and update interfaces for the library catalog and collection should enforce articulated policies for library data integrity and quality. Since searches for information may well depend on databases that are not part of what the librarian has chosen to include in the formal library catalog, the storage subsystem should also support queries which combine internal and external databases (This need is not commonly recognized, and is very difficult to satisfy as broadly as library patrons will want.). In summary, the document storage subsystem provides retention and catalog services and manages inter-machine communications, hiding them to the extent possible. Its implementation follows a client-server approach.

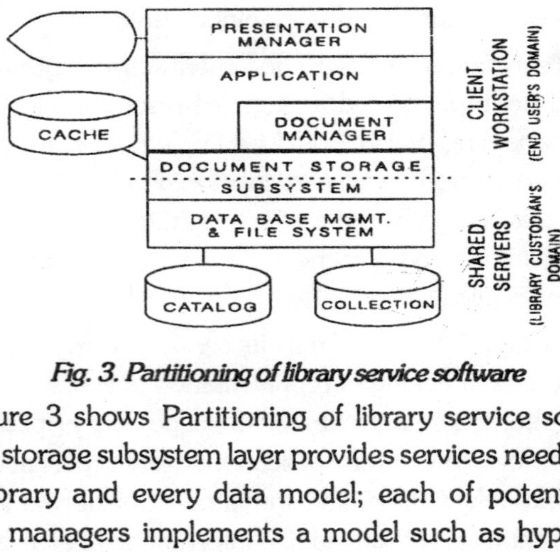

Fig. 3. Partitioning of library service software

Figure 3 shows Partitioning of library service software the document storage subsystem layer provides services needed by every kind of library and every data model; each of potentially many document managers implements a model such as hypertext or a service wanted by many enterprises. Application programs are workstation programs; the storage subsystem embeds needed inter-process communications.

To provide enough flexibility for all possible applications, the document storage subsystem interface is likely to have many primitive operators, making it somewhat difficult to program for ad hoc applications. This can be overcome with document managers which implement broadly interesting information access methods. For example, we see Mosaic (Hahn and Stout, 1994) as a document manager. The storage subsystem attempts comprehensive coverage of functional requirements in its domain; good document managers would offer less flexibility and fewer options, but would be much easier to explain and understand.

More generally, document managers give those services which vary among access occasions because different document types need different presentation and manipulation and because users have different objectives and preferences. Document editing, transformation, combination, and presentation, and other complex manipulations are conveniently implemented as document managers. In the architecture suggested by Figure 3, document managers execute in users' workstations.

Thus, in a practical system, each of many document managers embodies a *document model* – the set of concepts that create the digital analog of some collection of papers or other physical objects, or some information network invented for a particular application, such as hypertext (Haan et.al., 1992), or some flow of documents through a series of routine steps. In contrast, the document storage subsystem layer avoids modelling. Typical document managers interpret scanned data to create catalog entries automatically, manage interrelationships among documents, facilitate the most common search methods, and help move information among workers. For instance:

- A folder manager might include a scanning service for memoranda, letters, contracts, and financial records; such a manager would extract names, addresses and dates to cross-index information received (Malone et. al., 1987) and associate each document with a folder.
- A second document manager might manage moving pictures; it would communicate with its users in terms of movies, reels, and frames and depend on a storage subsystem with video delivery channels.

- A third document manager might feature CAD and be applied to maintenance records of university buildings; it would generate and display building plans with a graphic editor and maintenance contracts with a customized text editor.
- A fourth document manager might model what is found in a university library –books and pamphlets with individually viewable pages, loose collections of papers in folders, manuscripts, video tapes, and so on.

Generic document managers for applications like geographic information systems, and enterprise-specific ones administering conventions and document quality standards, may evolve over time. While a good document manager would support most library services in its domain, the storage subsystem interface is exposed to allow other applications to bypass document managers.

4. CONCLUSIONS

The potential advantages of a digital library over a paper library are similar to those of any digital database over its paper counterpart: faster addition to the data collection with better quality control, improved search functionality and faster access to information found, but also more freedom and reduced bureaucracy for individual users.

Achieving these advantages will depend not only on topics traditionally dealt with by computer scientists, but also on superb engineering for human usability.

REFERENCES

1. *Digital Library Initiative, FY 1994.* (1993). A joint initiative of the National Science Foundation, the Advanced Research Projects Agency, and the National Aeronautics and Space Administration, U.S. Government document NSF, 93-141.
2. Fox, E. (1987). Development of the CODER System: A TestBed for Artificial Intelligence Methods in Information Retrieval. *IPM*, 23(4), 341-366.
3. Fox, E. (1993). Digital Libraries. *IEEE Computer*, 26(11), 79-81.
4. Fox, E. and France, R. (1987). Architecture of an Expert System for Composite Document Analysis, Representation and Retrieval. *International Journal of Approximate Reasoning*, 1(2), 151-175.

5. Gladney, H.M. (1993). A Storage Subsystem for Image and Records Management. *IBM Systems Journal*, 32(3), 512-540. Part of what this paper describes has been realized in commercial products.

6. Gray, J. and Reuter, A. (1993). *Transaction Processing: Concepts and Techniques.* San Mateo, California: Morgan Kaufman Publishers.

7. Haan, B.J., et. al. (1992). IRIS Hypermedia Services. *Comm. ACM*, 35(1), 36-51.

8. Hahn, H. and Stout, R. (1994). *The Internet Complete Reference*, Berkeley, California: Osborne McGraw-Hill. Mosaic was written by M. Andreessen of the National Center for Super Computer Applications (NCSA) at the University of Illinois.

9. International Organization for Standardization. (1988). *Open Systems Interconnection, Reference Model, Part 2: Security Architecture*, ISO 7498-2. Geneva, Switzerland.

10. Malone, T.W. et. al. (1987). *Intelligent Information Sharing Systems.* Comm. ACM, 30(5), 390-402, 1987.

11. Nicholas Negroponte. (1995). "A Bill of Writes." *Wired.* 1995.

13

Expert Systems – Impact on Library Services

N. Santhi

ABSTRACT

Expert system represent one of the most advanced facets of Information Technology. In simple terms, an expert system stores large amount of data and disseminate it in a systematic way as required by the users. Generally, structure of an expert system consists of Facts and Heuristics. A model expert system consists of the following: Knowledge Base; Knowledge Acquisition; User Interface; Inference Engine; Explanation facility; and External Interface. The chapter deals with concept of expert systems and its impact on library services. The application of expert systems proved to be effectively useful and convenient for performing these functions like Circulation of Books and Periodicals; Reference Service; Selective Dissemination of Information (SDI); Current Awareness Service(CAS); Indexing and Abstracting Services. Further, it helps to save the time of the users.

Keywords: Knowledge Base, Knowledge Acquisition, User Interface.

INTRODUCTION

The industrial revolution led the society towards mechanization and automation. Invention of computer is a great contribution of the industrial revolution. Continuous Research and developments led the computer science to introduce Artificial Intelligence(AI) techniques. Artificial Intelligence is attempting to create machines that can replace physical as well as mental power and intelligence of human beings.

The AI techniques helped the computers to perform intelligent tasks such as diagnoses of diseases in medical science, solve differential equations in symbolic forms in Mathematics, automatic translation in Linguistics, Decision making in Management, analyse and design electronic circuits in Electronics etc.

The AI techniques include Natural Language Processing, Intelligent Retrieval from databases, Expert Consulting Systems, Theorem proving, Automatic programming and Robotics. The present article emphasis the impact of Expert Consulting Systems on Libraries and Information Services.

EXPERT SYSTEM

An Expert System is regarded as "the embodiment within a computer of a knowledge based component from an expert skill, in such a form that the system can offer intelligent advice or take an intelligent decision about a processing function. A desirable additional characteristic, which many would consider fundamental, is the capability of the systems on demand, to justify its own line of reasoning in a manner directly intelligible to the enquirer. The style adopted to attain these characteristics is 'rule based programming'.

In simple terms, an expert system stores large amount of data and disseminate it in a systematic way as required by the users.

Expert systems represent one of the most advanced facets of information technology. That is, they help the users in some of the most complex and least understood human information handling tasks like decision making, problem solving, diagnoses and learning. They perform it by storing a large amount of factual information on a subject areas together with lines of reasoning employed by human experts in that area.

Most of this material is supplied to the program at the time, it is written, but it also has facilities for adding to this base of information as it is applied in new situations. The subject expertise is provided initially by interviews, observations of successful practitioners on the subject.

STRUCTURE AND DESIGN OF EXPERT SYSTEMS

Generally, structure of an expert system consists of Facts and Heuristics. A model expert system consists of the following:

Knowledge Base; Knowledge Acquisition; User Interface; Inference Engine; Explanation facility; and External Interface.

The following figure indicate design of a model expert system:

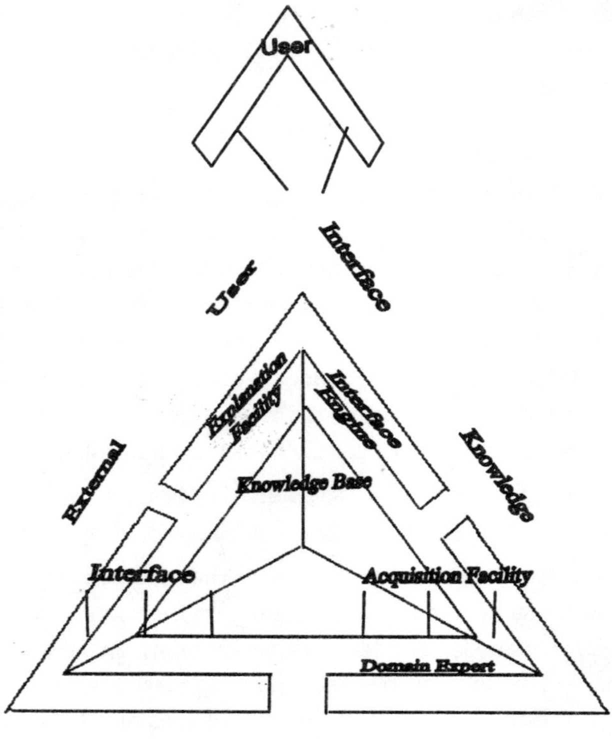

Knowledge Base

The core module of an expert system is Knowledge Base. It stores large amount of data relating to specific discipline. It represents knowledge through logic, frames, scripts, binary tables, semantic networks and on conceptual dependency. Such Knowledge representation deals with the structuring of the information, how to manipulate it to infer additional data and knowledge acquisition.

Knowledge Acquisition

The knowledge represented in the knowledge base has to be acquired from the subject experts. Subject experts make decisions based on qualitative and quantitative information. The expert has to translate the standard procedures and more difficult experience based heuristics into a form suitable for the expert system.

User Interface

It provides the user to communicate and interact with the system. An user normally interact with the system either for getting solutions to a problem, or to know the private knowledge(heuristics) of the system or for getting detailed explanations to specific queries. User may consult expert system for real world problems. The solutions, which an expert system gives is in the form of menus, graphics etc. Present day expert systems are not able to accept natural language from users, but the language, they will use for processing is very much user-friendly.

Inference engine

It is also called as "Rule Interpreter". The Inference Engine is that part of the program which reasons and determines how to apply the knowledge in the knowledge base to the queries presented at the user interface. The major task of the inference engine is to trace its way through a set of rules to arrive at a conclusion. The engine will trace the conclusion through forward chaining (Forward searching) or backward chaining (reverse searching). It reaches conclusion by firing rules. Firing of a rule causes two major things to happen:

- Triggers another rule, thereby a network of rules is triggered.
- Implies than an action has been carried out.

This adds new information to the database of inferred facts.

Explanation Facility

Getting answers to specific queries forms the explanation mechanism of an expert system. Explanation facility is actually a part of User Interface helps the user in the following ways:

- If the user is an expert, it helps in identifying what additional knowledge he is needed.
- Enhances the user's confidence in the system.
- Serves as a tutor in sharing the system's knowledge with the user.

External Interface

This provides the communication link between the expert system and the external environment. When there is a formal consultation, it is done through the user interface. The external interface with its sensors get the minute by minute information about the situation and acts accordingly. The real time expert systems are formed as part of the closed loop system. Such real time expert system are of immensely useful in industrial process controls, in nuclear plants, in supersonic jet fighters.

The communication subsystem, that is a part of the external interface, permits the system to communicate with a global database for its operation. The facts that have been inferred by the inference procedure are recorded in the global database called black board. Blackboard system contains:

- A global database from which different knowledge sources acquire data.
- A variety of knowledge sources
- A scheduler to control and coordinate the activity.

With the information in the Blackboard, different knowledge sources, which are in the production rule format get activated. The scheduler controls the sequence of execution of rules and every time a rule is fired, the result is saved in the blackboard. In this way, system proceeds to function. For performing these activities the system should have a good communication facility.

Another important constituent of the external interface is the Database Management System (DBMS). The DBMS serves as an archive for all the consultations, the system had with the user. The records of consultations will help in determining the scope of the information needed and disseminate the same.

The following is a list of systems that were developed to perform specific application:

CADUCEUS: It is Medical Expert system, and consists of programs that evaluate over 4,000 symptoms.

PROSPEKTOR: It advises on geological information

ALACRITY: It is a PC based expert system. It consists of 3,000 rules to provide expert advice on financial analysis and projections/

MACYSMA: It is developed for solving mathematical, scientific and engineering problems.

XPS-E: This system is developed for Production Planning.

EXPERTAX: It comprises 2,000 rules to advice on Tax Planning.

SRL: It is specialized in production control.

IMPACT OF EXPERT SYSTEMS ON LIBRARY AND INFORMATION SERVICES

Usually, an user will visit the library or Information Centre for the following purposes:

- To borrow books;
- To refer/borrow journals;
- To get information, he/she is needed.

As per the requirements of the users, the libraries and information centres provide following services:

1. Circulation of books and journals;
2. Reference service;

3. Selective Dissemination of Information (SDI);
4. Current Awareness Service (CAS);
5. Indexing and Abstracting Services.

The application of expert systems proved to be effectively useful and convenient for performing these functions. Expert system ease these functions as under:

Circulation of Books and Periodicals

Expert system would display a list of books and journals along with detailed bibliographic details. Further it is useful for recording issue and return of books accurately. It helps to locate specific book required by user through fast searching of circulation and accession records. It also displays about new arrivals of books and articles in journals on a pinpointed subject. Expert system also guide the user regarding searching for information needs. Expert systems also helps in maintaining library techniques such as classification and cataloguing.

Reference Service

It is a kind of service, where the Reference Librarian, or an Information Scientist answer and clarifies the users' queries by referring various information sources such as Encyclopaedias, Dictionaries, Catalogues, Biographies, Yearbooks, etc.

As already discussed, an expert system stores a large amount of information in Knowledge Base and answer to the users' queries through User Interface. The explanation facility helps the user to know more about the facts.

Selective Dissemination of Information

SDI is a service through which a retrospective search of large number of documents is made to get information on a micro topic in a discipline. It is very useful service for Research scholars and Scientists.

For instance, a Research Scholar who conduct research on Benchmarking in Management require SDI service. The librarian searches books, periodicals, information sources etc and provide a list of references to the Researcher. Now-a-days computers are being used for providing this service.

SDI is having two components Viz.

a) A Document database, which consists of information on books, periodicals etc.

b) User profile is a list of users who want information as per their varied requirements.

The matching function helps to supply the required information to the respective user.

An expert system helps to store large amount of the data and retrieves the same to the right user. The explanation facility is useful for getting detailed information on a topic.

Current Awareness Service

Through CAS an user can get the latest development in his/her area of interest. This service is given to the users to refresh the knowledge. Now, CAS is provided through current contents, circulation of books catalogues etc.

If an expert system is applied for providing this service, it explains about the information newly acquired, to the users.

Indexing and Abstracting

An Index provides information about the articles published in the various periodicals giving full bibliographical details such as author, title of the article, name of periodical, volume No., year of publication etc.

An abstract provides information regarding the articles published in various documents furnishing full bibliographical details along with brief summary(abstract) of the articles.

When the information about the published articles stores in Knowledge Base of an expert system, it helps to retrieve the bibliographical details of the articles along with abstract. In this way, it is useful for indexing and abstracting.

CONCLUSION

Even though technology made such a progress, the information society lagged behind. This is so because of the "Various challenges due to the lack of Information Professionals' skills Information Management skills and Up to date subject knowledge."

Therefore, now it is the duty of an information professional to know about the following:

- Information regarding development in technology
- Information needs of users
- Ability to collect and store information in computer and expert systems systematically
- Effective presentation,publication and retrieval skills
- Ability to evaluate information
- Methods of disseminating information

If the latest technological skills like expert systems applied for providing information services, the work of information professionals will become convenient, systematic and easy. Further, it helps to save the time of the users.

REFERENCES

1. Patterson, DW . (1990). Introduction to Artificial Intelligence and Expert Systems. New Delhi: Prentice Hall of India.
2. Janakiraman, V.S. and others. (1993). Foundations of Artificial Intelligence and Expert Systems. New Delhi, Macmillan India Ltd.
3. Johri, Amit and Janhari, B.S. (1993). Computer Today. Vol.1. Mumbai, Himalaya Publishing House, 1993.
4. Basandra, S.K. (1992). Computer for Managers, New Delhi, Global Business Press.
5. Laudon, Kenneth C. and Laudon, Jane P. (1999). Essentials of Management Information Systems. New Jersey: Prentice Hall of India.
6. Sadagopan, S. (1998). Management Information Systems. New Delhi: Prentice Hall of India.

14
Digital Libraries Development

Barada Kanta Mohanty

ABSTRACT

Information and Communication Technology has revolutionized the concept of libraries. As a matter of fact and looking to the greater demand and enthusiasm developed in this new generation each and every library is now-a-days getting digitized. A 'digital library' comprises of digital collections, services and infrastructure to support lifelong learning, research, scholarly communication as well as preservation and conservation of recorded knowledge. It is also a process of democratization of information.

Keywords: Digital library, Digitization, Digital libraries development.

INTRODUCTION

Digital library is a library which has all information in electronic formats. It provides an excellent opportunity to widely disseminate our documentary heritages and greatly increases access to library collections of rare documents as well as current research literature. The rapid growth of Internet and the increasing interest in development of digital library related technologies and collections accelerate the volume of digitization of printed documents. These large volumes of Digitized documents are made accessible online either through intranet or Internet channels to the end users to satisfy their information needs.

The term Digital Library has a variety of potential meanings, ranging from a digitized collection of material that one might find in a traditional library through to the collection of all digital information along with the services that make that information useful to all possible users. As there are many definitions of a "digital library," terms such as "electronic library" and "virtual library" are often used synonymously. A digital library is nothing but a large database for the people who are working on hypertext environment. It is an environment, which supports the full life cycle of creation, storage, preservation, dissemination and use of data, information and knowledge.

DIGITAL LIBRARY DEFINITION

A digital library is a library in which collections are stored in digital formats (as opposed to print, microform, or other media) and accessible by computers. The digital content may be stored locally, or accessed remotely via computer networks. A digital library is a type of information retriev

Roots of Digital Libraries

DLs have evolved from and are based on the techniques and principles developed by the early IR researchers such as-

Calvin Mooers (1950)

Perry (1951)

Taube (1955)

Information Retrieval Systems of 1980s

Salton's Automatic indexing and search systems (1960s)

Hypertext systems of 1980s

Digital Library: origin and evolution

Amongst the earliest examples of pre-Web DL efforts were:

CMU's Project Mercury (1989-1992)

The TULIP project (1993-1995)

CORE (1995)

ENVISION (1993)

Digital Library Initiative

Beginning in 1992-93, The US Govt. agencies, NSF, DARPA, and others initiated the digital library efforts in the US with massive funding resulting in 6 major DL initiatives

Digital Library Initiative II (1998-2002)

E-Lib programme in the UK

AI system. – Wikipaedia

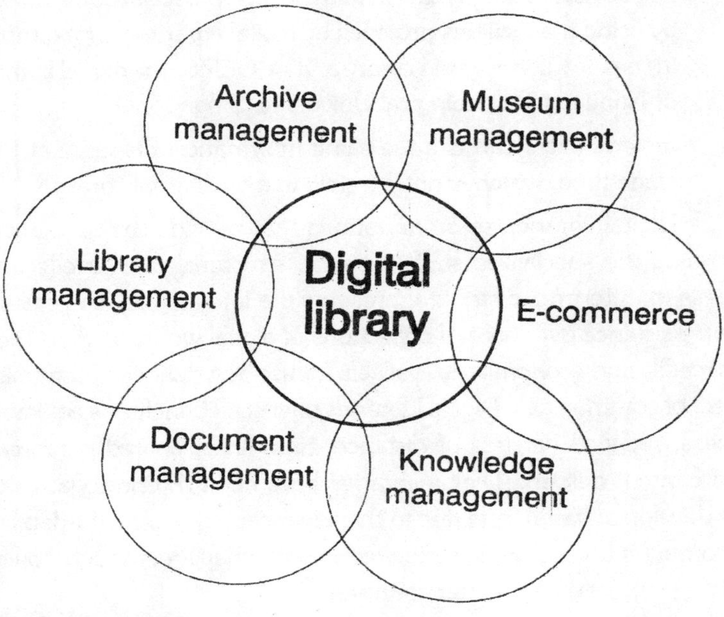

Digital library features

A digital library emphases the equitable and timely access to a vast access to a vast amount of diverse resources in a shared mode in a given specialty, lifting traditional barriers of time and space.

1. Digital library users may be distributed anywhere in the world and in some cases several different levels of services have to be designed to meet the needs of local as well as remote users.
2. Digital libraries are the digital counterparts of traditional libraries and include electronic (digital) as well as print and other (e.g. audio, video, graphics, animation etc) materials.
3. Digital library collections are not restricted to document surrogates but include digital.
4. A digital library has a unified organizational structure with consistent points for accessing the data.
5. Relation between digital libraries and information services are transparent to users.
6. Digital library users may build their own personal collection(s) by using the facilities provided by digital libraries, for example in the HeadLine hybrid library and in iGEMS, the digital library of Nanyang Technological University, Singapore.
7. Several users can use the same information resource at the same time, which is not possible in a traditional library.

Digital libraries as organizations that provide the resources, including the specialized staff, to select, structure, offer intellectual access to, interpret, distribute, preserve the integrity of, and ensure the persistence over time of collections of digital works so that, they are readily and economically available for use by a defined community or set of communities. Digital Libraries offer such benefits as equitable access, reduced barriers of distance, time lines, shared resources and content delivery. Digital libraries have been the prerogative of the developed world, and due to the advancements and affordability in computer and communication technology, they are, though slowly, getting importance in other countries.

Components of digital library: Regardless of whether the digital library has content by digitizing print medium or a collection of born-digital documents, building a digital library involves three following essential components. These 3 components essentially represent selection, access to collection and deliver information to users.

3 Essential Components of a Digital Library - Content, Delivery & Discovery

A. Content

The primary component of any digital library is of course, its content- it may be of born digital type or print converted to digital format. Whatever may be the case the quality of content should be appropriate to the purpose of setting digital library. Collection infrastructure consists of two components –Digital object & Metadata

Digital object - Compiling content into presentable collections is where librarianship shines. Collections are about the relationships between digitized objects; and librarians are specifically skilled to organize, describe, and present those relationships through the use of well-organized metadata. Collection development of Digital object involves the following steps -

1. Acquisition of collections available in digital formats: CDROM/ DVDROM. The Born Digital forms may be – Doctoral Thesis, Annual Report, Technical Report, Manual, In-house journal etc.
2. Conversion of existing print media into digital format. After scanning, Optical Character Recognition (OCR) software – Matrix (font based), Feature Extraction (structure & shape), Structural analysis (density gradation), Neural Networking (artificial intelligence) are used to make these fully digital form.
3. Metadata - For librarians just beginning their digital librarianship, metadata is synonymous with indexing, or cataloging, with the inclusion of technical information about the digital object itself

B. Delivery

Once a collection of digitized objects is compiled, it is to be delivered to library patrons. Delivery is the second essential element, and typically involves access to the collection either online through a web browser, or on a local machine through storage disks such as DVDs or CDs. Delivering collection online requires converting the digitization files and metadata into browser readable HTML. If collection is small and static, this could in theory be done through hand-coding the HTML in a text editor or program like Adobe's Dreamweaver. If collection is even fairly large, or you plan to add content to the digital library, it will need some type of delivery software. Delivery systems like D space, Greenstone, or E print automatically convert the metadata and digitization files of collection into HTML and manage changes to digital collection. These delivery systems available are called Digital Library Software. Some, like D space, Greenstone, are open-source; while others have commercial licenses. The available software varies greatly in its capabilities and features, so its important to match your content and project goals with digital library software that suits your collection well.

C. Discovery

This component is in addition and closely related to delivery component of a digital library. It is a way to discover the content within the digital library. Most digital library software will include indexing and search functionality. In addition to search, browsing is another popular discovery method. Browsing options generally use metadata categories, such as dates or titles, to organize and present the collection. The importance of an efficient discovery system is vital to any Digital Library. Search interfaces that are easy, intuitive, and fast returns really good impact to the value of the digital library. For many collections, especially text-based collections like newspapers, faceted search filters help users narrow search returns to quickly find what they're looking for. Also, pay particular attention to the search interface's speed and robustness. This plays a important role in the amount of time a user has to wait while the search interface assembles and displays the results. The faster the search interfaces the better, and as the collection grows, the results time should not be significantly impacted.

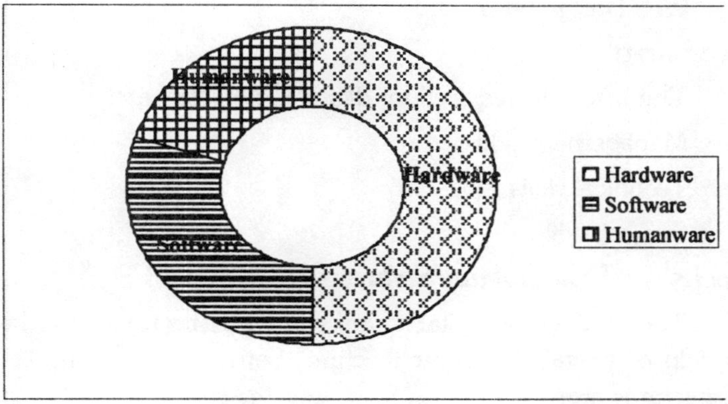

Hardware

1. Internet Connectivity
2. Computer servers
3. Scanners
4. Storage media: Hard disk tower and CDs
5. Digital camera
6. UPS
7. Converters
8. Networks
9. Multimedia interfaces

Software

1. Scanning of software
2. Adobe Acrobat reader
3. Optical Character recognition software
4. RDBMS(Relational database) which supporting the variety of Digital Databases like ORACLE, posgre SQL, My SQL etc.
5. Full Text Search engines to indent and provide access to digital resources.
6. Software: Comprises of operating software, LINUX

7. Web Designing S

Humanware

The key skills required for digital library staff are:

1. Management skills
2. Technical skills
3. Subject skills

Greenstone Digital Library Software

The concept of digital library can be better understood with the help of digital library architecture. Some of the digital library architectures are:

Architecture of greenstone digital library (GSDL)

Harvest

Architecture of NCSTRL (Networked Computer Science Report Library)

File structure

The Greenstone interface will accept different plugging (file extension like html, xml, ppt, doc and pdf etc.). The catalogue cards are represented by a simple HTML file by Greenstone. Each HTML file is associated with an XML file that contains the meta-data that Greenstone will be used in its indexing. Each HTML, XML file pair is placed in its own directory, whilst this helps to manage the data, this was mainly done because Greenstone requires the meta-data to have a specific file name, and for ease of managing this.

Steps involved in GSDL

- The collection configuration
- Creating user defined indexes or search index
- Building collection using GSDL

Greenstone digital Library

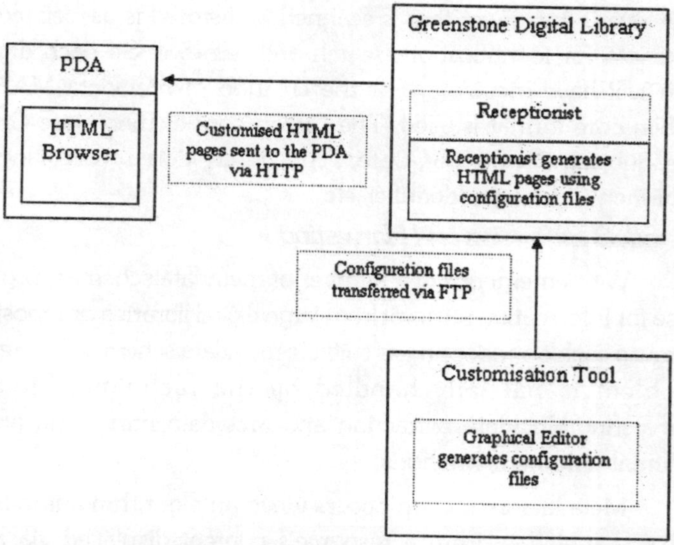

Digital library collection and development

In recent days the digital library process is rapidly changing and provides digital collections and services to their communities in a various ways. For developing the best possible systems for finding, identifying and using digital resources are distributed on the network. The digital resources are either deliberately created as a digital or created in parallel to print. Looking to this the Publishers are increasingly moving upward to XML or SGML format. In coming future digital libraries e-resources in electronic journals and electronic database and datasets would be in many formats.

Metadata : Metadata in its broadest sense is data about data. The process of metadata generation & maintenance in digital library development is very important. The traditional Catalogue is a form of metadata representation. Title, author, publisher, place of publication, year and etc are metadata for any printed document. With the card based cataloguing rules, from the ALA rules through

AACR2, each catalogue entry was a precise, unchangeable unit of the catalogue, a cell in a well-designed body. It involves with Conversion of existing print, audio and video in to digital format, then every document that is scanned and stored is associated with metadata for identification, search and retrieval. So each digitized item will have metadata. For the creation of metadata MARC or Dublin core format is used. The Dublin core elements are Creator, title, Subject, Contributor, Date, Type, description, source, language, publisher, Coverage, Identifier etc.

Metadata Extraction and Harvesting

With emergence of a number of metadata schemas, problems arise for information retrieval from large digital libraries or repositories because each one adopting its suitable metadata schema. This retrieval problem is partially handled by the technique Metadata Harvesting.Metadata extraction and Metadata harvesting are two different automatic methods.

Metadata extraction occurs when an algorithm automatically extracts metadata from a resource's content displayed via a Web browser. Metadata that are used for object representation are extracted from the resource content to produce structured ("labeled") metadata. These structured metadata are specific to Web resources and are extracted from the "body" section of a HTML or XHTML document.

Harvesting, the other automatic metadata generation method, occurs when metadata is automatically collected from META tags found in the "header" source code of an HTML resource or encoding form another resource format (e.g., Microsoft WORD documents). The "harvesting process" is dependent on the metadata provided by the content developer (humans) or by full or semi-automatic processes supported by web development software. For example, Web editing software(e.g. Dreamweaver and FrontPage) and selected document software (e.g., Microsoft WORD and Adobe) automatically produce metadata at the time of resource creation or updation. Metadata like, "format," "date of creation," "revision date," are automatically taken care by these software without human intervention. The software automatically converts the metadata to META tags (or other tag form depending on the document format) and places them in the resource header. These metadata not only aid searching, but can be harvested by a generator to create a structured metadata record.

The process of conversion of paper documents into digital format is mainly with the help of scanners. Printed text, pictures and figures are transformed in to computer accessible forms using a digital scanner or a digital camera.

Some of the important scanners being used for capturing digital images are.

- Kodak 5005
- HP scan jet 6300 C.
- Digital Camera-Zen ached Omani scan 3000 Minolta PS 3000,
- Microfilm Scanner-modekel m 500 SL, sunrise SRI-150

Storing

Digital resources can be stored in CD, DVD, Hard disk and tape. It is digitize will be in image, text, image and photographs after scanning is stores in the (joint photographic experts groups) JPEG and graphic interchange format (GIF). Basically two things can be used for storing of images taking into the size and can display the quality and size of the picture.

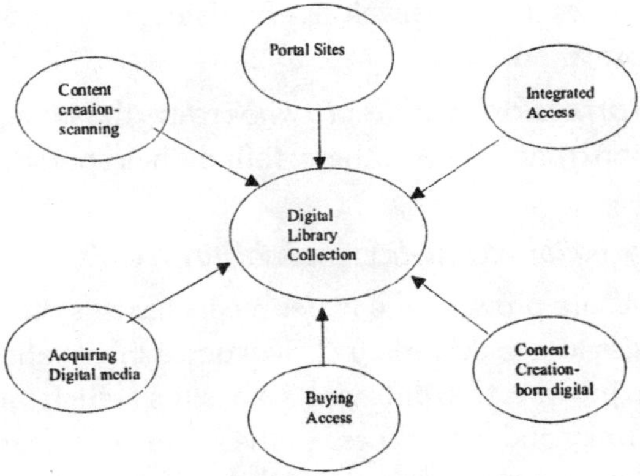

Fig. **Digital Collection Development**

Professional involvement in digital library development

Collection development

Organizing principles and techniques

Research and retrieval

User studies

End user training

Standards participation

Role of Digital Librarians

1. To handle the tasks of mass digitization, digital storage process and digital preservation.
2. To provide universal access and retrieval of digital knowledge, ultimately access to all
3. To disseminate digital information from computer-held digital information
4. To catalogue and classify digital documents and digital knowledge
5. To provide knowledge mining from the emerging knowledge warehouses
6. To organise the digital knowledge and information

Hybrid Librarian : to explore and provide integration of services and systems using the available appropriate resources to achieve the user's information desire

Information Architect : who creates the structure or map of information that allows others tofind their personal paths to knowledge.

Access to digital information availability on web

Web site provides the hyper media based systems that allow rapid access to a wide variety of networked information resources. One can browse the different web sites which are scattered geographically and have access to the major resources from which one can download the information. Some of the major portal sites or gateways that provides access to electronic resources are

http://www.edoc.com/

http://mcl.library.mi.us/

http://bubl.ac.uk/

Skills required for the digital librarian

Technical Skills (ICT Skills)

Operating systems

Dos

Windows

Windows NT

Unix

Linux

Packages

MS Excel

MS Access

MS Word

MS Power point

Knowledge of Library Automation Software

Management Skills

Research & Project management skills

Resource Management skills

Systems Management skills

Personnel & Financial management skills

Information Skills

Collection management skills

Digital reference and information service skills

Skills related to various types of user studies, user education etc

Impediments in the development of DLs in India

Lack of Financial support for technology and costs for digitization and technical infrastructure.

Lack of indigenous, efficient and effective library software package.

Lack of standardisation of both hardware and software

Problems in the conversion of the existing manual databases

Limits of network bandwidth and slow transmission speed

Digital libraries and its use

These functions and uses of the digital library in the context of users are that it

support multimedia content

provides a friendly interface

support publishing, annotation of new information

Issues and challenges

Digitization : Digitization is a process which does the work of converting of print and other materials. This process converts to a fixed or analogue issues like books, journals, photos, paintings and microfilms into electronic either through scanning and networking. A problem may arise with regard to naming identifiers and persistence. Digital objects can identify of naming. System of naming is permanent and lasting and the name cannot be bound with specific location. The scheme required unique identifier for digitization.

Building digital collection : Another aspect is most important issues in creating a digital library is building of digital collections. The major issues are the degree to which libraries will digitize existing material and acquire original digital works. How is the specific material to be digitized to be acquired or identified by a given library. Who collects and/digitizes which material could be based on factors such us collection strength, unique collections, the properties of user groups and skills of the staffs.

Preservation : Materials with regard to digitalized preservation technically not sound. Therefore preservation of the storage medium tapes, hard derives floppy discs bears a short life span. Preservation of such access to the content of the document regardless to the format.

Copyright : Digital library development is most important factor so far as to the copyright is concerned. The copyright exists from the fact of creation. This means without observing formality, original paperwork, or having any right, of one's own paper work cannot construed to be an author. In practice, it will of course be able to prove copyright, this copyright, with any proof or evidence, which will certify you, designer or creative are the author of this creation.

The deposit is to establish an absolute and indisputable link of your rights by establishing:

- The creator (author)
- The creation (the work, text, image, website, project ...)
- The date certain
- Subject originality

Technical architecture

Libraries always need to enhance and upgrade current technical architecture such as:

- Full text search engines to index and provide access to resources.
- Relation database that supports a variety of digital formats.
- E-management system

Open Archival Information System (OAIS) model

The OAIS is a relatively simple reference model currently under review (as an ISO Draft International Standard) that contains within itself the means to expand and adapt to most potential design requirements for long-term digital information holding and access.

Digital library architectures are very complex and designers tend to use their own terminology within the design process.

The OAIS is especially useful in the way it has brought together the terminology and concepts used to describe and compare digital library architectures within an understandable, commonly agreed and overall less complex framework.

Remodeling the strategy for digital library development

New models of information and knowledge services have to be found or invented. Libraries can either lead the way or being marginalized on the way.

i. Knowledge processing mechanisms are built within user information environment and embedded into user information processes to support knowledge discovery, knowledge organization and knowledge management.

ii. Digital objects in the research space are described, organized, interlinked and Integrated as an open knowledge grid.

iii. Collaborative mechanisms are developed for librarians to work together with researchers to develop the above structures and services, and to provide further value added and personalized services.

CONCLUSION

Digital information facilities are getting much attention the world over due to their intrinsic benefits over the prevalent paper based mode of distributing information. The advances in technology are increasingly reducing the gap between developing and developed countries. A very few of our libraries were able to use online information facility, a few more were able to procure and service CD-ROM sources in a stand-alone or network mode. Whereas when it comes to web, a large number of our libraries have been able to assimilate this technology either by using web information sources or by hosting them. Availability of qualitative contents in substantial quantity is the key to involve in full- fledged digital library development, where many of our institutions stilling. The widespread availability of suitable products in the market may enable our libraries to taste the virtues of digital information.

REFERENCES

BAWDEN, David and ROWLANDS, Ian. (1999)Digital Libraries: developing a conceptual Framework. *The New Review of Information Networking*, 5, 71-89.

Fox,E A and lumen, L (1993).Introduction and overs view to perspectives on Digital libraries.*JASIS* 44(8), 441-443.

Sharma (RS).(29.05.2002)Digital Libraries,Refresher Course in Library Science at academic staff college,Saurashtra University,Rajkot.

Smith,T.R.(1997). Meta Information in Digital Libraries., *International Journal of Digital libraries.*1,105-7

Cole Timothy W (2002)creating a framework of guidance for building good digital collections.*First Monday*,7(5) (http://www.firstmonday.org/issues 7-5/cole/ index.html).

Greenstein, Daniel I., Thorin, Suzanne Elizabeth. (2002) The Digital Library: A Biography. Digital Library Federation ISBN 1933645180. Accessed June 25, 2007.

Das Jaha, (march 2003) Greenstone Digital Library/software (GSDL) : a TUTORIAL 235-269P. In DRTC workshop on Digital Libraries.

15

Digital Libraries: Trends, Issues and Challenges

Bhanu Partap

ABSTRACT

This paper defines digital libraries, their function and characteristics, challenges and opportunities, evolution and origin of digital library initiatives, advantages and disadvantages of digital library, need and scope of digital library. This paper further discusses the various problems, challenges and issues involved in the design and development of digital libraries, focused on the Indian context. It also highlights the initiatives taken by various Indian libraries / organizations towards the development of digital libraries present scenario in India perspective.

Keywords : Digital libraries, Information and communication technology, Computers.

1. INTRODUCTION

Libraries are the repositories of the wisdom of ages stored in the form of recorded information for use of present and future generations. Digital technology has made it more easy and comfortable to apply this wisdom and use the collected information for further research and overall development of the society. Earlier, the main task of the librarian was just the material selection but now the same has been extended to the creation and maintenance of web sites, teaching specific references, fund raising and other tasks. Even when libraries have been restructured and divisions have been given new names like computer application division etc., the work is still perceived as belonging either to technical services, reference service or acquisition.

Digital Libraries (DL) are now emerging as a crucial component of global information infrastructure, adopting the latest information and communication technology. Technological advances in educational delivery and information provision through the use of ICT have impacted the way learners and educators acquire and deliver information and knowledge.

The primitive idea of 'library' connoted a storehouse of written document mainly based on clay tablets, palm leaves, waved wooden boards, papyrus role, etc. but with the advancement of knowledge in the human civilizations, the library has become the nerve centre of the civilized society. It becomes the sign and symbol of incentive to become dynamic and regarded the rich springs from which knowledge flows out to irrigate the wide fields of education and culture. It becomes an important medium of continuing self education.

The digital library extends the breadth and scale of scholarly and cultural evidence and supports innovative research and lifelong learning. To do this, it mediates between diverse and distributed information resources on the one hand and a changing range of user communities on the other. In this capacity, it establishes "a digital library service environment" that is, a networked online information space in which users can discover, locate, acquire access to and, increasingly, use information. Although access paths will vary depending on the resource in question, the digital library service environment makes no distinctions among information formats. Books, journals, paper-based archives, video, film, and sound recordings are as visible in the digital library service environment as are online catalogs, finding aids, abstracting and indexing services, e-journals and e-print services, digitized collections, geographic information systems, Internet resources, and other "electronic" holdings.

Historically, libraries have witnessed more technological change in the past decade than during the entire history since Gutenberg's printing press. Developments in computer hardware, software and the Internet have revolutionized libraries into "knowledge centers". More so, the profession itself has undergone a major 'shift' where the traditional library designations are being replaced by web-masters, e-resource managers, knowledge managers and the like. While some libraries are moving ahead by transforming their print collection into digital collection, some are developing their own digital collection while trying to preserve their traditional identity (hybrid), yet others are merely waiting to see what happens before proceeding further.

The new information technology is being used for a variety of functions. From the familiar web OPAC to online journal delivery system, people are accustomed to obtain information from their desktops. It is amazing to note that many of these technologies were not developed for libraries sake, but somehow these products are extensively used in all kinds of libraries. For instance, Xerox in 1950, Fax in 1983, CD-ROM in 1985 and the Internet in 1993, are some of the greatest inventions, which transformed the libraries. The impact of these technologies on libraries is so much that the people's perception of a library has changed altogether. Much of this is attributed to the technological developments in the fields of computer and communication technologies. However, It is heartening to know that even nine years after the first 'Library without walls' developed by the Los Alamos National Laboratory in 1994, the term "digital library" remains an abstract and amorphous thing to many library professionals in India.

2. DIGITAL LIBRARY

The term "digital libraries" have been associated with many connotations such as electronic library, hybrid library and virtual library.

We understand a digital library to be an electronic collection of real or virtual resources, which may also be available elsewhere. These resources must be whole works, with which humans can have a complete cognitive or affective engagement. A digital library may allow either online or offline access to the elements it organizes and houses, and may include multimedia as well as multilingual data. Although accessible online, a digital library is not identical to a website or a portal. However, while portals, specialized websites and search engines cover a wide range of subject areas, digital libraries are more narrowly focused around one or a specific group of disciplines. Digital libraries, moreover, attach content specific and highly descriptive metadata such as, descriptors or keywords to describe each item in the collection. Therefore, searches in a digital library can produce more useful results, save time and effort in searching, and in the best of cases browsers may directly access the text or multimedia content for which they executed their search.

3. DIGITAL LIBRARIES (DEFINITIONS)

Some of the definitions given by the computer 'gurus' are given below:

"Digital libraries are organized collections of digital information. They combine the structuring and gathering of information, which libraries and archives have always done, with the digital representation that computers have made possible." (Lesk)

"Digital library which looks and feels like a paper-based library but where items have been stored in digital form and stored for access in a networked environment which can be used by users in remote locations" (Stella Keenan).

"A digital library is a library in which collections are stored in digital formats (as opposed to print, microform, or other media) and accessible by computers. The digital content may be stored locally, or accessed remotely via computer networks. A digital library is a type of information retrieval system". (www.wikipedia.org)

Sun Microsystems defines a digital library as:

"The electronic extension of functions users typically perform and the resources they access in a traditional library" With digital libraries, an individual can:

- Gain access to the holdings of libraries worldwide through automated catalogs.
- Locate both physical and digitized versions of scholarly articles and books.
- Optimize searches, simultaneously search the Internet, commercial databases, and library collections.
- Save search results and conducts additional processing to narrow or qualify results. From search results, click through to access the digitized content or locate additional items of interest.

4. WHY DIGITIZATION

The two most obvious benefits of digitization are improved access and preservation of documents. It can be used by many users from different places simultaneously at any point of time and because of that the library does not have to purchase several copies of the same material, which saves money. Unlike printed and analogue library collections like papers, photographs, paintings, audiovisual materials, digitized collections are not damaged by extensive and frequent usage and it helps to prevent the document generation after generation. It is a great help for distant learners and those who do have opportunity to come to the library physically and use the resources. According to (Chowdhury and Chowdhury, 2004), the digitization of library materials provides us the following other benefits too.

- A digital library brings information to the user
- Improved searching and manipulation of information
- Improved facilities for information sharing
- Timely access to information
- Improved use of information
- Improved collaboration
- Reduction of the digital divide.

A large proportion of a digital library's collection comprises materials that are born digital, such as e-journals, e-books, internet resources, databases, and so on. In Indian aspect, library resources are in a printed format and needs to be digitized to include in the library collection for electronic use.

5. DIGITAL LIBRARIES – ADVANTAGES

Digital collections have a number of distinct advantages over traditional physical collections.

One of the largest is that they typically allow ***convenient access***, at all hours, to a wide variety of materials, from any location that provides Internet access. By offering different forms of access, digital libraries may also expand the potential user community, by offering, for example, more convenient access to disabled users, digitizing fragile materials for popular use, or offering access to remote populations. Offering open access to journals has been shown to further increase usage.

Cost is another significant motivation. Recent adoptions of digital libraries show that they can dramatically reduce the costs of some types of access. Although not yet uniformly less expensive than off-site depositories of paper materials, in the foreseeable future, for many materials, digitizing and distributing digital collections will be simply less expensive than maintaining the corresponding physical space.

Digital libraries have a number of other advantages. They can easily be replicated as a safeguard against loss. They can more easily be shared for collaborative work. They enable new forms of search, since both the metadata and the content of digital objects can be indexed. They enable new forms of information organization, since digital materials are not limited to a single location on a single shelf, and they can be included in many different cross-cutting virtual collections. They facilitate new forms of content, such as newspaper articles with interactive graphs, journal articles with embedded data and simulations, works that include accumulated commentary, and "mash-ups" intermingling content from multiple works in distinctive (and often dynamic) ways.

6. DIGITAL LIBRARY DESIGN

Architecturally, a digital library system typically includes four types of components: repositories, catalogs, identifier systems, and user interfaces. This is sometimes called the Kahn-Wilensky architecture. Repositories store the raw bits comprising each digital object contained in the library. Catalogs support search, by indexing information in the digital objects, and metadata describing them. Identifier systems provide a framework for identifying and locating objects. User interfaces bring together the functions of the other components to perform services for the users – such as, searching, browsing, visualization and delivery.

Many other components, services, and agents are also often incorporated into digital library architecture, such as:

- Discovery services that provide a mechanism (such as a central directory) by which interfaces to the digital library system dynamically discover the services that are available for the user.
- Security services to support authentication of users (perhaps by recognizing authentication from another party), provide framework for making authorization decisions, and secure communication services
- Presentation services that assist the user in viewing complex digital objects that are not otherwise easily viewable at the user's desktop or in a browser. This may include on-line systems for data analysis, reformatting services, and streaming media players.
- Software agents, that run independently of the main digital library system, and which perform additional services with respect to the library's content.

7. CREATING DIGITAL LIBRARIES

There are 5 stages in building digital libraries. These are 1)

Selection of documents and Scanning, 2) Storage & management, 3) Search & Access, 4) Distribution, and 5) Rights management. In digital library parlance, duplicating the printed publications into digital format is called 'retrospective conversion', while creating new digital information is called 'e-publishing'.

Before we venture into digital libraries, we must remember that a lot of information is already available in digital form over the Internet. Once the necessary permissions to tap this information is obtained, it can be used as remote (off-site) information, or may be downloaded to local hardware (on-site). Many think that every printed book in the library can be digitized, unaware of the copyright law that does not permit books to be converted just like that into digital format. We tend to forget the copyright statement on the back of the title page of every book - *"No part of this book may be produced, stored in a retrieval system, or transmitted in any form or by any means electronic, mechanical, photocopying, microfilming, recording or otherwise, without written permission from the publisher"*. Further, some publishers, particularly Learned Societies & Associations offer their publications in digital form. Sometimes, selection of material becomes the most crucial part of digital library rather than creation. In other words, documents (in all forms) published by the concerned university or its library may be digitized to start with, and later acquire other sources.

The documents in a digital library are called 'items' or 'objects', which contain data or the 'content' that is stored in the form of 'repositories'. The description of the stored data/information is known as 'metadata' or 'properties' of that data. Almost every type of information can be represented in digital form including text, pictures, music, computer programs, databases, models, video and a combination of any of the above. Every digital 'object' needs to be identified by a name, a time stamp and the owner, so as to establish the legal ownership.

In the past, a major problem with digital library implementation was the need to deal with a variety of computer hardware owned by different users. Today, the web has defined the standard interface, which everyone must support. Some models of digital library involve scanning of printed material into images, particularly for retrospective conversion; others involve ASCII-based text. In principle, much of the image-scanned material can be converted through Optical Character Recognition (OCR), but there are still other materials, which are provided as images and which may be hard to search. With the advent of new technologies and standards, the various conversion problems that we face today may disappear in future.

8. DIGITAL LIBRARIES AND TRADITIONAL LIBRARIES

Digital library functions, in so far as they purport to organize information, may be compared with traditional library functions. A common human artifact, such as a bound book, loses value when simply scanned into bits. In library context, where organization, access, protection, and preservation are important business functions, digitization technologies are starting points for a complicated set of computational processes that in the first instance reconstruct the cultural, conventional, and intuitive significance, structure and external relationships that defined the original artifact.

8.1. Comparison of Digital and Traditional Library Capabilities

Digital Library Capability	*Traditional Library Capability*
Capture	Acquisition and collection development
Catalog and Index	Cataloging rules and bibliographic control
Store	Stacks, inventory management and shelf lists
Search	Public card catalog
Protect	Patron privileges & circulation rules consistent with public law and policy
Retrieve	Loan management and interlibrary loans

Having made these comparisons, it must be emphasized that neither in the United States nor in Japan is the digital library regarded as a technology related to library automation or the provision of integrated library systems for operating traditional. None of the digital library projects were based on library automation technologies.

9. PHYSICAL AND DIGITAL LIBRARIES

Why a digital library is called a library at all? This question has been addressed by various members of this research community and discussed the notions of collection, information sources, and place with respect to physical libraries and how these notions might carry over into the digital realm. It is considered how work practices in physical libraries might be used in the design of digital libraries. The physical library can provide the starting point for discussing the elements and domains of digital libraries. An element of a library is a constituent part of the library. A domain of the library is the universe from which the library materials are drawn.

9.1. Elements

It is helpful to consider three broad classes of library elements: data, metadata, and processes. *Data* are library materials. *Metadata* are information about the library and its materials. *Processes* are active functions performed over library elements. For example, a book in a library may be thought of as being data of that library. An index over book titles (in a card catalog, for example) may be thought of as library metadata. The act of a librarian helping a patron find a book by suggesting the use of the card catalog may be thought of as a process.

9.2. Domains

A physical library deals primarily with physical data, whereas a digital library deals primarily with digital data. Of course most modern libraries deal with both, but it is useful for sake of discussion to consider hypothetical "all-physical" and "all-digital" libraries as foils.

The magnitude of differences between physical and digital analogs may be related to the accuracy of the physical/digital translation. A spectrum of translation quality certainly exists. Without more research into the effects of translating material between physical and digital form, it is difficult to know the accuracy of such translation.

In summary, though both physical and digital libraries may be thought of as sharing certain goals and of consisting of elements that may be classified similarly, the domains of the two types of libraries differ. Digital libraries will deal with translated physical elements, conceptual elements of the physical library adapted to the digital realm, and completely new digital elements with no apparent physical library analog (e.g. hyper novels). Differences between physical library and digital library elements have created many open problems concerning how to adapt the tradition of the physical library into the digital realm.

10. TECHNICAL ISSUES

10.1. Meta-data Standards and Protocols

Metadata, or "data about data," is a critical element for searching information through a database especially, when the information available in an invisible space like the Internet, unlike a conventional library. The function of metadata is to standardize the structure and content of indexing or cataloging information. Conventional libraries practise Meta data standardizations in the form of non-automated taxonomical systems. However, among the diverse standards that have been tested and tried and at present, there are a few universally recognized standards of classification that are being used around the world for digital resource management purposes. A brief summary of existing worldwide meta-data standards is as follows. The International Standards Organization's (ISO) Metadata Working Group has a related standard, ISO 11179, Specification and Standardization of Data Elements. It may also be made available to private sectors, civil societies and citizens. The American National Standards Institute (ANSI) has established the NCITS L8 (formerly X3L8), the *National Committee on Information Technology Standards.* The committee covers naming, identification, definitions, classification, and registration of metadata. The World Wide

While metadata standards are protocols *per se*, metadata systems are those that describe a set of metadata elements such as Title, Author, Rights, Date and so forth for a given digitizable material. For example, Dublin Core, MARC, DESIRE, SHOE, XML are metadata systems, of which Dublin Core is more widely adopted around the world.

It also has official standing within the WWW Consortium and the Z39.50 standard. Dublin Core metadata is endorsed formally by governments in three countries for promoting discovery of government information in electronic form, and Dublin Core is under consideration as national information standard in at least five others.

At present, digital library initiatives in India make use of Dublin Core for web-based publications, Encoded Archival Description (EAD) for archiving and Visual Resources Association (VRA) for visual data. Consortia such as the INFLIBNET and INDEST are involved in developing Indian metadata standards and software applications as part of the Open Archives Initiative Protocol for Metadata Harvesting (OAI_PMH).

10.2. Software Issues

Greenstone is a digital library software used for building and distributing digital library collections, organizing information and publishing it on the Internet or on CD-ROM. Produced by the New Zealand Digital Library Project, it integrates functions such as metadata, full text search and retrieval, multilingual support, support for multiple document formats and administration. Greenstone is open-source software, issued under the terms of the GNU General Public License. The aim of the software is to empower users, particularly in universities, libraries, and other public service institutions, to build their own digital libraries. The Indian Labour Archives was one of the first Indian digital library initiatives to use Greenstone. In India, at present, Information Library Network (INFLIBNET), a consortium incubated under the rubric of UGC, is actively involved in Library Automation, Database Creation, Software Development, Human Resources Development, Information Services and Networking. They have developed a software SOUL based on relational database management language, which is used for cataloguing, archiving as well as enabling online public access of resources.

10.3. Digital Rights Management

Given the vulnerability of materials accessible over the public access networks like the Internet, issues of IPR of material over the digital domain has become a serious concern. Digital Rights Management involves ways in which the digital library operators manage issues of IPR, those of ownership of material made available on the digital library, how one controls access to as well as dissemination of copyrighted material. Several methods of managing digital rights do exist nowadays from which one could choose to adopt the more convenient one for their purposes. Examples include, (i) charging a fee for the use of material as part of a copyright fee if that is mandatory, (ii) act as a middleman for other libraries so as not to get involved in these issues and to let the source organization deal with its IPR. (iii) holding restricted access to resources using user authentification method for those paid/registered users. This can be enabled using magnetic swipe cards, biometric methods or simple online security software that pops a username/password dialog box (iv) withholding original material and sending photocopies to the addresses. Of course, this works only at a local level and also for only an automated library that provides access to its catalog online and allows.

11. TRENDS IN DIGITAL LIBRARIES

The extrapolation of something today and its transformation into the reality of something tomorrow has been the tendency. To adapt the new ways and means or to resist the change in information handling and services is visualized through the cross sections of the technological insight. There have been massive changes in the nature of recorded knowledge akin to the revolution associated with printing. The librarians need to have parallel touch with the cutting edge developments even as the book as a source of knowledge becomes extinct .It ought to be augmented by some other media. While discussing the scope of the paper, the basic speculations are struck on electronic technology for preserving literature. The subtle thoughts contained in the existing sources need to be galvanized to correlate the imagination the images to the mind.

12. ISSUES AND FUTURE TRENDS

Although digital libraries have yielded significant benefits and gained rapid adoption, a number of significant challenges are foreseeable. A digital library is, as Arms aptly points out, far more than a collection of digital objects, systems, and software. He identifies a number of core digital library principles, paraphrased here:

- Digital library technology exists within a legal and social framework.
- Digital library concepts are obscured by technical jargon.
- Software systems should be separated from digital library content.
- Persistent identifiers are a basic building block in the digital library.
- Different forms of an object may be necessary for storage, delivery, display, and use.
- Repositories should preserve the information in digital objects.
- Users want access to intellectual works, not digital library technology and objects.

Many of the trends and challenges surrounding digital libraries are corollaries of these basic principles. One of the largest challenges is preservation. Archivists face a new paradigm in the digital age. Previously, much of archiving physical object centered on maintaining them in their original forms. This is neither necessary nor sufficient for works in digital form. Both hardware storage media and software file formats are constantly evolving, and thus digital objects must be frequently migrated from one media and format to another in order to ensure future usability. At the same time, these reformatted objects may need to be carefully checked in order to ensure no intellectually significant information is lost in the reformatting ("Universal numeric fingerprints" offer a possible approach to solving this problem). Complex dynamic objects such as data-driven websites and software pose particularly difficult technical challenges.

In addition, the responsibilities and rights of institutions with respect to archiving and disseminating digital materials are often hazy. The elimination of the requirement to register or even to include notices of copyright by the Copyright Act of 1976 implies that copyright applies automatically to almost all digital works. The act's extension of copyright from dual 28 year terms to the life of the author plus fifty years (changed in 1998 to life plus 70 years) implies that newly created digital objects are likely to remain under copyright until long after any systems capable of displaying them have disappeared. Moreover, many libraries may need to take on additional preservation responsibilities, in order to ensure that one publisher's demise does not wipe out swathes of important content. In order to manage digital works over time, to cite those works, and to copy them, those objects need to have identifiers that are unique and persistent. Another issue that has generated concerns among researchers, educators, activists, and librarians is the wide variation in the quality and coverage of content in many digital libraries.

Information scientists who study web search have suggested that a number of more inadvertent biases may also be present in current digital libraries. Wouter [2004] find a bias in both content selection and search results weighting that tilts toward more recent material. This "recency bias" occurs, at least in part, because new material are "born digital" and thus easier to include in digital collections; current journal articles and other similar content demands a price premium and is thus more profitable for the publisher; search engines and digital libraries often do not retain copies of previous versions when material is updated; and search engines may explicitly weight recently updated material more heavily. The increasing 'Googlization' of information seeking suggests that users are not becoming more critical of search systems. Underlining this, in a recent large survey, two thirds of college students reported that they started their research projects with a Google search and held Google to be as trustworthy as their library. Furthermore, almost one third of the student respondents reported that they did not validate the results of web searches against any print sources.

The economic pressures on libraries are created in large part by the disintermediation of publishers and end-users made possible by network technology, and also, in part, by changes in the intellectual property rights regime associated with digital materials. Both driving and driven by the changing intellectual property regime, the increasing use of digital rights management (DRM) software to restrict access to digital materials complicates the libraries dual roles in disseminating information and in preserving it. In the past, libraries would typically own a physical copy of the works that they purchased, and could make a straightforward decision as to whether to circulate it or preserve it, or even to duplicate portions as "fair use." DRM moves libraries from a position of ownership to a more limited and ambiguous position, since, fair use notwithstanding, it may place limits on such things as how many times an object can be viewed.

The issue of "orphan works" is a telling example of the unintended effects of intellectual property law, and a serious problem for libraries. "Orphan works", are works for which the current copyright status or copyright holder is unknown. These works constitute a significant portion of works of some types and for some periods, especially: photographs that are embedded in other works, and older films, books and music that have not yet clearly entered the public domain.

For scholarly libraries, the costs of academic journals have become an increasingly important issue, due to a dramatic increase in prices. Exacerbating this increase, publishers have adopted the practice of 'bundling' electronic access to large groups of journals together, which makes it more difficult for libraries to be selective in their subscriptions. As a reaction to this, and to take advantage of the opportunities that the Internet offers for widespread distribution, a movement toward "open access journals" has arisen.

These technological, legal and economic trends underscore fundamental changes in the role of the library, as well as in the form of its contents. Possession of information by a library, which was once a primary measure of institutional success, is becoming less important – individuals may soon have the equivalent of large libraries in their pockets. At the same time, the ability to facilitate an individual's search for, access of, and collaboration with information is becoming much more important. Such facilitation is not straightforward, however.

12.1. Archiving & Preservation issues

In a traditional library situation, books, journals, CDs, Videos, etc are taken care of by periodic cleaning and dusting. When some of these documents become brittle or damaged, some effort is made to repair and restore them using old methods. There is no guarantee that the life of these documents can be extended forever.

Millions of such valuable documents stored in libraries all over the world, continue to decay and crumble over time. There is a need to save these resources in a cost-effective manner and preserve them for future generations. Libraries face challenges to preserve not only the paper-based records of humankind, but also to save vital information in a variety of formats for future generations. A wealth of information is now available in digital form, and vital data on magnetic tapes is degrading daily, key electronic information about the early days of the Internet and the Web has already been lost.

There are a few methods in practice to preserve digital information. One method is to take full backups, maintain off-site duplicates and 'mirroring'. Another way is to adopt data migration strategy where the data is moved (migrated) to another 'improved' media. Sometimes data created using old software (or earlier version) cannot be read because of 'software obsolescence'. In such cases we need to preserve the old software and/or recreate the original data if necessary. In addition to all the above, access to the digital information should be fully 'secured' to avoid loss of data due to vandalism or 'hacking'.

Since information comes in different forms such as plain text, images/pictures, sound recordings and video films, we need to select the most appropriate file format to create and store them. There are various file formats for each type of data. For example Postscript & PDF for page description; TIFF, JPEG, GIF, PNG and PCD for images; HTML, XML & SGML for structured documents; AU, MP3, WAV,

RAM & MIDI for audio, etc, The Digital Library Federation (DLF) recommends standard naming conventions for the digital objects.

12.2. Copyright and IPR Issues in Digital Libraries

Basic copyright law for printed works is almost 300 years old. It is unlikely that we need some adjustments to be made to the copyright model to make digital libraries and hypertext publishing environments as commercially viable industries. Because of the ease of reproduction (copying) of digital works, the protection of the intellectual rights of the creators of the original information becomes more important. It is apparent that the issues of copyright and intellectual property rights are still in the formative stage with regard to electronic access. At present, it would be wise for the digital library to view solutions in the same light that they view the issues in a traditional library setting.

Among the important issues to libraries are digital fair use, registration, digital preservation, moral rights, data base protection, and liability for plagiarism, libel, and incorrect information. Various rules such as "fair use'' have meant that for traditional printed books most use in research libraries is permitted without additional charge beyond the original purchase. This situation is likely to get much more confusing, partly because digital information may not have the permissions associated with paper, partly because multi-media information already has different rules from printed paper, and partly because there are many revisions in the law under consideration.

The current copyright laws allow libraries to copy deteriorating materials for preservation purposes, but only to make facsimile copies. It is proposed that the next change in law permit digital copying for preservation, which may not be certain. The problems with non-print material have already become tough to tackle. For example, there is no "fair use" on recorded music, so that libraries can make copies of published sound recordings without obtaining permission. Video material is often involved in great many complex copyright difficulties, and little of it is actually old enough to be in the public domain.

The most difficult issue to date has been the definition of the library's user community. Many libraries serve their user community consisting of corporate bodies, alumni and even members of the general public. Publishers are particularly anxious that remote use be limited to students, staff and faculty of an academic institution. Traditionally, libraries have not been responsible for the content of the books issued to their patrons. In a digital world, it is not clear whether this will change. There are at least three issues: plagiarism, libel and tort liability. The plagiarism risk is that a change in the law may make people other than the original publisher responsible for copyright violations.

As of today, there are not many National or International copyright laws pertaining to the use of digital documents. However, the recent American "Digital Millennium Copyright Act (DMCA)" of 1998, extends copyright protection to electronic materials and upholds the Fair Use Clause and the First Sale Doctrine. The recent "Information Technology Act –2000" will be a guiding step to us in India. Once, more and more people start using the digital material for fair (or unfair) use, any lapses or 'leaks' in the system would come to the surface and the law will take its course.

13. DIGITAL LIBRARY STANDARDS

Since information comes in different forms such as plain text, images/pictures, sound recordings and video films, we need to select the most appropriate file format to create and store. Unlike traditional libraries, which use simple standards of classification, cataloguing and indexing such as UDC, DC, LC, AACR2 and ISBD; standards for creating digital libraries are more technical and complex. Hence, it becomes essential to adopt various international standards for the creation, storage and delivery of digital information.

There are various file formats to store each type of data. For example Postscript & PDF for page description; TIFF, JPEG, GIF, PNG and PCD for images; HTML, XML & SGML for structured documents; AU, MP3, WAV, RAM & MIDI for audio, etc, The Digital Library Federation (DLF) recommends standard naming conventions for the digital objects. Dublin Core Metadata is one such method that describes a resource or contains data about data. Various National and International agencies are involved in developing standards for representing electronic documents, such as Digital Library Federation, W3 Consortium, etc.

Dublin Core Metadata Element Set is a standardized, descriptive metadata method to locate networked resources. Metadata formats such as Dublin Core, MARC, IAFA, TEI, and GILS, describe an object in a standardized format that by using the Warwick framework interchange can be brought together and appended to the online document.

Dublin Core uses a controlled vocabulary and at least 21 classification schemes such as UDC, DDC 21, ICC, and LCCS to describe each element. Each of the 15 elements is optional and can be repeated. Each element has a limited set of qualifiers (attributes) that may further refine the meaning of the element; qualifiers cannot broaden the meaning of an element. Dublin Core's suitability depends on how close the metadata resembles text document metadata and whether the metadata file format (HTML, RDF/XML, W3 Consortium's RDF, PICS) can be interpreted by search engines. Metadata elements can be contained in a record separate from the document or embedded directly into the document.

The second step in creating a digital library is the actual scanning (or converting the text/image into digital format) of printed documents, which is most laborious and time-consuming. The scanning is usually done on a good, high-speed, high-resolution scanner. Nowadays, special scanners are available in the market, which can scan both sides of the page in a book. Further, the commercial digital library software available in the market can perform all the jobs right from scanning to hosting the content on the web. It is worth preparing a 'work-flow' to enter all the relevant information describing the document for the purpose of Indexing.

Information in digital form is normally hosted locally (Intranet) or globally (Internet), depending upon the need. In most cases it is hosted on a web server so that users can access the content over the

Internet. Since digital library is web-based, it should support all the existing web browsers like Internet Explorer, Netscape, Opera, etc. Along with the problems of security, digital libraries are also vulnerable to many 'technical hardships' like hardware failures and 'crashes'. Careful planning in locating the computer servers, mirroring the data and a good disaster recovery plan can avoid such catastrophes.

As said earlier, digital libraries do not confine to any geographical location. They are accessible over the Internet from anywhere and by anyone on all the 365 days of the year. However, all digital libraries may not be 'free for all', or some information is available only for a 'fee'. Depending upon the need, these restrictions can be set into the system by their producers. If access to some information is going to be only on payment, the necessary licensing, security and accounting procedures have to be built-in to the system. E-commerce software such as 'VeriSign', are available for this purpose.

14. DIGITAL LIBRARIES CHALLENGES

Digital Library mediates between diverse and distributed information resources on the one hand and changing range of user communities on the other. It offers information service that is a networked online information space in which users can discover, locate, acquire access to and, increasingly, use information. Today's digital library systems are capable of making available information or knowledge through various means and format. Books journals, paper-based archives, video, film, and sound recordings are as visible in the digital library service environment as are online catalogue, findings aids, abstracting and indexing of documents, e-journal, e-books, digitized collection, geographical information systems, Internet sources and other "electronic holdings".

Opportunities of access are now beyond the boundary of desktop and laptop PCs. Digital Libraries can now be accessed through mobile phones and PDAs, and libraries can integrate services to include providing information services via Mobile SMS and MMS services.

Configuring access to a world of information owned or manages only part is an integral part of constructing a digital library services environment. Accordingly digital library will not only be known to the extend and nature of collections its own but it is important to establish a defined set of information to be made available including value added services that they layer on top of overlapping electronic collections.

Increasingly, digital library services are not simply about opening up access to and use of information. It may include the following features:

- Supports the full range of administrative, business, and curatorial functions required by the library to manage, administer, monitor and ensure fair use of its collections whether in digital or non digital formats, whether located locally or offsite.
- Integrates (and interfaces with) information repositories that are characterized by open-access shelving, high-density bookstore, and availability via interlibrary loan, and include data services and digital archival repositories.
- Manages information about collections and items within collections often throughout their entire life cycle.
- Incorporates patron, lending, and other databases, and integrates appropriate procedures for user registration, authentication, authorization, and fee-transaction processing.
- Evolve into a networked learning space, providing access to and a curatorial home for distance and lifelong learning materials.
- An electronic information space that supports very different views and very different uses of the library.
- Designed for the library's patron as well as for its professional staff and with an eye on the needs and capacities of those who supply it with information content and systems.
- Evolving as the library's defining function and as such is developed with a view to its financial and organizational sustainability.

- Built in the full knowledge that information technologies will continue to change rapidly as will our understanding of how they can be used to support education and cultural engagement.

15. DIGITAL LIBRARY INITIATIVES IN INDIA

During the past few years, India has seen several Digital Library initiatives at the institutional, organizational and at national levels. Some of them are quite successful while others are making significant progress.

Some of the major initiatives on Digital Libraries in India are furnished below:

- 'Archives of Indian Labour' at the V.V. Giri Institute of Labour (http://www.indialabourarchives.org/sources/ jnu.htm)
- Indian Institute of Science NCSI (http://vidya-mapak.ncsi.iisc.ernet.in/cgi-bin/library)
- Indian Institute of Management Kozhikode (http:// intranet.iimk.ac.in/cgi-bin/library)
- Search Digital Library SDL at DRTC Bangalore (https:// drtc.isibang.ac.in/index.jsp)
- Nalanda Digital library, National Institute of Technology (NIT) Calicut (http://www.nalanda.nitc.ac.in)
- Vidyanidhi Project (http://www.vidyanidhi.org.in)
- Million Book Universal Digital library Project - Carnegie Mellon - IISc – ERNET (http://www.dli.ernet.in)
- Indira Gandhi Centre for the ARTS (IGNCA Digital Library) - (http://ignca.nic.in)
- INDEST, Ministry of HRD, GOI (http://paniit.iitd.ac.in/indest)
- National Tuberculosis Institute (NTI), Bangalore (http:// ntiindia.kar.nic.in/)
- Rajiv Gandhi University of Health Sciences, Karnataka (RGUHS) http://www.rguhs.ac.in/dl/index.html)
- Traditional Knowledge Digital Library (TKDL) – (http:// 203.200.90.6/tkdl/langdefault/common/home.asp)

- Indian School of Business (http://www.isb.edu/lrc/index.html)
- Indian Institute of Technology, Kharagpur (http://www.library.iitkgp.ernet.in/usr/elib/digital.htm)
- E-Prints at IISc: www.ncsi.iisc.ernet.in
- TIFR Digital Library Initiative: www.tifr.res.in/~library/
- Center for Education and Documentation: www.ced.org
- CSCS Media and Culture Archive: http://www.cscsban.org/html/media_archive.htm
- INFLIBNET: Information and Library Network Centre: www.inflibnet.ac.in
- Digital South Asia Library: http://dsal.uchicago.edu

16. CONCLUDING REMARKS

So, a digital library is a collection of information that is stored and accessed electronically. Digital libraries offer expanded access to information at all levels of complexity — from recipes to research. These libraries have made it possible for experts to access information far more rapidly and efficiently, and lowered the bar to non-experts who are working to find information of all sorts. Currently, however, such libraries offer only a portion of the collections available at large traditional libraries, and significant institutional and technical challenges remain to be overcome.

A digital library serves the same purpose, functions and goals as a traditional library. The 'digital' part of the term indicates merely that the material is stored digitally and accessed over the Internet. Librarians and administrators of digital libraries should remember that their job is to serve as 'intermediaries' of knowledge who can form a bridge between the authors and users of the 'information society'.

The future of the library will consist of books, bytes and buildings. Whether information comes in the form of print on paper, microfiche, streaming video, or digital text, the library will continue to collect mankind's intellectual, scientific and artistic achievements, and the record of humanity's triumphs and failures. The most important contribution of web technology in the library and information service sector has been the creation of digital library that allows users to access digital information resources from virtually anywhere in the world.

If digital libraries are to achieve their full potential, they need to be usable and *used*— by people for whom information retrieval is not generally the main goal.

REFERENCES

1. Borgman, C. L. (1999). What are digital libraries, who is building them, and why? In T. Aparac (Ed.), Digital libraries: Interdisciplinary concepts, challenges and opportunities, pp. 29. Zagreb: Benja.
2. Chowdhury, G. G. and Chowdhury, S. (2004). Introduction to digital libraries. London: Facet Publishing.
3. Garrett, John and Waters, Donald (1996). Preserving Digital Information, Mountain View, CA: Commission on Preservation and Access and Research Libraries Group joint publication.
4. Gerhart, Susan L. (2004). "Do Web Search Engines Suppress Controversy", *First Monday* 9(1). URL: <http://firstmonday.org/issues/issue9_1/gerhart/index.html>
5. Greenstein, D. (2000). Digital libraries and their challenges. Library Trends, Vol. 49(2); pp.290-03.
6. Griffin, Stephen M. (1998). NSF/DARPA/NASA Digital Libraries Initiative: A Program manager's Perspective, D-Lib Magazine (July/Aug).
7. Guthrie, K.M. (2001). Revitalizing older published literature: preliminary lessons from the use of JSTOR. In J. MacKie-Mason and W. Lougee (eds), *Bits and Bucks:* Economics and Usage of Digital Collections. Cambridge, MA: MIT Press, URL: http://www.si.umich.edu/PEAK-2000/
8. Haji Awang Suhaimi Bin Haji Abdul Karim and Miss Lim Bann Dih. Uniting E-Libraries and E- Learning: Challenges and Opportunities for VILIS Brunei.
9. Jolly, Surabhi (2005). The Digital Technology: Yet to Take Off. 3rd Convention PLANNER -2005, Assam University, Silchar, 10-11 Nov., 2005.
10. Kuny, Terry and Cleveland, Gary (1996). Digital Libraries: Myths and Challenges. Paper delivered at the 62nd IFLA General Conference - August 25-31, 1996. www.ifla.org/IV/ifla62/62-kuny.pdf
11. Lesk, Michael (2005), Understanding Digital Libraries (2nd Edition), San Francisco: Morgan Kaufman.

12. Licklider, JCR (1965). Libraries of the Future, Cambridge, MA: MIT Press.

13. Lyman, Peter (1996). What Is a Digital Library? Technology, Intellectual Property, and the Public Interest, Daedalus, Vol. 125, pp. 1-33.

14. Rao, M. Koteswara (2004). Digital Libraries: Challenges, Opportunities & Implications. Paper presented at the SIS 2004 Conference - 22-23 January 2004, IIT Madras, Chennai- 600036, India.

15. Sood, Aditya Dev and Chandrasekharan, Uma (2004). Digital Libraries in India: a baseline study. Educational Development Center Center for Knowledge Societies.

16. Sun Microsystems. (2000). *Digital Library Trends*. http://www.sun.com/products-n-solutions/edu/whitepapers/pdf/digital_library_trends.pdf

17. Wang, Mei-yu. (2003). The Strategic Role of Digital Libraries: Issues in e-Learning Environment. *Library Review*. Vol. 52(3); pp. 111-116.

18. Wilinsky, John (2005). *The Access Principle*, Cambridge, MA: MIT Press.

19. Witten, H. Ian and Bainbridge, David (2002). How to Build a Digital Library. San Francisco: Morgan Kaufman.

20. Wouters, Paul, Iina Hellsten, and Loet Leydesdorff (2004). "Internet time and the reliability of Search Engines." *First Monday* 9(10).

21. www.wikipedia.org/

16

Access to Open Access Journals in Library and Information Science

Dr. Anna Kaushik

ABSTRACT

Open access platform provides a gateway to access electronic journals free of cost but these journals available on different portals in various subjects. This chapter aims to discover volume and publication patterns of open access journals in library and information science available on Directory of Open Access Journals. The results of this study demonstrated that majority of journals published by universities, from United States, in English language, in the year of 2005 and having three key words. This chapter would be helpful to keep track towards growth and publication patterns taking place so far of open access journals in library and information science subject.

Keywords: Open access journals, library and information science, electronic journals

INTRODUCTION

Open access resources are very popular in this era and used in every field. Nowadays open resources have been proven their significance and open for all that can be accessed free of cost on the web. These resources may include electronic journals, websites, web 2.0 technology and so on. Electronic journals play imperative role particularly in research and development activities in different levels such as academic, social, economic and others as well.

Perhaps, open access movement came into existence in 1960s but adequate development was noted in 1990s when new internet and information communication technologies were emerged and several open access initiatives took place. Among different open access initiatives, two initiatives viz. Budapest Open Access Initiatives (BOAI) and Public Library of Science (PLoS) played key role in lifting up huge platforms and networks for open access model. Morrison [1] described that open access as a one of the most critical open movement for scholarly communication. Wikipedia[2] claimed that first open access journal was published in late 1980s (2012). Suber [3] defined open access literature as "digital, online, free of charge, and free of most copyright and licensing restrictions". Willinsky [4] identified nine flavors of open access journals. These flavors are: 1) e-print archive (authors self-archive pre- or post-prints), 2) unqualified (immediate and full open access publication of a journal, 3) dual mode (both print subscription and open access versions of a journal are offered), 4) delayed open access (open access is available after a certain period of time), 5) author fee (authors pay a fee to support open access), 6) partial open access (some articles from a journal are available via open access), 7) per-capita (open access is made available to countries based on per-capita income), 8) abstract (open access available to table of contents/abstracts, and 9) co-op (institutional members support open access journals).

However, open access journals can be defined as journals which provide free access to their available literature altogether with facilities to download, print and use without any legal restrictions.

As a consequence, publishers of paid electronic journals started to provide a free copy of their respective online journals and many leading LIS publishing agencies were opened their e- journals on the open access platform for example, especially, in India two leading LIS e-journals namely Annals of Library and Information Studies and DESIDOC Bulletin of Information Technology are now available on open access platform and can be access free of cost which were earlier available in paid mode. Simultaneously, many open access portals, institution repositories and directories have been developed which facilitate users to get free access to various scholar literatures published in different e-journals in library and information science domain according their own respective policies related to open access publishing literature.

LITERATURE REVIEW

Way [5] conducted a study for examining open access availability of full text articles in top 20 library and information Science journals using Google Scholar. A bibliometric study was conducted by Mukherjee [6] using 17 fully open access electronic journals in the field of library and information published during 2000-2004 which found that average increment of 23.75 articles per year, team research was not very common in LIS OA publishing, male authors were keener than female authors and open access journals covered a wide range of topics in library and information science subjects. Walters and Linvill [7] examined the characteristics of 663 open access journals in field of biology, medicine, economics, history, computer science and psychology and discovered that more than 2,700 articles published per year and medicine and biology field have large numbers of open access journals in comparison to other four subjects. A review study was exclusively carried out by Gupta [8] on different kind of open access and non open access bibliographies available in LIS marketing using diverse parameters such as authority, scope, arrangement, methodology, currency, accuracy and subject coverage. Mukherjee [9] expressed the trends of open access journal publishing in the field of library and information science by language, top-level-domain, country and time through which he identified 124 LIS open access journals which either partially or fully free accessible on the web but out of 124 identifies open access journals, 12 OA journals were found creased their publication and rest 112 open access journals found presently accessible freely. Results of his study depicted that most of open access journals in the field of library and information science were available in English language and published from either academic or organizational domain and from developing countries such as United States of America (USA) and United Kingdom (UK). Xia [10] ranked the position of library and information science related open access journals which published during the selected period between 2004 and 2008 by using h-index tool and found that open access journals have gained momentum supporting high-quality research and publication and open access journals have been ranked as high as the best traditional print journals. His study also encourages LIS professionals to be a part of open access movement and publications. Mukherjee [11] examined the hyper- linking patterns of references cited web based scholarly electronic articles of 17 open access library and information science journals published during the period of 2000-2004 in terms of language, file format, source and top-level domain. Scholarly impact LIS open access journals with help of Google Scholar was investigated by Mukherjee [12] using 17 fully open-access journals published during 2000 to 2004 in the subject of library and information science and on the junctures of quantity of articles published, subject distribution of the articles. Yuan and Hua [13] measured the scholarly impact of 97 LIS open access journals on the basis of citations and links and revealed that LIS open access journals have become a significant component of the scholarly communication system. Liu and Wan [14] analyzed the publication trends of227 open access scholarly journal articles retrieved from LIS databases such as Library and Information Science Abstracts, Library Literature, Social Sciences Citation Index and Bailey Jr.'s bibliography from 2000 to 2005 through which general works, library science journals, viewpoint articles, library professionals, and U.S. authors were found maximum in numbers. Singh and Niadu [15] explored the benefits of library and information science related electronic open access journals. Ghosh's [16] study expressed that open access (OA) programs adopted by libraries in various institutions and provided a list of relevant literature and resources in the library advocacy setting, with regard to the ongoing needs of OA repositories in India and his study further discovered that a proactive approach in information handling and collaboration with information technology staff and academics are essential for building open access model. Gupta [17] investigated growth and patterns of LIS marketing literature published in two well known databases namely Library and Information Science Abstract (LISA) and Library and Information Science and Technology Abstract (LISTA) during the selected period from 1970 to 2005. Lyons and Booth [18] evaluated the status of open journals articles published in early 2009 in the subject of business and management which available on a wide variety of websites, including repositories, author profile pages, open access journals, and so on. Hemantha Kumar et al. [19] assessed contribution of agriculture and food sciences subjects towards open access journals in India perspective and found that in respect of number of open access journals and revealed that India has 5th and 11th position in the Directory of Open Access Journals (DOAJ) and in Directory of Open Access Repositories (Open DOAR) respectively. Hawkins [20] investigated characteristics of 28 electronic journals in field of information science and found majority of authors belong to United States of America and United Kingdom countries, only 26 articles have authors from more than one country, about 2/3 of the articles connected to academic institutions and among seven online databases, only Information science Abstract covers all 28 selected journals. Gupta and Jain [21] mapped the growth of LIS marketing periodical literature in terms of articles published in India through Indian authors either in Indian or foreign publications and by foreign authors on India during the period of 1980-2008 year-wise, prominent author-wise and productive journals-wise and discovered that total 125 items were published, maximum 14 articles published in 1998, author self came out as most prominent author with 10 articles and DESIDOC Bulletin of Information Technology considered as most productive journal which contained 20 articles during the above said period but their study mainly includes paid LIS journals and only two open access journals such as Annals of Library and Information Studies and DESIDOC Bulletin of Information Technology.

Objectivities of the study

The study consists following objectivities:

- To identify the open access journals in library and information science.
- To examine growth of identified open access journals on the subject.
- To investigate publication patterns of open access journals listed under the banner of library and information science in DOAJ portal.

Methodology

The search was made through Google search engine (www.google.com) by using "open access journals in LIS" search term, in order to find out open access journals in library and information science subject. Further, directories such as Directory of Open Access Journals (DOAJ) (Lund University Library), (http://www.doaj.org/ljbs?cpid=129) web portals accessed and searched. Through this effort, 135 open access journals in library and information science subject were found under the umbrella of social sciences- Library and Information Science. Further, every identified open access e-journal thoroughly checked for discovering the open access journals in library and information science area. Finally, 135 open access electronic journals in library and information science field, were discovered. This study was carried out during certain period from November 8, 2012 to December 8, 2012. Besides this, a database was developed in Micro Soft Excel which consists different fields like title, author, journal name, publication year, keyword etc., in order to analysis of growth and publication patterns of LIS open access electronic journals by using different corpus such as publication patterns, authorship patterns and related bibliographical phenomena.

Results

Year wise publications

Table 1 : Year wise publications

Years	Number of Journals	Years	Number of Journals
1911	1	2001	2
1975	1	2002	4
1985	2	2003	6
1987	1	2004	10
1991	2	2005	14
1993	1	2006	13
1994	2	2007	9
1995	4	2008	3
1996	8	2009	6
1997	5	2010	4
1998	8	2011	11
1999	11	2012	1
2000	6		
		Grand Total	*135*

Out of total 135 open access journals found on library and information science in DOAJ, Table 1 showed that majority of journals were published in two years (2005 and 2006) in which most productive year was noted as 2005 in which 14 open access journals were published and slightly low (13) number of open access journals were published in 2006. Apart from this, in both years 1999 and 2011 equal numbers (11) of open access journals were reported publish and very little less number 10 and 9 journals were published in two years intervals 2004 and 2007 respectively. It is surprise to discover that very low publication of journals were noted in beginning year 1999 and at the end year 2012 in which only one open access journals was came under this directory (DOAJ).

Country wise publications

Table 2 : Country wise publications

Name of Countries	*Number of Journals*	*Name of Countries*	*Number of Journals*
Argentina	1	Lithuania	2
Australia	2	Mexico	1
Brazil	16	Netherlands	3
Bulgaria	1	New Zealand	1
Canada	7	Pakistan	1
Chile	1	Peru	1
Colombia	1	Poland	2
Costa Rica	1	Puerto Rico	1
Croatia	3	Romania	1
Cuba	2	Slovenia	1
Czech Republic	1	South Africa	1
Denmark	2	Spain	10
Egypt	1	Sweden	2
France	2	Switzerland	1
Germany	6	Taiwan	4
India	5	Turkey	2
Indonesia	1	United Kingdom	7
Iran	1	United States	36
Italy	3	Venezuela	1
		Grand Total	***135***

Journals published from different countries present their research and development activities taking place in the respective countries, Table 2 demonstrated that highest volume (36) of open access journals in library and information science area published solely from United States followed by Brazil (16) and Spain country (10) but slight less numbers of journals (7) were observed form two countries namely Canada and United Kingdom. While only one open access journal was contributed in DOAJ portal form 18 countries out of total identified 38 counties which made contribution in open access journals in library and information science area.

Language Covered

Fig. 1. Language covered

Perhaps, most of literature in world published in English language but open access journals in library and information subject clubbed with Directory of Open Access Journals (DOAJ) published in English language as well as other languages, Figure1 depicts that majority 74 percent means almost 100 open access journals on the subject were published on English language and 26 percent journals published in other languages. Moreover, it is interesting to discover that out of total 135 open access journals found from this study, 66 journals were published only in English language, 34 journals available in English as well as other languages and 35 journals purely published in other than English language so called non- English open access journals.

Publishing Agencies

Table 3 : Publishing agencies

Universities	Individuals	Special Institutions	Libraries	Associations
58	7	44	2	24

Table 3 showed that majority of journals (58) were produced by universities around the world closely followed by special institutes (44 journals) that include research and development institutions, research labs, information agencies and other agencies/institutes which involved in special activities, library associations including other that library related associations that produced (24 journals) and seven journals published on individual level while few journals (2) published by libraries.

Subject coverage

Table 4 : Subject coverage

Subject covered	*Number of Journals*
Library and Information Science - Medicine (General)	2
Arts in general -Library and Information Science — Visual Arts	1
Computer Science - Library and Information Science	4
Law - Library and Information Science	1
Library and Information Science - Business and Management	1
Library and Information Science -Computer Science	5
Library and Information Science -Education	1
Library and Information Science -Education — Business and Management	1
Library and Information Science -History — Computer Science	1
Library and Information Science -Media and communication	1
Library and Information Science -Medicine (General)	2
Library and Information Science -Social Sciences	2
Media and communication -Library and Information Science	1
Medicine (General) - Library and Information Science	3
Philosophy - Library and Information Science	1
Religion - Library and Information Science	1
Science (General) - Technology (General) - Library and Information Science	1
Technology (General) - Library and Information Science - Business and Management	1
Library and Information Science	105
Grand Total	*135*

Being the all journals related to library and information science subject, each open access journals consist at least "library and information science" subject but inclusion of other subjects. It is also found that majority of journals (105) categorized only in "library and information science" subject and rest 30 open access journals contained other than library and information sciences subject whereas out of 30 above mentioned journals, 14 journals started with other subjects first and 16 were started with Library and information science subject (first) plus other subjects after words.

KEYWORDS

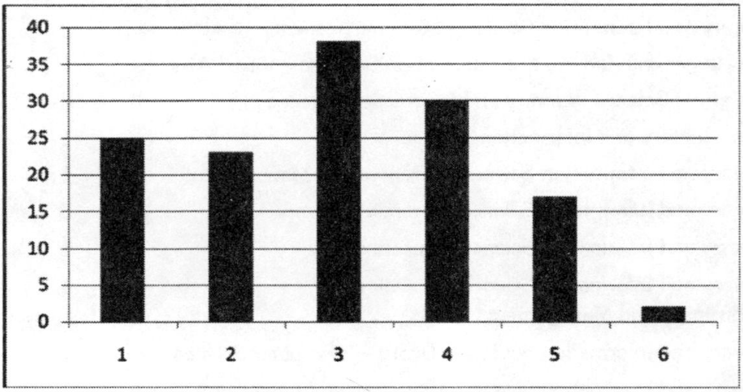

Fig. 2. Key words covered by journals

Figure 2 shows about number of keywords open access journals having with their respective coverage area in which the maximum journals (38) contain only three keywords which nearly followed by 30 open access journals that having four keywords but 25 open access journals in library and information science area consist only one keyword and closely lower number of open access journals(23) having two keywords while minimum only two open access journals comprise six keywords which is maximum number of keywords were noted during the access of open access journals in library and information science subject. It is interesting to note that 12 open access journals contain only one keyword "library and information science" in contrast to other keyword of open access journals.

DISCUSSION

Table 1 reported that open access journals were stared from 1911 with very low quantity only (1) and also ended with the same quantity (1) in the current year 2012, but good numbers of journals were included in the five years viz. 1999, 2004, 2005, 2006 and

2011. Among these just mentioned five years, 2005 year was emerged as most productive year in terms of publication of open access journals in library and information subject. It is also recommended that publisher of paid databases and journals should publish some journals in open access mode and include in such valuable portals (i.e.DOAJ) in respect to build productivity of open access journals in LIS sector.

It is interesting to discover from Table 2 that large number of open access journals in library and information science produced by United States in comparison to other identified thirty eight countries across the world. Thus, it is necessary to produce more LIS related journals on open access platform especially from those countries which have less number of journals.

It is found by Figure 1 that most of open access journals on the subject are available in English language inclusion of other languages. Therefore it is needful to mention that all open access journals should published in English language whereas other languages may also be incorporated along with English language one as English language is a world's most common and known language in information communication as well as in writing perspectives.

It is noticed from table 3 highest quantity of journals were product of universities in comparison to other publication agencies identified for this study but low frequency of journals were noted from libraries therefore it is suggested to libraries to product more open access journals in library and information science domain.

The main responsibility of publishing agencies of open access journals is to apparently express subject coverage of the journals so that users can know the depth of subject coverage in first look.

Though open access journals listed in library and information science subject in Directory of Open Access Journals (DOAJ) have different keywords of their respective journals nature and subject coverage but it is necessary to mention for all journals editors to develop and indicate appropriate keywords for their respective journals so that the scope, nature and connected topics with in the journal will be clearly identified at a glance for the users.

It is perceived that some journals listed in DOAJ portals had been ceased but start again with new name, hence there is also scope for published agencies to restart their ceased journals on open access platform. At the last, this study also suggests to produce one stop point for LIS open access journals on the web so that users may have access all open access journals from one place rapidly.

CONCLUSION

This study provides a picture about open access journals in library and information science subject with in Directory of Open Access Journals by different viewpoints. Analysis of the open access journals revealed that majority of open access journals available in English language and published from United States but while viewing through year-wise productivity it is found that very low frequency noted in current year (i.e. 2012) therefore it prime duty of library and information agencies and publishing agencies to be part of open access journals and product more journals on open access platform. The further research may be carried out on open access journals in LIS domain on the following issues:

- Study of open access journals in particular time frame intervals
- Development of open access portals and their evaluation
- An analysis study that based on causes enforcing to publishing agencies for adopting open access models for their products.
- Study of attitude and satisfaction of LIS professionals' towards submitting and publishing their own intellectual creations to open access journals.

REFERENCES

1. Morrison H. (2009). Open access, *in Scholarly Communication for Librarians,* Chandos Publishing, Oxford, pp. 103-134.
2. "Open-access journal" available at http://en.wikipedia.org/wiki/Open-access_journal (accessed 10 December 2012).
3. Suber, P. (2007). Open access overview: focusing on open access to peer-reviewed research articles and their preprints, available at http://

www.earlham.edu/~peters/fos/overview.htm (accessed 14 December 2012).

4. Willinsky, J. (2003). The Nine Flavours of Open Access Scholarly Publishing, *Journal of Postgraduate Medicine*, 49 (3), pp. 263-267.

5. Way, D. (2010). The Open Access Availability of Library and Information Science Literature, *College and Research Libraries*,71(4), pp. 302- 308.

6. Mukherjee, B. (2009). Scholarly research in LIS open access electronic journals: a bibliometric study. *Scientometrics*, 80 (1), pp. 169–196.

7. Walters, W. H. and Linvill, A. C.(2011). Characteristics of open access journals in six subject areas. *College and Research Libraries*, 72 (4), pp. 372-392.

8. Gupta, D. K.(2008). Bibliographical literature on LIS marketing: a review. *Annals of Library and Information Studies*, 55 (4), pp. 308-316.

9. Mukherjee, B. (2008). Open access scholarly publishing in library and information science. *Annals of Library and Information Studies*, 55 (3), pp. 212-223.

10. Xia, J. (2012). Positioning open access journals in a LIS journal ranking. *College and Research Libraries*, 73(2), pp. 134-145.

11. Mukherjee, B. (2009). The hyper linking pattern of open-access journals in library and information science: a cited citing reference study. *Library and Information Science Research*, 31(2), pp. 113–125.

12. Mukherjee, B. (2009). Do open-access journals in library and information science have any scholarly impact? : a bibliometric study of selected open-access journals using Google Scholar. *Journal of the American Society for Information Science and Technology*, 60 (3), pp. 581–594.

13. Yuan, S. and Hua, W.(2011). Scholarly impact measurements of LIS open access journals: based on citations and links. *The Electronic Library*, 29 (5), pp. 682 – 697.

14. Liu, Z. and Wan, G. (2007). Scholarly journal articles on open access in LIS Literature: a content analysis. *Chinese Librarianship: an International Electronic Journal*, 23 available at: http://www.iclc.us/cliej/cl23LiuWan.htm (accessed 15 December 2012).

15. Singh, R.P. and Naidu, G.H.S.(2011). Open access to e-journals in library and information science. *SRELS Journal of Information Management*, 48(2), pp. 165- 180.

16. Ghosh, M. (2011). Advocacy for open access: a selected review of the literature and resource list. *Library Hi Tech News*, 28 (2), pp. 19 – 23.

17. Gupta, D. K.(2007). Literature on LIS marketing: growth and pattern. *Annals of Library and Information Studies*, 54(1), pp. 32-36.

18. Lyons, C. and Booth, H. A. (2011). An overview of open access in the fields of business and management. *Journal of Business and Finance Librarianship*,16 (2), pp. 108-124.

19. Hemantha Kumar, G. H., Srinivasa, V., Bhaskara, R. M. and Chandra, B.T.(2012). India's contribution to agriculture and food sciences through open access literature. *DESIDOC Journal of Library and Information Technology*,32 (1), pp. 53-58.

20. Hawkins, D. T. (2001). Bibliometrics of electronic journals in information science. *Information Research*, 7 (1), available at http://informationr.net/ir/7-1/paper120.html (accessed 20 December 2012).

21. Gupta, D. K. and Jain, A.K.(2009). Marketing of library and information services: a study of periodical literature. *Annals of Library and Information Studies*, 56 (4), pp. 217-226.

17

Challenges in the Management of E-Journals in Academic Libraries of India

Abhijit Chatterjee

ABSTRACT

This chapter deals with challenges and issues faced in management of electronic journals in the academic libraries of India and at the end some important suggestions and recommendations are also incorporated.

Keywords: E-journals, academic libraries, management

1. INTRODUCTION

We are now living in the information society where much of the information consumption habit of the users are gradually changed with the advent of the computer and associated technologies. The users flooded with the much of the information which is available through Internet. But the authenticity of the information remains questionable to the users also. The trend of using Internet for quick retrieval of information often found in the libraries also. The libraries are now emerged as information hub in the recent era. The Internet is become major driving force.

Traditionally libraries preserve print documents which are very difficult for searching for the users. With the advent of new tools and techniques it is now possible to find out the electronic representation of the documents in digital form. Recently electronic versions of books, journals, CD-ROMs are available to the users. Among all these digital tools e-journals proved as most important and valuable tool for the academic and research community. Now-a-day libraries have to deal with not only printed documents rather their electronic counterparts also.

2. BACKGROUNDS

We are in the verge of the time where advancement of the society taking rapid pace. The advancement of information and communication technology takes such a shape which is difficult to believe few years ago. The academic sector has the most influence with these changes. The information and creation and consumption habit of the users changed drastically. Present society provided the opportunities to access and retrieve on-line electronic/ digital information which is very easy to handle. In this scenario, use and management of information and knowledge becomes extremely crucial for the steady development of the society. Following are some of the basic reasons for adopting E-Journals as important media for communication:

- The developments in scientific publications posed new challenge for the libraries. The retrieval and access are very much important in scientific publications. People from science need different mechanism to access quickly the findings of the journal articles. Therefore the e-journals may solve these issues.
- The quick increase of journal price over the world throws the challenge to the academic libraries with their limited budget.

Therefore the sharing among the different academic and research communities need a common digital platform which is very easy to share among the peers. Sharing of the journal article possible when the content is available in digital format.

- Now-a-days the users want information in a transportable and communicable form. E-Journals are available in transportable and communicable form and thus increase the usage of the articles.
- Keeping and managing the e-journal resources accessible for use by future generations will require conscious effort and continual investment. Managing and accessing e-journals become most crucial questions for the organisation in future. It needs continuous and hard effort by the stake holders.
- Any user having access to Internet can now have access to e-journals, as publishers are able to deliver them directly to the users' desktops. The access, browse and retrieval of e-journals become easier for the users as it is available in single desktop.
- E-journals are becoming popular and more effective with the growth and expansion of the Internet. E-Journals become more popular with the increase of the use of internet among common people.
- There have been clear transitions from print to online media due to the advancement of technology. The Libraries are now termed as information centre where users want information service rather than reference service is expected from the library professionals.

The above activities are quickly take place in the libraries of our country. The trend shows there have been quick and steady increase of the usage e-journals. Therefore the Library and Information Professionals should take proper action to fight against the different issues or problems associated with the management of e-journals

3. E-JOURNAL

The term Electronic Resource used as the broader term in

digital world. The word Electronic journals or E-Journals express the same meaning and the words are used synonymously. There are different words used interchangeably such as Electronic serials, Online Journals, and Electronic periodicals, Virtual journals the Paperless Journal. Still there is no accepted standard definition exists for electronic serial publications.

3.1. Definition

D. Scott Brandt defined e-journals as "In its broadest definition, an electronic journal is some grouping of information which is sent out in electronic form with some periodicity".

Gail Mcmillian stated "any serial produced, published and distributed nationally and internationally via electronic networks such as Bitnet or the Internet".

James and cook define e-journals as a " digital periodical that publishes on the Internet and www".

Shackel defined e-journals as one which involves using a computer to aid the normal procedures whereby an article is written, reefed, accepted and published.

Lancaster[1] also defined that an electronic journal is one created for the electronic medium and available only in this medium.

Rowland & Jagtar singh (1998) gave quite comprehensive definition of an electronic periodical as something that appears at regular intervals, is distributed electronically and is not restricted to a closed user group, has an identifiable title and editor(s), and contains discrete items with named authors.

According to Harrod's Librarians' glossary[2] (2005), an electronic journal is "a journal which is available in electronic format; a physical, printed version may also be available".

Smith[3] (2003) defines e-journal as 'any journal that is available online, including both electronic only journals, and journals that are available both electronically and in print'.

Bombak et al. (1992) define e-journal as 'a publication whose primary means of delivery to subscribers is through computer files.'

In simple words e-journals is journal whose contents are available online at regular interval and accessible through internet. It may have print version also.

3.2. Features

Print journals and electronic journals are two important counter parts of each other. These two are independent entities of the library collections. Following are the basic features of the electronic journals:

- Electronic journals are digital copies of the print journals.
- It occupies less space than the print copies of journals.
- It is possible to provide multiple access simultaneously through e-journals only.
- E-journals are accessible to anybody regardless of geographical barriers through proper compatible software and browser services.
- It eradicates time-consuming printing and mailing process and therefore takes less time to publish and distribute.
- E-Journal able to accommodate more article than the print version
- It is possible to avail e-journals through online portals or CD-ROM.
- It is possible to get e-journal in colour figure and graphics at no extra cost.
- It is the possible to access individual articles by the users by making pay-per-view that is pay for the required articles, if they do not want to subscribe to the entire journal.
- E-journals are available more economically than the paper ones, because the main costs of preparing the text, the review process and other such procedures are less expensive due to the costs of printing and mailing print copies.
- Quick access and retrieval become one of the most interesting features of the e-journal.
- An electronically published article can very easily contain a

link, which facilitates e-mail communication with the author or the editor.

- E-journal can contain hyperlinks to cited articles and other information sources such as related journals or websites.
- Searching facilities in e-journals are very effective and fast. E-journals provide excellent search facilities with every issue in which user can search articles not only by title, author, keyword but can also use boolean operators for searching.
- E-journal can never be never missing from the shelf at any time and several people can read the same article at once from separate workstations.
- It is possible to assess hits in electronic journals and thus find out the impact of their scholarly work for promotion.
- Through e-journal it is possible to prepare usage statistics which can be generated by using accepted standards.
- Through e-journals the problem of serial crisis can be solved and to share the resources among libraries.
- Libraries can provide better information service by using e-journal retrieval facilities available in India through consortium.
- Portability of e-journal is one of the interesting features of the electronic resources.
- Greater number of access and print of article is possible in case of e-journal.

3.3. Need

The facilities of the e-journals in academic environment are manifold. Its benefits will be touched the every corner of the academic institutions. The advanced technologies of the e-journal provide wonderful opportunity to browse and search texts in the documents. Following can be considered basic needs of the e-journal in the technology environment.

Support searching capabilities : The searching and browsing in print version of journal is quite tedious for the users. It is possible for the users to find the relevant portions of the articles. Therefore texts in e-journals can be effectively used by the users. Indexed e-journals can provide value addition services to the users. E-journals provide wide search option (by author, title, keywords, etc), so users can easily and quickly search and retrieve the desired articles.

Don't require physical processing : E-journals do not require much of the tasks like that required in the print journals e.g. ordering, receiving accessioning etc. But in case of e-journals there is not require physical processing which required for the print version of e-journals and thus reducing the work burden from the library staff.

Save physical space : The collection of the library will increase day by day with the introduction of new subjects in different fields. With this increase the physical space of the library gradually decreases with the increase in the collection in size and shape. E-journals help to reduce the physical space in the library and thus reduce the physical load of the professionals.

Contain multimedia information : The e-journal may contain multimedia information which can be very effective for the user understanding of the subject matter. It is quite easy understanding if it is available in multimedia form.

Value Added Resource : E-journals appeared as the value added resource to the organisation. Different new features are available in e-journals which are not available in print version. The features like citation, links etc are available in e-journals which added value addition to the resources.

Shelving Space : E-journals do not require any physical space. It is available regardless of the availability of the network systems in the organisation. Thus physical selves do not required in this case. This may lead to the reduction of the shelving space. E-journal saves shelving space in a library because it requires no space, thus it does not require human resources for shelving and rectification.

Users' Satisfaction : It is frequently found that the users of the e-journals remains more satisfied than the print counterpart. It users becomes more satisfied due to its portability and easy mode of searching and browsing information.

Easy Handling : The handling and maintenance of the e-journals are quite easy for the users. It is quite difficult for the users to access and the print materials. But there are no hazards for handling the electronic versions of the same journals as it does not involve any tough procedure.

Remote Access : The print version of journals are held and accessed in the libraries only. But in case of e-journals it is possible to access by the users remotely. The access may be provided by either through IP Authentication or Password Authentication.

Multiple Accesses : Print journals can be accessed by one user at a time as it has only one copy. The unique benefit of the e-journals is to provide multiple accesses to the different users simultaneously.

Easy to Use : The e-journal is quite easy to use only the basic literacy of computer is sufficient for the users to use the resources. There are no hard rules associated with the use of e-journals. Users can easily browse and download the electronic versions of the journals

Reduced Cost : Most of the academic libraries especially college and university libraries unable to subscribe important journals for their students due to the huge cost involved in the print journals. Rather the libraries have to be quite selective in order to subscribe the core journals. Due to the low cost of e-journals if taken in bundle, many libraries able to take the opportunity of subscribe these journals. Besides publishers sometimes offer discounted price for the developing countries.

Avoid Missing : Print copy of the journal is quite difficult to handle due to its physical nature. Print journals are usually sent through post. Sometimes the copy is not reached to the library or for several other reasons. Therefore the supply system creates problem for both the subscriber and publisher. E-journals able to eradicate these problems. The hard copy of a journal can also be missed or lost by theft from the library anytime. But such problem will not occur in case of subscribing e-journals.

Accommodate Unique Features : E-journals provide unique features like links to related items to increase its usability and access. It is also available in different format like PDF, PDF/A, HTML etc which enable for the publisher to accommodate different new features for the users.

Cost Savings : E-journals do not require regular maintenance like that of the print journals which required physical processing, binding, cleaning and making the documents accessible to the users which include different types of expenses at different stage.

Time Saving : Now-days the users want specific information from the users. The quick delivery of services becomes possible with the help of electronic information. The electronic journal helps to quick delivery of information in electronic from thus saves the time of the users.

Improved Service : The e-journals help to provide users better and improved services. It is possible to provide digital based services with the help of e-journals. The services of the users become more modernized in the present age.

5. MANAGEMENT OF E-JOURNALS

With the advent of internet E-Resources emerged as one of the important driving force in knowledge sector. Among these resources Electronic journals forms the major part of the digital collection in most of the academic libraries. Introduction of electronic resources in academic libraries made a strong and continuing impact on library and information services. Now library staff have to deal with the E-Resources which is very difficult to handle for the professionals. The increasing information communication technology and digital revolution in the Library and Information centre has posed challenges to the library professionals to handle such technological advancement. Thus slowly the management issues of handling and managing of the electronic journals have crept up. Therefore it is the need of the time for the professionals to gain knowledge about the different issues that have come up when dealing with the e-journals. Rajender Singh Bist[4] has broadly categorised the management of E-Journal in three respects. These are:

- Selection related issues.
- Acquisition related issues.
- Access related issues.

5.1. Selection of Electronic Journals

Selection of the e-journals is most important part as it reflects the nature of the organisation. Therefore it needs judicious thinking and planning from the Library and Information professionals. The selection of the resources should be based on the objective of the organisation and clientele served. But what kind of selection methods will be adopted depends upon the need of the organisation. Thomas E. Nisonger[5] has raised the following questions in terms of selection of e-journals:

What does selection of an electronic journal mean?

Selection of e-journals implies different meaning in different contexts. It may state the selection of the titles of the e-journals or the selection of mode of providing access to the users. From the organisational point of view, it is the method of choosing title from the available resources.

Which library staff select electronic journals?

The selection of the e-journal must be the most important and valuable duty for the Library and Information professionals. Thomas E. Nisonger[6] described two methods. One is based on format while the other based on subject. Under the format-based approach electronic journals would be selected by separate staff with expertise in automation and electronic resources rather than the same staff that select traditional materials. In contrast, under the subject-based approach selection of electronic journals would be done by the same collection development staff that select traditional resources. Whatever methods may be adopted these selection should be done by appropriate and experienced staff. The demand and need of the user community will also be kept in mind.

How are selectors trained?

The staff members of the library who are involved in the

selection procedure of the resources should be well acquainted with the demands, services and objectives of the organisation. There is every need to properly train the selectors. In case of format based approach the selection is done by the expert in electronic resource. In case of subject based approach there is need training for the subject expert as he may lack skills in electronic resources. But whether the training is actually required is become questionable. The methods and contents of the training are other areas of concern for the library authorities.

What selection criteria are used?

What kinds of criteria are used to select the e-journals is important task for the librarian and library committee. There may be different categories of criteria for selecting print and electronic journals. But the criteria should be organisation dependent. Usually the libraries use the same criteria as used during the selection of the print resources. Besides these criteria the libraries may also judge the criteria like technical compatibility with the library's hardware and software, user interface, the amount of training required, whether the journal is archived, and the e-journals data format are some criteria's to be used.

How does a library budget for electronic journals?

Allocating budget for the electronic journals is one of the most difficult tasks for the librarians. Since the entire things are new to the professionals it is quite difficult to assume the increase of the price rate of the e-journals. Therefore it is better to make separate budget for the e-journals.

What process is used in selecting electronic journals?

Thomas E. Nisonger[7] described three tier process of selection of e-journal. First, ***Identification*** is the most important task as it involves in identifying the availability of the resources. It enables to choose the proper items from the available resources. This is most difficult stage as there is no single complete database of e-journals available in the market. Secondly, ***Evaluation*** of the identified e-journals in terms of the factors like subject content, language of publication, accuracy, currency, indexing, authors' credentials, editorial board membership, publisher's reputation, whether it is refereed, overall scholarly quality, and audience. These can be considered as the traditional mode of evaluation criteria. On the other hand whether it is available in online, CD-ROM, or networked; whether PDF, ASCII, Postscript, HTML format will be available. Besides this technical compatibility with the equipment and amount of training for the staff are important evaluating criteria. Thirdly, ***Selection*** stage, here the decision regarding the selection needs to be taken. The decision regarding the selection will be based upon the user needs, the objective of the institute, collection development policy and budgetary considerations.

5.2. Acquisition Related Issues

Acquisition of e-journals includes several complex procedures and the main difference between the acquisition of printed and digital journals is that the former are purchased outright, whereas e-journals are acquired under licenses. In contrast to print journals it is very much difficult to control the digital issue of the e-journals. E-journals can never be received rather than the accessed. Acquisition of E-journals in academic libraries is quite complicated process issues which needs to be take care properly. Rajender Singh Bist[8] referred the few important issues of e-journals which need to be addressed. These can be considered as important acquisition activities of the e-journals:

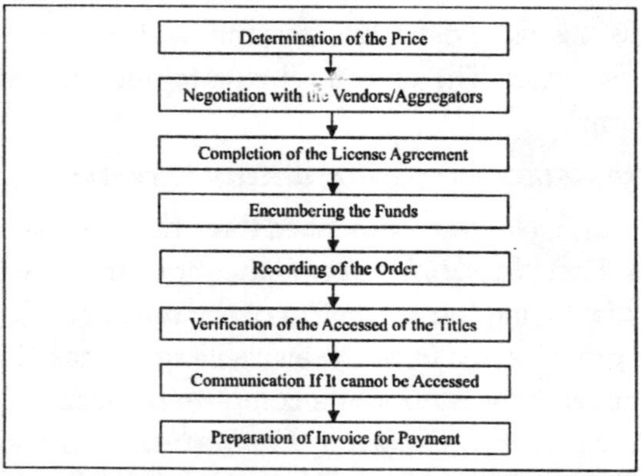

Diagrammatic Representation of Acquisition Activities of E-Journals

Issues in Acquisition of E-Journals

Ownership/ Access rights : Print versions of journals do not have the problems of ownership but in case of e-journals the problems of ownership arises. When the subscription of journals discontinued the librarian kept the previous copies, whereas in case of e-journals sometimes they may not be available for access or cannot be retained when discontinued. This becomes serious issue to the library authority. Librarian must sign the proper agreement which should ensure perpetual access for the uses.

Licensing : A license usually takes the form of a written contract or agreement between the library and the owner of the rights to distribute information. Typical licensing issues include method of calculating payment, restrictions on use, and what happens upon termination etc. Every library needs expert staff and an office that handles and maintains a file of license agreements. It is necessary that the professionals closely review the agreement and clear all the doubts at the time of signing the agreement.

Budgeting : The budgeting of the journals is crucial for the information professionals. In many cases the e-journals initially are free with the print journals. How much budget of the library will be dedicated to the e-journals is serious question for the librarians. Moreover the proportion of e-journals that are free will inevitably decline. There are two theoretical approaches to budgeting,

Pricing Options : It is usually found that e-journals cost more then their print versions. There are dual pricing structures for many online journals that are separate for individual and institutions. Another pricing mechanism is based on the size of the service population, frequently based on the number of library users. What kind of pricing models will be opted will be based on the need of the organisation.

Weeding and cancellation : The weeding of e-journals will be vital questions of the library professionals. The duty of the professionals is to decide which will no longer provide access that is the journal can be stopped. This has to be done keeping in view the user needs. If the library has a dual print and electronic subscription, then it could be decided to cancel the print version keeping in view the cost or budget and space on self. A library presumably would not wish to cancel the print subscriptions until it had confidence in archiving strategy for electronic ones.

5.3. Access Related Issues

E-journals require proper set–up for building the electronic collection. Access to the subscribed e-resources is crucial questions for the vital issues. The task of the librarian is vital in this regard. They must ensure that the technical issues have been addressed and sorted, before the service is implemented. If the access is the web based and domain in nature, providing IP ranges is fairly straightforward. However, password verification is a requirement of some systems, and libraries have to decide who will have access to these passwords within the institution or organizations, will users be logged on individually, or will certain users such as faculty members be given passwords to use as needed. Libraries must also consider that, if anything will appear in the libraries OPAC, will the OPAC reflect just title, electronic address or both. Will there be a link in the OPAC or the library website. If the journals are accessible from offsite, whether through a proxy server or other means, that support exists in the library and the institution for offsite users. Moreover staff will need time for familiarization and training for using the electronic resource and finally providing access. Broadly access can be ensures either through IP ranges or login and passwords.

Multiple IP Addresses: is a group of Internet protocol (IP) addresses. Every institute and organization, libraries having its own web servers sets a single or multiple IP addresses from their internet service provider (ISP). It is also called as static IP address or group of addresses, which are unique in the Internet domain. This number or numbers provided to the publishers at the time of registration will enable the librarians to get online access which is domain restricted, in other words member can access the journals only within their organizations. Whenever the request for article is made, the server at the other end recognizes the request by IP address of the sender. Access is denied in case of mismatch. Most of the publishers prefer to provide access through this method. However, the library not having its web server may seek access through the user name and passwords.

Password Access: Accessing journals through passwords has a plus point, that the members can access the requirements from anywhere, however the misuse of passwords is a consideration. The best option for the access is through IP address. The member need not always remember the password and secondly the access is restricted only to the domain thus preventing unauthorized use.

6. CHALLENGES

The e-journal is the gift of the technology. The tremendous up gradation and advancement virtually changes the way of scholarly communication among the peers.

Incompleteness in coverage: The journal should be complete in coverage. Advent of the e-journal creates problems in this respect. It is almost impossible to make complete coverage with the use of e-journals

Authentication issues: Access is one of the prime challenges for the library personnel. Access will be given to e-journals based on some authentication procedures. It may be either through IP Authentication or by Password Authentication. It is the duty of the library to decide what kind of access will be given to the users and accordingly take security measures in order to avoid unauthenticated users.

Archival issues and long term preservation: The access of the e-journals are not available in the during the any time span of the organisation. It may be limited within the fixed time bound of the publishers. Therefore it is better to archive the electronic resources and preserve properly for the posterity. But the way to do it remains a challenge for the library professionals.

Less control over the object: The main source of the e-journal is from the gateway of the publishers. The use of e-journals may give the users a feeling that it is available within the organisation. Since it is mostly controlled by the publisher, the library authority has less control over the object. Therefore any problem for accessing the documents required the help of the publishing authorities. The library hardly feeling any kinds of ownership over the subscribed objects.

Awareness of the technology: Technology is gradually changing in every respect in this world. It is quite tough for the librarians to keep the staff as well as the users updated about the latest technologies which are used in accessing and retrieving information. To make them aware regular arrangement of different workshops and seminar is the tough task of the librarian in the existing library environment.

Differences in the use of technology: Sometimes technology becomes the barriers of using the e-journals. The types of technology used by the library may not match the technology used by the publisher community which creates serious problems for the library authority. Thus the challenge of the professionals is to keep the current system updated as per the need of the publisher.

Temporary unavailability: The e-journals must be accessible to the user groups to the regardless of the time and space. It is sometimes found that the resources are temporarily unavailable due to the several reasons. The reasons may be on the part of the library or publishing community. But it is the responsibility of the authority to immediately make the resources available without hampering the users at any time of the day.

Technical problems: There are several problems arises in accessing, retrieving and archiving the e-journals for the users. Since these problems are new to the staff it appears as the challenges for the library personnel. Technical problems may consist of any kind of problems which associated with the availability of electronic journals.

Skilled manpower: The problems arise in processing and handling e-journals is serious question for the problems. There is no special training given in these matters. Therefore the scarcity in skilled manpower is the actual case in academic libraries. The staff became experiences with the handling of the more and more electronic journals. the challenge of the professionals to create a fresh set of experienced candidates for the posterity.

Huge expenses: E-journal requires huge initial expenses for making the infrastructure. Therefore incurring great expense in the beginning of implementation of digital library system for accessing e-journals in the prime challenges for the library. Later the expense for maintaining will gradually decrease. But starting the project with the huge expenses becomes challenge for the academic libraries.

Need special equipment: There is need to be proper infrastructure for maintaining the collection of the e-journal. There is need to have proper equipment for maintaining collection. The access and retrieval of the resources need special equipment. The purchasing the standard hardware related to the work also a matter of concern for the academic libraries.

Compatibility among different publishers: It is found that different publishers provide different interfaces for accessing the e-resources. It is quite difficult for the professionals to create a standard platform which enables to accept all the technologies of all the publishers. The compatibility among the different publishers is challenge for the library professionals.

Inadequate promotion and training: E-journals required proper promotion and training. But most of the academic hardly organise promotional activities in respect to e-journals. This is also a true challenges of the information professionals.

Concern about copyright: It is easier for the professional to restrict violation in case of print version of journals. But in case of e-journals it is quite difficult for the library authorities to control. The users of the e-journals can easily browse and download in a limited time period which again the violation of the Copyright.

Difficulties in browsing than paper journals: Browsing e-journals need the basic commuter literacy. Print journals do not need any kinds of user expertise. Anybody can easily use and access the information as we are habituated with the media we are using. But e-journal is separate medium for the users in the academic library and therefore needs more concrete effort and which ultimately remains challenges for the professionals.

Incorporation with paper journals: The print and electronic journals are two different media of the scholarly communication. Therefore the making decision regarding which of the journals will be available only print and what journals will be available in print medium is a serious questions and remains challenges to the library authority. Sometime it may also need of the organisation to keep both the print and electronic copy of the journals. The decision regarding the proportion or combination of the print and electronic journals is question of concern for the library authority.

Require complex licensing agreements: The access and subscription of the e-journals involved complex licensing agreements. But the library professional do not have the knowledge about this areas. Therefore the professionals should acquire the knowledge about the different issues and clauses that may included in the agreement and act accordingly. In near future the licensing issues will be one of the major challenges for the library professional in academic libraries.

Low bandwidth: Bangladesh has already been connected to the Information Super Highway through submarine fibre optic cables in 21 May 2006. However till date the benefits of the fibre optic cables have not reached to the users level. The current bandwidth is not sufficient for the Internet dependent works in the country.

Insufficient computers and computer user: Computers are becoming popular in Bangladesh, but the country is still lack of computers and computer literate users. The number of computers in the country is about 0.5 million (Khan, 2004). Many senior researchers and educationists do not know how to operate the computer. This has led to them being not interested in using ejournals in the libraries.

Lack of Internet connectivity and users: The country has only 2.43 million Internet users (Islam and Rahman, 2006). Even many organisations and libraries do not have any Internet connection, which is a vital barrier for ejournals subscription in Bangladesh.

Uninterruptible Internet connection: Bangladesh's dial up and broadband connection are frequently interrupted due to technological disruptions of Internet service provider and so often cables are cut down by the theft of wires.

Lack in infrastructure development: Although e-journals are less expensive than print journal, the former require good infrastructure such as adequate number of workstations with Internet connection, high bandwidth, laser printers, dedicated web servers, Uninterruptible Power Supply (UPS). Many libraries cannot afford the high cost of this equipment.

Perpetual access: It was found in the study that the ejournal publishers/suppliers do not give access to the e-journals after the end of the subscription period, or do not provide the CD-ROM/ DVD version of the journal.

Continuous training and orientation: Prospective users of e-journals need orientation and training programmes frequently and it is the responsibility of the library to organise training programmes that require special resources person and proper planning.

Complex search techniques: Search syntax and techniques are different from one publisher to another. So it is complicated for the users to capture different search techniques of different journals and to know which search techniques are applicable for a particular e-journal site.

Lack of promotional activities: The academic world around us changing very fast and cope up with this technology you need to accept technology and its advancement. E-journal is one such kind of gift of the technology. But there is a need of constant promotional activities of the e-journals in the colleges and universities to promote the usage of e-journals. This kind of activities will not require in case of print journals. Therefore it is the duty of the information professionals to promote e-journal to its prospective users. But there is lack of realisation of the need for promotional activities and therefore work accordingly. It is rarely found that college and university libraries organise promotional activities for the user group.

7. SUGGESTIONS AND RECOMMENDATIONS

Building and maintaining resource based collection is the need of the day. The modern users of the library are quite different form the previous years. The librarian realising the true nature of the services the infrastructure should be made. Following are some of the important recommendations for removing the challenges in building and maintaining the electronic journal collections:

- Increase the number of Computers in the organisation
- Increase the number of Computer with Internet connection
- Good Speed of Internet connection
- Printing facilities of the e-journals
- CD-write facilities
- Staff orientation and training at regular intervals
- User orientation programmes organised solely by the library authorities
- Maintain own portal or website for providing the access of the resources
- Links to E-journals in the library's site
- Providing facilities for the Remote Access to the e-journals
- Prepare separate processing section of the e-journals
- Providing perpetual access to the users
- Separate experienced staff for the e-resources.
- Try to understand the core issues of access to the e-journals.

8. CONCLUSION

The field of library and information services have been revolutionised with the introduction of ICT in the collection. E-journals appeared as the one of the strong pillars for the academic libraries. Many libraries all over the world have already replaced print journals with e-journals. The academic libraries in India are in the verge of accepting e-journals as most important resource. Therefore it is the duty of the librarian to take proper care of these issues and remove the necessary challenges in the library.

REFERENCES

1 Lancaster, F.W. 1995. "The Evolution of Electronic Publishing". Library Trends, 43(4): 518-527.

2 Harrod's Librarians' Glossary and Reference Book. Accessed January 18, 2010. http://lisdpt.community.officelive.com/Documents/HarrodLibrariansGlossary.pdf

3 Smith, E.T. 2003. Changes in faculty reading behaviors: The impact of electronic journals on the University of Georgia. The Journal of Academic Librarianship, Vol. 29, no.3: 162-168.

4 Rajender Singh Bist. Managing And Handling Electronic Journals : Some Issues. 3rd Convention PLANNER -2005, Assam Univ., Silchar, 10-11 Nov., 2005

5 Thomas E. Nisonger, (1997),"Electronic journal collection management issues", Collection Building, Vol. 16 Iss: 2 pp. 58 - 65

6 Thomas E. Nisonger, (1997),"Electronic journal collection management issues", Collection Building, Vol. 16 Iss: 2 pp. 58 - 65

7 Thomas E. Nisonger, (1997),"Electronic journal collection management issues", Collection Building, Vol. 16 Iss: 2 pp. 58 - 65

8 Rajender Singh Bist. Managing And Handling Electronic Journals : Some Issues. 3rd Convention PLANNER -2005, Assam Univ., Silchar, 10-11 Nov., 2005

18

Medical Libraries Useful Online Resources and Utilization Demand in Age of Communication and Information Technology

Mukesh Chand Bharti

ABSTRACT

Medical libraries are in very dynamic position today due to the adoption of information and communication technologies (ICT) are on the increase in India higher Medical libraries of learning. The paper examines the role played by the medical library and the information and communication technology (ICT) tools in medical research. The study highlights the role of the medical libraries and their on line resources are very useful in meeting the information needs of health professionals. The study also define various kind of information technology tools such as search engine, social networking tools different medical links that can be used by physician and health information professionals in information seeking. The study advocated the formation of consortium by medical libraries in India and national Medical Library (NML) India providing very useful platform to medical libraries to developing their powerful medical healthy on line information environment. Guides to medical resources and internet searching tips are recommended in the study and will be played very vital role.

Keywords: Medical libraries, online resources, information communication technology.

INTRODUCTION

Information is an essential part of our daily life and without information knowledge stem never make progress. Information Technology is studying in many areas of our education systems and majorly it comes from the applied engineering science. It is a branch of computer engineering that is becoming a rapidly growing field and perfectly using in Medical on line resources searches.

The world book dictionary (2008) described information as knowledge given or received in some facts or circum-stances. Raji (2008) sees information as processed data that is purposeful and meaningful to a user.In other words, various businesses and professions in every sphere of life rely heavily on information. Jiyane and Mostert (2010) further asserted that both developed and developing countries are investing in information and communication and its technologies for improving life styles and business practices.

Information system services serve the objectives of their parent bodies. The library deals with the acquisition, organization, processing, storage and dissemination of information. The advent of information communication technology has revolutionaries' information systems which are now linked to one another and to the larger organizations.

We have combined our leading search technology with powerful productivity tools to help users save time in their research process, so they can focus on the output of their work to answer important patient questions, uncover new theories, and make groundbreaking contributions to their field.

To stay ahead of the increasing rate of scientific and medical research output today, you need one destination where you can conduct all your online research in order to do your work efficiently and effectively. Search and discover current full-text e-journals and e-Books, as well as bibliographic information, plus manage your results and all of your research documents.

ROLE OF THE MEDICAL LIBRARY AND HEALTH ORGANIZATIONS IN INFORMATION DEVELOPMENT & SEARCH

Medical libraries are regarded as a special library whose sole objective is for the purpose of providing the information and knowledge resources. As a repository of knowledge, libraries in medical institutions ought to play a leading role in knowledge-based information management. Essentially, the information professional (library staff) is to use his professional skills of information access, retrieval and packaging coupled with computer literacy to provide support services to researchers especially in the area of bibliographies compilation, literature searches of relevant health information, and clinical information in aid of medical users. The past two decades have witnessed a tremendous increase in the availability and use of online resources not only in India across the World. These sources include online databases, articles, thesis, online public access catalog (OPAC) e-conference, e-mail, discussion forums, full text data-bases, books, scholarly websites, pre-print and archives and bulletin boards amongst others. Despite the increase in use of electronic information resources in developed countries, access to published biomedical journals is a major problem for researchers and scientists in lower income countries; especially in Asia one major initiative to solve this problem was the introduction of World Health Organization's led health internet work to research initiative (HINARI). Launched in 2002, HINARI provides health workers and researchers with free or low cost access to a collection of over 3800 online full-text articles of the world's leading biomedical journals from many of the largest publishers of scientific, technical and medical (STM) journals. Also, available through HINARI are databases and other information resources covering medicine, Nursing and Dentistry and Health Science.

All targeted at health workers, researchers and others in not-for profit institutions in developing countries (Press Release figures, 2006). HINARI is targeted at government offices, educational institutions and not-for-profit organizations involved in health care, research, teaching and policy making for free.

WHO : Envisioning better health for all Indians, Mr Ghulam Nabi Azad, the Hon'ble Minister for Health & Family Welfare, Government of India launched WHO's new Country Cooperation Strategy with India (2012-17) along with Dr Nata Menabde, WHO Representative to India on 29 June 2012.

Present at the launch were Mr P K Pradhan, Secretary, Ministry of Health & Family Welfare (MoHFW); Mr K Desiraju, Special Secretary (Health Administration), MoHFW; and development partners including representatives from other UN agencies, World Bank, USAID, CDC, Norway India Partnership Initiative and Rotary International.

Reflecting the shared vision of the two partners, it is for the first time that the Country Cooperation Strategy (CCS) has been developed jointly by the Ministry of Health and Family Welfare (MoHFW), Government of India and the WHO Country Office for India (WCO).

Promoting access to and utilization of affordable, efficiently networked and sustainable quality services by the entire population.

ICMR : The Indian Council of Medical Research, New Delhi, the apex body in India for the formulation, coordination and promotion of biomedical research & literature, is one of the oldest medical research bodies in the world and helping in use of e-sources.

IHO (Indian Health Organization) is on its way to building the finest health care network in India, working with select medical practitioners & helping in information development.

CONSORTIUM DEVELOPMENT IN INDIA

The consortium is a latin word, meaning 'partnership, association or society' and derives from consors 'partner', itself from con-'together' and sors 'fate', meaning owner of means or comrade. Library consortium is a community of two or more information agencies and have formally agreed to coordinate and cooperative of two or more libraries/information agencies which have formally agreed to coordinate, cooperate or consolidate certain function" to achieve mutual objectives it is an association of group of libraries to achieve mutual benefits.

Many Medical consortiums are developing in India for e-resources of medical and health science and making easy platform to search information and supporting to medical users. A study conducted during 2004 various consortia models are practiced in India: ***Open Consortia, Closed Group Consortia, Centrally Funded Model, National Consortium, Publisher Initiatives*** mostly consortium as all the models and using as perfect tool of information search. Some useful e-consortium as INDEST, UGC INFONET, CSIR, ICMR, MCIT Consortia CSIRL, DAE, IIM Consortium and FORSA EBSCO MEDLINE.

UGC has initiated the UGC-INFONET E-Journal consortium is a great boon to academia in the country,Under the consortium, about 494 full text scholarly electronic journals in Medicine and open access databases like PubMed Central, Biomed Central, High wire Press and Public Library of Science, Directory of online journals etc can be accessed.

EBSCO Publishing (http://www.epnet.com) has joined with the Open Society Institute, a part of the Soros Foundations Network, to create the Electronic Information for Libraries Direct (EIFL Direct) consortium. The largest information consortium in the world, EIFL Direct encompasses libraries in 39 countries included in the consortium are 27 countries in Central and Eastern Europe and the former Soviet Union, 10 countries in Southern Africa.

Medical Consortium in India

1. ERMED Consortium

Recognizing the need for sharing of information in biomedical research and development in India through Online Networking the ICMR, New Delhi has taken keen interest in establishing ERMED-India Consortium. 39 centrally funded Government Institutions including 10 Director General of Health Services libraries + 28 ICMR Libraries and AIIMS library are selected at the initial stage as its core members. The consortium will be coordinated though its headquarter set up at the NML. JCCC (Journal Custom Content for Consortia) has been launched by ICMR Head Quarters.

2. National Medical Library Consortium

National medical library, New Delhi has taken up a pilot project for linking 25 Government Medical College Libraries in the country. National Medical Library has set up a network of health science Libraries in India. With the support from WHO, it has 6 regional medical libraries and 8 resource medical libraries in the country. National Medical Library is also the national focal point of HELLIS Network set up by the WHO in Southeast Asia in 1982.

3. HELINET

Health Science Library and Information Network (HELINET), an electronic resource sharing consortia concept was adapted by Rajiv Gandhi Institute of Health Sciences, Karnataka (RGUHS) in 2001 to network all health science libraries in Karnataka. It is the first health university in the country started in 2003 as a collaborative effort to network 25 medical colleges in the state for promoting e-journal access and resource sharing. HELINET has grown to be the single largest library consortium in the country by membership. Today, HELNET is reaching out to 666 medical colleges in the state under university's umbrella.

4 NTRMEDNET

The Digital Library Consortium (named as NTR MEDNET) of NTR University of Health Sciences, Vijayawada, Andhra Pradesh with the libraries of all affiliated colleges was inaugurated on 12-10-2005. Under this Consortium the E-resources are available for the 345 member colleges.

Some other essential e-databases for Medical Libraries:

InfoTrac Medical Collection: http://go.galegroup.com

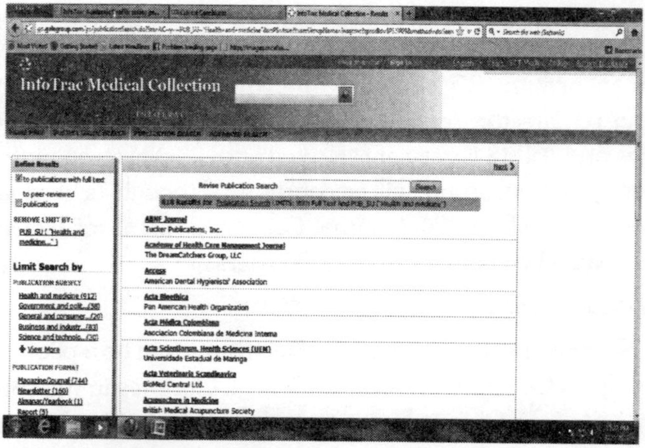

EJ-Server: http://w ww.ejserver.com/

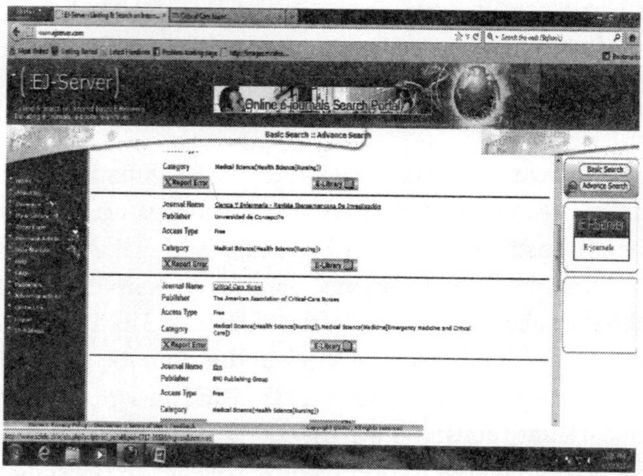

ScienceDirect: http://www.sciencedirect.com/science/journal

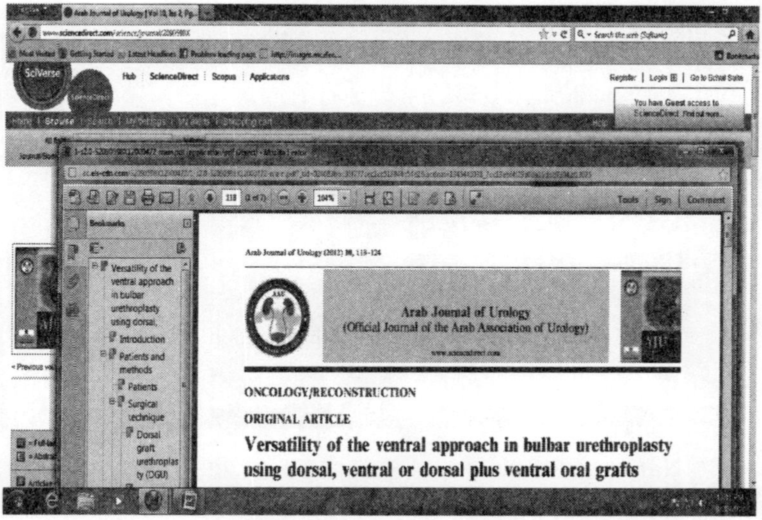

Wiley Online Library: http://onli nelibrar y.wiley.com/subject/ code/000041

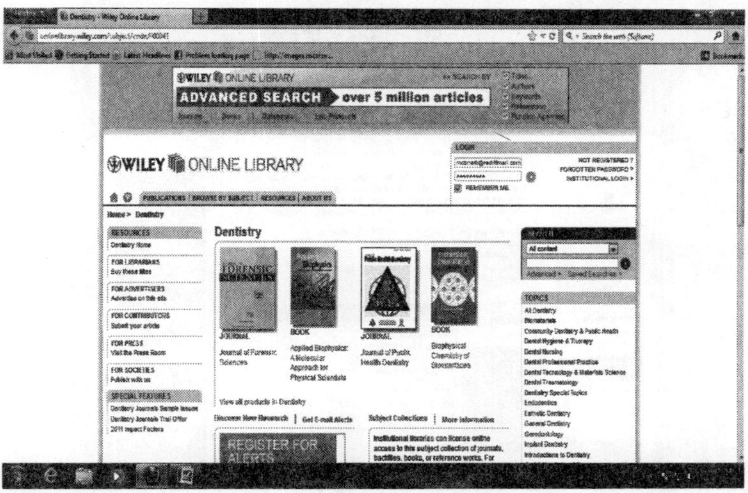

Quintssecse International e-books & Journals: http://www.quintpub.com/journals/journals

Nature Publishing e-Books & Journals: http://www.nature.com/siteindex/index.html

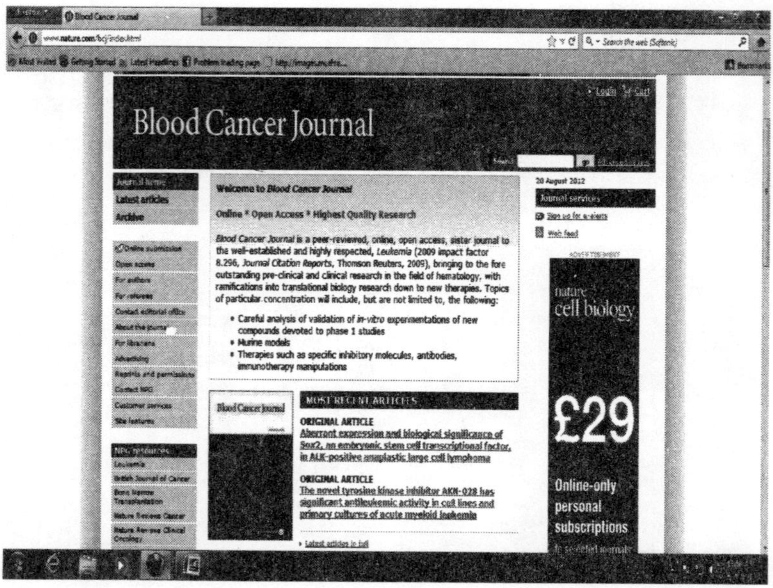

OvidSP: http://www.ovid.com

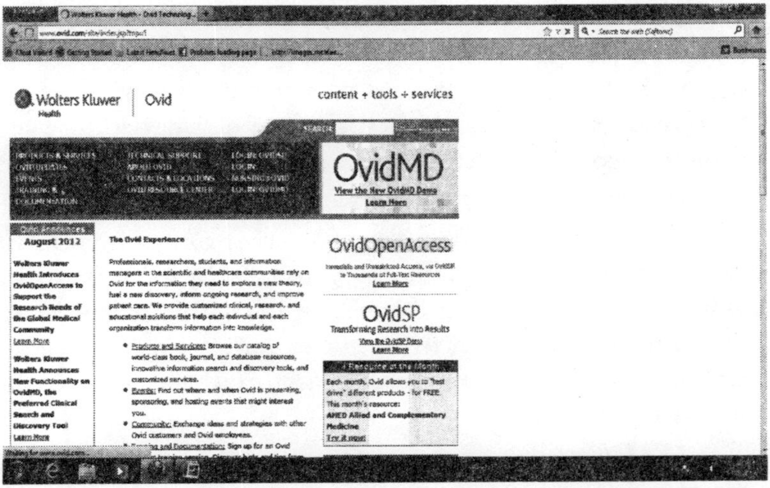

The Medical information resources are found on the internet in various forms:

- Documents
- Pictures & Graphics
- Audio and video files
- E-Books
- E-Journals
- Software
- News directory services
- Library catalogues
- Databases
- Blogs
- Junks

Medical information and use of ideal search engines:

Search engines are the tools that provide subject access to websites. There are many search engines available but all of them search differently and none of them search the entire World Wide Web. Basically, there are four types of search engines:

1. Directory search engines : These search engines operate like a library card catalog. Although they allow word or term searching, the websites included in the directory have been studied and organized into topics and sub-topics. A good example of a directory search engine and two of the best to select for a beginning search are Yahoo (www.yahoo.com) and the www.virtual library (http; /vlib.org).

2. Robot/spider search engines : The majority of the existing search engines employ a technology in which a robot or spider (software) searches through the web or the search engines own database to capture search terms. As a result, a large number or responses are given to the searchers, many of which are not useful e.g. (www.google.com).

3. Meta search engines : Meta search engines are also referred to as "search engines of search engines". This is because they send a search query to several search engines at the same time and display the result found by each search engine. This simplifies the work of the searcher and also allows for comparisons between search engines on their work with a particular topic. Example is (www.dogpile.com).

4. Specialized search engines : Specialized search engines for websites in a particular area only, for Oduwole et al. 3 example, law, medicine, education. Some can only be used to search for sites originating in a particular country or using a particular language country or using a particular language, e.g. (www.education. world.com) and Google scholar (www.scholar.google.com).

Useful links for Medical Information Search:

- http://www.free-ebook-download.net/medical-book/
- http://drebooks.blogspot.com/
- http://downloadfreemedicalbooks.blogspot.com/
- http://medchrome.com/downloads/ebooks/free-medical-ebooks-download-...
- http://www.medicalebooks.net/

- http://theonlinegk.wordpress.com/2009/11/15/free-download-full-text...
- http://www.free-ebook-download.net/video-training/24094-medical-ebo...
- http://www.medcastle.com/more-than-200-medical-books-free-download....
- http://www.filestube.com/m/medical+books+free+pdf
- http://ebookee.org/index.php?tag=61
- http://freeonlinebookstore.org/medicalScience.html
- http://freemedicalebooks.blogspot.com/ -
- http://medicalebooks-aslam.blogspot.com/
- http://medicalebooks-aslam.blogspot.com/

National Cancer Institute

- http://www.cancer.gov/
- http://www.medscape.com/
- http://www.ncbi.nlm.nih.gov/pubmed/
- http://www.proquest.com/en-US/catalogs/databases/detail/medline_ft.shtml
- http://medicalbooksfree.com/
- http://www.freemedicaljournals.com
- http://www.clinicaloptions.com/
- http://www.ama-assn.org/ama/pub/medical-journals.page?
- www.youtube.com/sgulcso
- http://www.ivimeds.org
- http://www.cebm.net/
- http://ebm.bmj.com/
- http://www.gfmer.ch/000_Homepage_En.htm
- http://www2.cochrane.org/reviews/
- http://acpjc.acponline.org
- http://emedicine.medscape.com

- https://www.mededportal.org/?from=mep2
- http://www.eperc.mcw.edu
- http://www.healcentral.org
- http://www.merlot.org
- www.similima.com
- www.medicalebooks-aslam.blogspot.com
- www.innerbody.com
- www.blog.cardiacforum.org
- www.mediconet.blogspot.com
- www.freedentalbooks.blogspot.in
- www.fourthmolar.com
- www.medclip.com
- www.cetl.org.uk

REFERENCES

MEDLINE Overview [Homepage on the internet]. US National Library of Medicine. [Last cited 2007 on May 19]. Available from: http://www.ncbi.nlm.nih.gov/entrez/query/static/overview.html#Medline.

Eysenbach G, Till JE .(2001). Ethical issues in qualitative research on internet communities. BMJ.323:1103-5 .

Adefule Y (2009). Promoting Learning and Research Trough Library Automation and Digital Archiving. Paper delivered at the International book fair, University of Lagos, June 2010.

Agbonlahor RO (2008). Internet Resources. in A.P. Olayinka, L,. Popoola, and A. Ojebode A (Eds). Methodology of Basic and Applied Research. Ibadan: The Postgraduate school, University of Ibadan, Ibadan, pp. 153-171.

Ajegbomogun F, Oduwole A, Agboola T (2008). Consortium Building for Cataloguing and Classification of Nigerian University Libraries: Problems and Prospects. Gateway Libr. J., 11(2): 65-73.

Ajuwon GA, Olorunsaye OJ (2009). Utilization of HINARI resources among Researchers and Clinicians in Health Institutions in South-Western Nigeria. Ibadan: College of Medicine, University of Ibadan, Ibadan.

Alexander B (2006). A New wave of Innovation for Teaching and Learning? "EDUCAUSE Rev., 41(2): 32-44.

Jethwani KS ,Chandwani (2007).The internet: Revolutionizing medical research for novices and virtuosos alike. Students Corners,Vol-54/1:49-51.

Digital Library Initiative — phase 2, (http://www.dli2.nsf.gov/index.html)

Ambati, V.; Sankar, P.; Pratha, L.; and Jawahar, C. 2005. Quality management in digital libraries. In Proceedings of 1st ICUDL.

Bainbridge, D.; Thompson, J.; and H.Witten, I. (2003). Assembling and enriching digital library collections. In Proceedings of the 3rd ACM/IEEE-CS joint conference on Digital libraries, 323–334.

S.G. Hombal, K.N. PrasadS.G. Hombal, K.N. Prasad.(2012) Digital Copyright Protection: Issues in the Digital Library Environment: JLIT. 32(3),07-10.

19

E-Book : Ideal Communication Media for Learning and Knowledge Dissemination

Dr Tabasum Maqbool

ABSTRACT

Paper discusses the concept of e- book and major projects specially developed with regard to e-books and its applications.

Keywords: E-books, portals, projects.

INTRODUCTION

The history of online books traces back to 1945, with the idea of Memex, a design envisaged by Vanaevar Bush, and continues to present day with the electronic reader such as rocket e-book and electronic book reader applications, such as acrobat reader and Microsoft reader. The Memex was to be a storage and retrieval device using microfilm storage. The machine would augment human memory by allowing the users to make links, or "associative trials", between documents. ***(Massachusetts Institute of Technology, 2002).*** Dream of Bush was nurtured by Michael Hart with the inception of Project Gutenberg. A project dedicated to converting public domain books and documents in to ASCII files which over the years inspired number of other such projects in different parts of the world. The next stage in evolution of e-book industry was the creation of CD-ROM that allowed easy access and storage of electronic information. These early efforts led to the current crop of online books, readers and online book applications.

Since the inception of the online books, a number of projects started by various educational institutes like libraries, universities, colleges etc. resulted in the access of online books on the Web via directories, databases, archives, subject gateways, etc. The functional differences in how a book is made available online are profound, with varying levels of ease of reading, copying, repacking, extracting, storing, and using as an archival copy. Some formats are a threat to current publishing paradigms; others (like page images) are digital representations of the current paradigm.

Online books are generally presumed to represent the leading edge of innovation in the presentation and dissemination of information. After all, online books use the latest Internet technology to disseminate ideas which for centuries have been available in print. They can reach potentially enormous academic and lay audiences in a fraction of the time and at a fraction of the cost of printed books.

Some confusion persists about what the term Online or e-Book refers to. Any definition of terms would be slightly problematic until technology and practice settle down long enough for language to catch up. To get a better understanding of online books, some of the researchers and authorities who worked in this direction are quoted in proceeding lines.

Thomson (2009) portray online books as

"a complete book that is made available through the

Internet. Online books are different to regular e-books because they are available directly on Internet, as opposed to a download"

In view of ***Crowston and Williams(2000)***

"An online book is a sequential list of chapters, each linked to the next, with a table of contents pointing to each chapter; and a hyper-document has a pattern of densely interlinked pages".

From the above definitions one conclude that online books are those books where the text is in digital form of words and images to be accessed through internet and viewed on a desktop/notebook/ dedicated portable device or read on all types of computers. The technology now has made it possible to read whole book to the user thus making online books one of the strong medium for the future publishing industry.

FEATURES OF E-BOOKS

Online books are gaining momentum with widely accepted features. The below mentioned features make them popular among masses:

i. They are accessible anywhere 24X7.

ii. Now a day's users not only view images, graphics and multimedia, even entire book is narrated to the user.

iii. Purchasing of foreign books is time consuming but in online format it is accessed quickly.

iv. They cost less than the average conventional books one buys from bookstores.

v. Online books catch the interest of the modern youth and help children to develop a love of reading due to multimedia capabilities.

vi. Never go out of print.

vii. Allow the authors to self-publish and distribute their own books inexpensively.

viii. Help a user to find that quote in seconds (by search through text)

ix. Helps user to annotate or highlight important text

x. Can be customized by the readers to suit their specific interests and tastes e.g. allow users to choose different fonts (text) sizes in which they wish to read the eBook.

xi. Enhance accessibility as these can contain/create links between multiple eBooks.

xii. Very much beneficial for visually impaired readers who can switch to audio mode and listen to an eBook.

xiii. Reference material in eBook format can be easily updated

E-BOOK TYPES

EBookson the basis of format can bebroadly classified in following types:

i. Plain text eBooks

These eBooks exist in plain text format, are small in size and require ASCII standards and are ASCII text files interchangeable and readable on Unix, Macintosh, DOS, Windows and other systems.

ii. Hypertext Markup Language

These electronic files are based on Hypertext and can be read using web browser. These files support a wide range of standards and their display can be complicated.

iii. Kindle eBooks

These eBooks are based on a proprietary file format (Amazon kindle) and can be read using a Kindle eBook Reader. These books are delivered over a wireless system known as Whispernet.

iv. PDF FILES

These ebooks are based on Adobe portal Document Format (created using Adobe Systems) and require Acrobat reader to view the files.PDF files can contain brochures; magazines; product manuals; even an entire books and can embed fonts, images and other documents.

v. MobiPocket Books

These eBooks have an extension "Mobi", using Mobipocket which is based on XHtml open eBook standards. These files can be read by Mobipocket Reader and created by Mobipocket Creator. These files can also be read by popular eBook readers like the Amazon Kindle and many smart phones that support the format.

vi. EPUB BOOKS

These eBooks are based on an open eBook standard format i.e. ePub (electronic publication) that has great compatibility across a wide range of readers like; Kobo Reader, Apple iBook, Barnes and Nook, Sony Reader, Bebook etc.

vii. DAISY BOOKS

Daisy are "Digital Talking Books" (Audio) mainly meant for visually impaired readers, blinds etc. using an open standard format "DAISY" based on MP3 and XML language. DAISY books provide user three important features viz, Multimedia, Navigation, Synchronization.

viii. Multimedia Books

A multimedia eBook is media and book content that utilizes a combination of multiple book content formats. These eBooks include a combination of text, audio, images, video, and/or interactive content formats.

ix. Audio Books

These electronic books are available in recorded form.

Growth of Free E-Book Portals

Progressive development of information and communication technology during recent years has introduced a transformative shift in reading as well as learning manners. Nowadays, dedicated e-textbook applications (i.e. eBooks) and portable personal libraries are forming a new trend for reading and learning. Using popular free eBook portals, users can quickly and easily access the Internet and download information/various interesting books during travels.

EBook portal is simply a starting point into vast ocean of

EBooks where users are able to use and exchange eBooks and videos freely. By Free eBook we mean a publication that involves no direct costs to acquire, access, read, copy or use. These include can include any reading material like textbooks, fiction books, poetry books, audio books etc. Project Gutenberg is the first producer of free eBooks which was founded by Professor Michael Hart in 1971***(Project Gutenberg, 2012)***. The second initiative in the field of free eBooks was the Online Books Page which was founded by John Mark Ockerbloom in 1993 at University of Pennsylvania ***(Ockerbloom, N.A)***. After Online Books Page various other free EBook portals came to the forefront like "Internet Archive" that was founded by Brewster in 1996 at San Francisco ***(Internet Archive, 2001)***. World Digital library was created by Library of Congress in 2009 at UNESCO headquarters in Parisand others like Manybooks.Net is owned by Matthew McClintock and launched in 2004 ***(Many Books.net, 2004)***, Google Books is a service of Google Inc. and was introduced at the Frankfurt Book Fair in October 2004 etc.

Major EBook Projects and Portals

A number of projects have been launched for the books to make them available online on the Web. An exponential growth of online books has made them more favourite among the internet users. Some of the distinguished online book projects are discussed in the following lines.

The Project Gutenberg

http://www.gutenberg.org

The Project Gutenbergthe first and largest online library of free electronic books started in 1971when Michael Hart was a student at the University of Illinois (USA). He set up Project Gutenberg with the goal of making available for free, and electronically, the largest possible number of books whose copyright had expired. This ground-breaking project became both the first Internet information site and the world's first digitized library. Michael himself typed in the first hundred books. When the Internet became widely-used, in the mid-1990s, the project got a boost and an international dimension. Michael still typed and scanned in books, but now coordinated the work of dozens and then hundreds of volunteers in many countries.

The increase in the online books available through Project Gutenberg is clearly seen as the number of electronic books rose from 1,000 (in August 1997) to 2,000 (in May 1999), 3,000 (in December 2000) and 4,000 (in October 2001). Project Gutenberg had 5,000 books online in April 2002 and reached 10,000 in October 2003,with the support of 1,000 volunteers around the world making 350 new books available every month. As on May, 2009 there are 28,000 free books available in the Project Gutenberg. Users have shown great interest in this project as the number of books downloaded monthly has crossed 2 million mark.

The Million Book Project

http://www.ulib.org/

The Million Book Project (2009) (or the Universal Digital Library), led by Carnegie Mellon University School of Computer Science and University Libraries, digitized more than a million books. Working with government and research partners in India and China, the project is scanning books in many languages, using OCR to enable full text searching, and providing free-to-read access to the books on the Web. As on May 2009, they have completed the scanning of 1.5 million books in 20 languages: 970,000 in Chinese; 360,000 in English; 50,000 in Telugu; and 40,000 in Arabic. Most of the books are in the public domain, while permission has been acquired to include over 60,000 copyrighted books (roughly 53,000 in English and 7,000 in Indian languages) accessible online.

The Open Content Alliance

http://www.opencontentalliance.org/

The Open Content Alliance OCAwas founded in 2005 is a consortium of organizations contributing to a permanent, publicly accessible archive of digitized texts. It is collaborative project of Yahoo!, the Internet Archive, the University of California, the University of Toronto and others. The OCA is, in part, a response to Google Book Search. OCA digitizes copyrighted works only after asking and receiving permission from the copyright holder ("opt-in"). While Google Book Search digitizes copyrighted works unless explicitly told not to do so ("opt-out"). So far OCA has digitised scanning of over 750,000 books, 300,000 of which are now part of the Internet Archive's online collection.

Google Book Search

http://books.google.com/googlebooks/

Google didn't lack behind in the online book market. It launched its online books programme in 2004 by the name of "Google Print", now known as "Google Book Search" with an attempt to scan the contents of the books available in famous libraries of the world. It quickly grabbed the attention of the user community from all over the world initially five major university libraries of the world namely University of Michigan, Harvard University, Stanford University, the New York Public Library and Oxford University, became part of the programme which is now expanded to 28 library partners. Besides, the book search interface is now available in 35 languages. Over 10,000 publishers and authors from more than 100 countries are participating in the book search partner program. ***(Google Book Search, 2009)***

Bookshare

http://www.bookshare.org/

Bookshare is an online accessible digital library for print disabled readers. Bookshare has over 50,000 books as on July 2009 in its collection, contributed by volunteers (who scan and upload the books to the site) and by major publishers (who send digital versions of their books to the collection). Bookshare has more than 60,000 users as on July 2009.It is a project run by Benetech, which is a non-profit organisation based in Palo Alto, California, USA.

Internet Archive (IA)

http://www.archive.org/

The Internet Archive (IA) is a non-profit organization dedicated to building and maintaining a free and openly accessible online digital library, including an archive of the Web, software, movies, books, and audio recordings. To ensure the stability and endurance of the Internet Archive, its collection is mirrored at the Bibliotheca Alexandrina in Egypt, so far the only library in the world with a mirror.

The IA makes its collection available at no cost to researchers, historians, scholars, and the general public. It is a member of the American Library Association and is officially recognised by the State of California as a library.

The texts collection includes digitized books from various libraries around the world as well as many special collections. As of September 2009, the Internet Archive operated 18 scanning centres in five countries, digitizing about 1,000 books a day, financially supported by libraries and foundations.

Between about 2006 and 2008 Microsoft Corporation had a special relationship with Internet Archive texts through its Live Search Books project, scanning over 300,000 books which were contributed to the collection, as well as financial support and scanning equipment.

Rare Book Room

http://www.rarebookroom.org/

Rare Book Room is an educational website for the repository of digitally scanned rare books made freely available to the public. Starting around 1996 the California based company Octavo began scanning rare and important books from libraries around the world. These scans were done at extremely high resolution using high-quality equipment, with some pages at over 200MB each. Theseare sold by Octavo as commercial products on CD-ROM. In 2006 the "Rare Book Room" website was created which contains the complete collection in medium to medium-high resolution freely available to the public through a web browser or as a PDF file. As on 2009 over 700 books are reported to be scanned.

The online books are revolutionizing the publishing industry through the rapid proliferation of digital reading material in the market place. Online books are the most important developments in the world of literature since Gutenberg Press. They have become a key driver for the information that used to be a part of the traditional books in print formats having a number of limitations. These help in disseminating the ideas that have been available only in print. They can reach potentially enormous academic and general audiences in a fraction of the time and at a fraction of the cost compared to that of printed books.

Ebrary

http://www.ebrary.com

Ebrary was founded by Christopher Warnock and Kevin Sayar. The vision is to build bridges between islands of information and facilitating the migration of valuable, authoritative information to the Internet through libraries. The core aim of Ebrary is to evolve symbiotic relationship between libraries, publishers, booksellers and consumers. At present, Ebrary offers access to more than 40,000 full-text books and other documents from over 180 of the world's leading academic, trade and professional publishers. Currently more than 1000 libraries throughout the world subscribe to Ebrary.

Questia

http://www.questia.com/

Questia, the one of largest online library provides access to online collection of books, journal articles, magazines and newspaper articles. It provides access to around 10,000 books from around 300 renowned publishers. One can search each and every word of all of the books and journal articles in the collection. Users can read every title cover to cover. Undergraduate, high school, graduate students, and internet users of all ages have found Questia to be an invaluable online resource.

CONCLUSION

The emergence of eBooks as a central part of the information experience requires libraries to think differently about how to meet the needs of their users. While eBooks may not absolutely replace print books in the near future, but users are rapidly adopting them as complementary to print books. Users value the convenience and ease of access that eBooks provide and are engaging in new forms of book content to take advantages of growing eBook collection available online via umpteen portals dedicated to this cause. Libraries can exploit the popularity of its unique combination in two ways one by educating larger population of users about availability of free eBook portals available and secondly thereby overcoming ever squeezing of funds of library. So this is a win-win situation not only to users but for library as well.

REFERENCES

Crowston, Kevin.,& Williams, Marie (2000). Reproduced and Emergent Genres of Communication on the World Wide Web. *The Information Society*, V16:201–215. Retrieved October 23, 2012 from http://citeseerx.ist.psu.edu/viewdoc/download?doi=10.1.1.84.3388&rep=rep1&type=pdf

Internet Archive. (2001). Frequently Asked Questions. Archive.org. Retrieved on 27th September, 2012 from http://archive.org/about/about.php

Manybooks.Net. (N.A). ManyBooks.net the best eBooks at the best price: free.*Manybooks.net.* Retrieved on 10th October, 2012 from http://manybooks.net/about/

Massachusetts Institute of Technology.(2002). Hypertext. Retrieved February 06, 2012 from http://inventors.about.com/gi/dynamic/offsite.htm&site

Ockerbloom, John Mark. (N.A) .The Online Book Page.Retrieved on 16thoctober, 2012 from http://onlinebooks.library.upenn.edu/aboutolbp.html

Project Gutenberg.(2012). Free eBooks by Project. Retrieved on 10thoctober, 2012 from http://www.gutenberg.org/

Thomson, Robert (2009). Reading Online Books Through The Internet. Retrieved October 23, 2012 from http://b4tea.com/internet/reading-online-books-through-the-internet

20

Managing Library's Corporate Culture for Organizational Effeiciency and Enhanced Service

Ramveer Sagar
Dr. D. S. Thakur

ABSTRACT

This paper is critical analysis of managing the library's corporate culture to enhance organizational efficiency, productivity, and efficient service system. It seeks to sensitize the library managers through divergent views and opinions how they can manage the corporate culture of their organizations, and to apply the basic principles of corporate culture management to library management. In response to the emergence of Information and Communication Technologies (ICT) that have brought changes to libraries, the paper explores the management of change in libraries corporate culture, especially in this era of ICT.

Key Words: Corporate Culture, Library Management, Culture Organization, Technology

INTRODUCTION

Academic interest in corporate culture is evidence by the level of attention it has received over the last few decades. The relationship between corporate culture and performance has been the subject of abundant research in several fields, including strategic management, organizational behaviour, and industrial organizations. While this topic is rich in studies, many researchers concur on the fact that there is no agreement on the precise nature of the relationship between corporate culture and performance.

Corporate culture is a component in the achievement of an organization's mission and strategies, the improvement of organizational effectiveness, and the management of change. Culture is rooted in deeply held beliefs. It reflects what has worked in the past. It is pattern of shared beliefs, attitudes, assumptions and values, which may not have been explicitly articulated. Corporate culture shapes the way people act and interact and strongly influences how things get done. It encompasses the organization's goal's behavioral norms, and dominant ideologies. Culture can be expressed through the organization's myths, heroes, legends, stories, jargon, rites, and ritual.

Libraries managers live within the corporate culture. They must understand it as a basis for diagnosing and solving problems and for managing the culture in times of change or during crises.

Culture is manifested in the forum of norms, the unwritten rules of behavior and values, what is regarded as important expressed as beliefs on what is best or good for the organization and what ought to happen. Values can be implicit or articulated in value statements. The value set of an organization may only be recognized at the top level, or shared so that the enterprise could be described as values-driven. Corporate culture is a system that is continuously affected by events and influences over time. These drive from the organization's external environment and from its internal processes, systems, and technology. [1]

1. MANAGING CORPORATE CULTURE

Because corporate culture is based on taken- for-granted assumptions and belief, it can be elusive concept. They may not be a single culture, but a number of culture s spread throughout the organization, and this does not make "managing" the corporate culture easier. There is no such thing as a "good" or "bad" culture, but only cultures that are appropriate or inappropriate.

The strength of culture clearly influences its impact on corporate behavior. Strong cultures have more widely-shared and more clearly expressed beliefs and values than do weak ones. These values will probably have been developed over a considerably period of time and they will be perceived as functional in the sense that they help the organization achieve its purpose. [2]

2. LIBRARY AND CORPORATE CULTURE

The library is an organization that has existed for centuries and has formed its own particular culture, which has not been static. In many cases a parent institution or organization, objectives determines the library's purpose and functions. The library is an organization where professionals, paraprofessionals, and other specialists work with a common objective that is, making information available to library patrons. The professional librarians are the key actors in creating library culture, and they have principles, rules, and guidelines for service, while being guided by professional ethics.

3. CHANGING CORPORATE CULTURE

Culture is not static. As the external factors that influence culture change, so culture will change. However, culture change will be slow, unless there are some major shocks to the organization. As Handy (1986) commented "experience suggests that a strong culture makes a strong organization, but does it matter what sort of culture is involved? Yes, it does. Not all cultures suit all purposes or people. Cultures are founded and built over the years by the dominant groups in an organization.[3]

4. DEVELOPING CORPORATE CULTURE IN LIBRARIES

For the libraries undergoing restructuring, management issues are now as important as technical processes and operations. Libraries are developing their mission statements, objectives and strategies to cut costs and enhance services; they are reorienting their services keeping in view their customers requirements. They are trying to have strategic alliances with other libraries for building collections and providing enhances services to their users through resource sharing. Privatization of some of the sections, e.g. reprography and the internet access is just happening at some libraries to improve efficiency, eliminate problems and achieve the desire quality of work. To achieve the time target of project-based work, some libraries are even getting the work done through outsourcing, e.g. retro conversion of card catalogues, introduction of RFID technology.[4]

5. TYPES OF CORPORATE CULTURES

The most useful typology has been developed by Charles Handy. Handy's categorization develops:

5.1. Power Culture

As one that is centrally controlled by powerful individuals. They tend to lack formal rules and decisions are based upon powe: relationships. People in the power culture organizations tend to be "power" minded, risks takers, loner and pretty "thick- skinned" .See Fig.1.

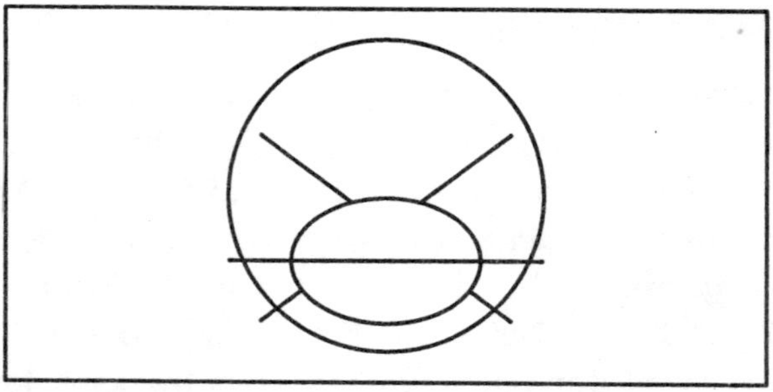

Fig. 1. Power Culture

5.2. Role Culture

Another name for a bureaucratic organization with clear lines of accountability, authority and communication channels. They tend to be stable and secure environments with people adapting to roles using accepted methods. See Fig.2

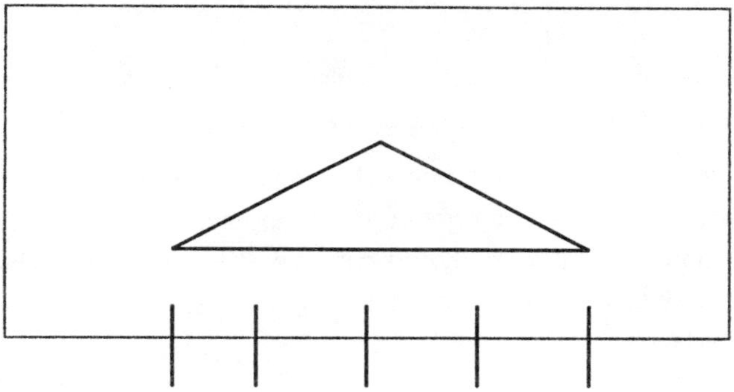

Fig. 2. Role Culture

5.4. Task Culture

Which is job –or-project-oriented. Experience and team working are highly regarded and give a power base. People on the whole like working in task. Fig. 3

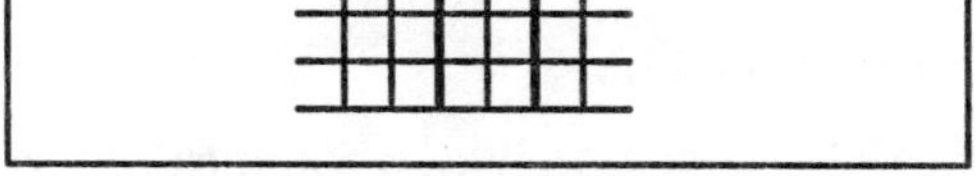

Fig. 3. Task Culture

5.5. Person Culture

Where the organization exists to serve the needs of individuals. People pursue their own development before that of the whole. Individuals tend to be irresponsive to conventional power system and hence cause managerial problems when they exist alongside the other culture dimensions mentioned previously. See Fig. 4

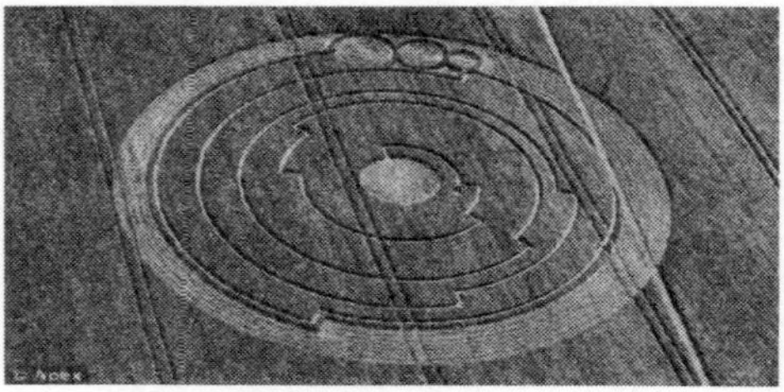

Fig. 4. Person Culture [5]

As handy points out, none of these cultures is right or wrong. Any one of them could be right in particular circumstances. This rule applies generally when analyzing cultures. It is neither possible nor desirable to impose on an organization a culture which is inappropriate to its needs.

6. CULTURE SHAPING FACTORS

Although each enterprise's special blend of elements develop a unique culture, a comparison of many enterprises identifies seven culture shaping factors (Plunkett and Attner, 1994:265):

- Key Business Processes
- Employees and other tangible assets
- Formal Arrangement
- The dominant coalition
- The social system
- Technology
- The external environment.

Each of these factors is in itself a complex concept and none is independent of the others. Their dynamic interaction shapes the corporate culture.

Key Business Processes: At the core and fundamental to every enterprise are the processes employees follow to gather information, make decisions, communicate, produce a product or service and manage work flow. The enterprise is defined by how leaders communicate to employees, how they share their decision making and how they structure the flow of work. The business processes affect and are affected by the other six factors that influence corporate culture.

Employees and other tangible assets: An enterprise's resources, like employee population, plant and offices, equipment, tools, land, inventory and money, are used by the enterprise to carry out its activities. These are the most visible and complex of the factors that influence culture because their quality and quantity determine much of the enterprise's culture and performance.

Formal Arrangement: The formal arrangements that organize tasks and individuals constitute another factor that affects corporate culture. These arrangements include the structure of the enterprise and its procedures, rules and specific mandated behaviors.

The dominant coalition: An enterprise's culture is intensely impacted by the goals, objectives, strategies, personnel characteristics and interrelationship of its leaders, who form the dominant coalition,. The leadership style of the enterprise leaders determines how employees are treated and how they feel about themselves and their work.

The social system: The social system contributes norms and values to the corporate culture. Components like employee relationship, the grapevine and the informal organization are also parts of the social system. Because people are the enterprise, their relationships define the enterprise's character.

Technology: The principal technological processes and equipment that employees use also affect corporate culture. For example, the utilization of technology plays a role. The question to ask regarding technology is: Is a machine or process intended to replace human labour or enable employee to enhance their skills and productivity? The answer to this question sends a message about the value of employees in the enterprise.

The external environment: An enterprise's external environment includes forces outside its boundaries that interact directly and indirectly with it. These forces might be suppliers, markets, competitors, regulators, organized labour and other elements outside an enterprise. These forces affect the goals, resources and processes of an enterprise. Clearly these elements shape the enterprise's culture in many ways.[6]

7. CORPORATE CULTURE IN INDIA

IT is now widely accepted that economic development cannot be adequately grasped unless the role of 'non-economic factor' is taken into account. This recognition, however, has generated a controversy over the precise role assigned to 'non-economic factors' in development. There 'non-economic factor' e was a time when under the influence of Schumpeter's ideas on entrepreneurship were considered more important than 'economic factors'. Schumpeter's argued that the entrepreneurship almost defied the laws of economic to give the critical push necessary for the economic to give the critical push necessary for the economy to attain higher levels of efficiency.[7]

CONCLUSION

Rapid changes are taking place in the information environment and managing change in the libraries and information centers is the greatest challenges of libraries. Library personnel play key role in managing the process of changes in the libraries.

Culture helps account for variations among organizations and managers, both nationally and internationally. It helps to explain why different groups of people perceive things in their own way and perform things differently from other groups. However, all members of staff help to shape the dominant culture of an organization, irrespective of what senior management feels it should be. Culture is also and determined by the nature of staff employed and extend to which they accept management philosophy and policies or pay only "lip service". It is therefore necessary that library managers live within the corporate culture. Understand it as a basis for diagnosing and solving problems and for developing new policies or procedures. And they may well be involved in managing the the culture in times of change or during crises.

REFERENCES

1. Armstrong, M (1991) "A hand book of personnel management practice" 4th ed. London: Kogan Page.
2. Sachin, E. H. (1983) "Organizational dynamics. Summer
3. Burnes, B (1991) .Managerial competency and new technologies: don't shoot the piano player—he's doing his best. *Behavior and Information Technology*, 10(2),91-109.
4. Malhan I.V. (2006). Developing corporate culture in the Indian university libraries: problems and challenges of change management. *Library management*, 27 (67), 486-493.
5. Handy, Ch. (1993) .Understanding Organization. Penguin Group, England
6. Ndleela, L. T. and Toit, A.S.A. Du (2000). Corporate culture as a foundation for successful knowledge management, 1(4).
7. Panini, M (1988). Corporate culture in India. *Economical and political weekly*, 23(35) (August 27), M86-M94

21

Digitization of Library Materials

Anil Kumar Siwach

ABSTRACT

Digitization is the conversion of materials or analog media into electronic form for creating digital collection. The digitization of library materials is now an established technology, and has been instituted throughout the world in programmes which convert holdings to digital form in order to allow wider access and better preservation. Digitization improves access to library resources. By digitizing library collections, information will be accessible to all instead of a select few. It is incumbent upon the library community to develop a carefully reasoned approach to the selection of library materials for digital conversion that is fiscally responsible to both itself and its parent institution.

Keywords: Digitization, Selection, Preservation

INTRODUCTION

The developments in the information, communication and web technologies have had a profound impact on every sphere of life and libraries are no exceptions. The most important contribution of web technologies in the field library and information service sector can be said to be the creation of digital library that allows users to access digital information resources from virtually anywhere in the world. Digitization in libraries is today's response towards a faster delivery of information to its users via internet or intranet. Digital conversion of Library materials has advanced rapidly in past few years. Digitization is one of the hot topics in librarianship today. To build a "Digital Library" requires that the content of a collection be available electronically.

DIGITALIZATION–MEANING

Digitization is the process by which analogue content is converted into a sequence of 1s and 0s and put into a binary code to be readable by a computer. It refers to the process of translating a piece of information such as a book, journal articles, sound recordings, pictures, audio tapes or videos recordings, etc. into bits. Bits are the fundamental units of information in a computer system. Converting information into these binary digits is called digitization, which can be achieved through a variety of existing technologies. A digital image, in turn, is composed of a set of pixels (picture elements), arranged according to a pre-defined ratio of columns and rows. An image file can be managed as a regular computer file and can be retrieved, printed and modified using appropriate software (Arora, 2010). Digitization process converts archival materials from formats that can be read by people (analogue) to a format that can be read only with the help of machines (digital). It is a process of taking a physical object (analogue contents), and taking photographs of or scanning the item and transferring the photographs into a digital medium. It is also a process of archiving born digitals into the institutions collections.

The process of digitization involves two major sets of activities: (1) the process of digital conversion where by the source materials are converted into digital form, and (2) the processing of digitized information, which involves several activities related to the storage, organization, processing and retrieval of digitized information (Chowdhury & Chowdhury, 2004). Digital information has common characteristics and qualities regardless of whether the content is stored on DVD, CD-ROM or other digital storage media: it can be linked to other materials to create multimedia; it is not dependent upon spatial or temporal barriers, or hierarchies; it can be stored and delivered in a variety of ways; and can be copied limitless times without degradation of the original. Digital data can be compressed for storage; meaning that enormous amounts of analogue content can be stored in a computer drive or on CD-ROM. Digital content can be browsed easily, and can be searched, indexed or collated instantly. Most importantly, it can be linked to a whole web of other content, either locally or globally via the Internet (Hughes, 2004).

WHY DIGITIZE

The growth of information and telecommunication technologies, web technologies and database technologies has compelled library and information centers to use them effectively to render better services. The expansion of global computer networks and high-speed access to the internet has led to a proliferation of digital content, delivered to increasing number of computer users worldwide (Hughes, 2004). There are several reasons for libraries to go for digitization. Some of these are highlighted here:

User Needs : The prime reason for digitization is the need of the user for convenient access to high quality information.

Usefulness : Digitizing a document in print or other physical media (e.g., sound recordings) makes the document more useful as well as more accessible.

Preservation : Digitization allows people to read older or unique documents without damage to the originals.

Accessibility : Digital information can be made accessible to existing users as well as distant users through the computer networks over the Internet.

Reuse : Digital documents can be converted into different formats; for example to use images in a slideshow and to adopt the content for a different purpose.

Multiple Usages: Digital information can be used simultaneously by several users at the same time.

ADVANTAGE OF DIGITIZATION

Some important advantages which digitization offers are as follows:

1. Broader Access : Digitization enables greater access to collections of all types. Availability of information in digital form enhances its delivery to a wider community as compared to its analogue counterpart. Digital materials can be made available to a broader audience than those who travel to the library to see the analogue collections, and access can be expanded to non-traditional audiences such as lifelong learners. Whatever the audience, their access to the materials is enhanced by the advantages of the digital format (Hughes, 2004).

2. Collection management : The availability of materials in digital form can help in overcoming the gaps in the existing collection. Digitization can also be a means of creating resources that can be used for different unforeseen purposes in the future.

3. Boost to research and education : The potential of this technology to enhance teaching, research, lifelong learning, or any number of possible goals that digitization is intended to achieve is huge and it will have a vital role to play in the e-learning environment.

4. Preservation of materials : Developing a digital surrogate of a rare or fragile original object can provide access to users while preventing the original from damage by handling or display (Hughes, 2004).

5. Saves space : The digital information takes less space for storage.

6. Digitization increases the scholarly value of source materials.

7. Providing access to digitized collections can help publicize the materials to other departments and peers, in other institutions around the world and demonstrate the importance of the collections.

8. Digitalization promotes international digital collaborations.

SELECTION OF MATERIAL FOR DIGITIZATION

Selecting materials for digitization is more complex than is selecting materials for the purchase or licensing of born-digital materials, because it involves expending resources for items that are already in the library's collection rather than acquiring new ones. In theory, a library would choose to digitize existing collection items only if it could identify the value that is added by digitization and determine that the benefits outweigh the costs (Smith, 2001). Before digitizing anything, it is important to establish procedures and criteria for selecting the material to be digitized. The decisions you make will depend on the particular aims and resources of your project, but it is vital that you develop some clearly defined criteria to guide the selection process.

The process of selection of material for digitization involves identification, selection and prioritization of documents that are to be digitized. The factors that need to be kept in consideration during selection of materials for digitization may include the following:

Vision and Mission : Selection of materials for digitization should be aligned closely with the mission and goals of the parent institution. It is important to see how does the digitization of the collection fit in with the wider aims and objectives of the group, department or institution.

Collection Policy : The policy for collecting and preserving content may be defined by law or by policy documents created within the collecting institution. These vary in detail and scope, from general legal obligations to detailed treatments of specific documentary types. Any selection for digitization should firstly fit these policies. The explicit aims, purposes and characteristics of the collection evidently have a direct influence on the selection of these documents.

Document Value : The intrinsic and use value of the document is necessary to analyze. The Intrinsic documentary value is primarily defined by content and context. Greater value is attributed to documents for which the authenticity and integrity can be ensured and the provenance is clear. The value of an item may be expressed in terms of its ability to meet these needs, bearing in mind, however, that the potential differences between current, intended and actual use require frequent re-evaluation (Ooghe & Moreels, 2009).

User Needs : In addition to evaluating the collection, it is important that an assessment of your users and their needs is undertaken. This might take a number of different forms (survey, focus group, analysis of previous usage), but it must establish who the potential users are, what parts of the collection they're likely to be most interested in, and how they might want to use the resources once digitized.

Budget/ Finance : The single most influential factor for selection is the financial framework of an initiative. Amount of finance available will be a key factor in selecting the documents for digitization.

Cost Benefit Analysis : For each sum used to digitize a part of the collection, another part will have to remain untouched. Similarly, finances used for digitization can't be used for new acquisitions. The criterion 'cost of loss' implies weighing the benefits of selecting larger parts of the collection against the significance of documents that are more costly to digitize, and weighing the cost-benefits of digitization against those of collection care.

Legal Restrictions : Legal restrictions on the reproduction (both in analogue and digital form) and the distribution of documents considerably affect the choices of material to be moved into publicly and often internationally accessible collections. Legal issues therefore represent some of the most important guiding factors in digitization. The materials selected should be in the public domain due to date or circumstances of publication or the library should have copyright permission to use the materials for this purpose.

Physical State of the Material : In general, priority should be given to material for which the content is likely to become inaccessible in the short- or mid-term. Such inaccessibility may be caused by physical decay. Documents most likely to physically disappear are usually prioritized, while fragile documents may be selected to reduce the danger of further decay caused by handling. However, when documents cannot be digitized without risk of loss or further damage, an institution might opt to delay selection in hopes of finding a safer method of digitization before the document disappears (Ooghe & Moreels, 2009).

Digital Multiplicity : If an organisation generates contents, strategies may be adopted to capture data that is "born digital". If documents are available in digital form, it can be easily converted into other formats. Considering the financial and logistic impact of digitization, it might be proposed to give lower priority to material that has been digitized elsewhere or that is available elsewhere in a better copy. This choice should also depend upon institutional differences in accessibility and legal restraints on the respective multiples. Close cooperation between institutions is necessary in order to map possible overlap between collections and to decide whose multiple will eventually be selected.

TOOLS FOR DIGITIZATION

The tools required for digitization can be listed as follows:

Hardware

1. Computer Systems
2. Scanner
3. Digital Camera

Software

1. Image editing software
2. File compression software
3. OCR Software

DIGITAL CONVERSION PROCESS

The digital conversion process includes the following:

1. Document
2. Data Capture
3. Data Processing
4. Storage

5. Indexing and processing
6. Retrieval and display

Document : They include the materials which need to be digitized like text, photographs, diagrams, charts, maps, colors, images, etc. They exist either in print or non-print form or also as single unit or collection.

Data Capture or Scanning : Data can be entered manually or we can use scanners for capturing the image. Capturing page image format is comparatively easy and produces a reproduction of its original maintaining page integrity and originality.

Data processing : The text in the convertible document may require conversion of diacritics or special characters; images may need enhancements, amplification or compression. To make the document text searchable it need to be OCRed. OCR (Optical Character Recognition) programs are software tools used to transform scanned textual page images into word processing file. OCR or text recognition is the process of electronically identifying text in a bit-mapped page image or set of images and generate a file containing that text in ASCII code or in a specified word processing format leaving the image intact in the process (Arora, 2010).

Storage : The digitized information needs to be transferred from the hard disc of scanning workstation to an external large digital storage medium, which may be hard disk, magnetic tape, optical CD-ROM, or networks with workstation to access.

Indexing and processing : Digitized documents need to be processed using standards, protocols and indexing systems. Metadata application should be a major component of the digital information processing. Dublin Core standard is adopted internationally to create Meta data of digital resources. Dublin Core recommends a minimal of 15 data elements to describe any documents.

Retrieval/Display : It is the process that uses an array of technologies for browsing, displaying and applying packages that ultimately helps in access. Most of the document management systems provide elaborate search possibilities including use of Boolean and proximity operators and wild cards and refining the search strategy.

CONCLUSION

The objectives of digitization initiatives differ from organisation to organization but the primary objective is to improve access. Some of the forces that prompted digitization include the proliferation of electronic information, the desire to access materials in remote locations, the quest for collaboration, partnerships and resource sharing, and the ever increasing cost of preserving analogue materials. A document can be converted into digital format depending on the objective of digitization, end user, availability of finances, etc. The most significant challenges in planning and execution of a digitization project relate to technical limitations, budgetary constraints, copyright considerations, lack of policy guidelines and, lastly, the selection of materials for digitization. Digitization, like other collection-development strategies, works to the extent that it supports the mission of an institution. Without a clear sense of how digital projects may fit an institution's mission, it is difficult to build a strategy for sustaining them.

REFERENCES

Arora, Jagdish (2010). Digitization: Methods, tools and technology. In Tariq Ashraf, Jaideep Sharma and Puja Anand Gulati (Eds.) *Developing Sustainable Digital Libraries: Socio-technical perspective* (pp. 40-63). Hershey: Information Science Reference.

Bhalekar, Dipak Krushnarao and Deshmukh, Prashant P. (2005). *Needs for digitization of library: Technology & supporting format.* Paper presented at 3rd Convention PLANNER -2005, Assam Univ., Silchar, 10-11 Nov., 2005.

Chowdhury, G. G. and Chowdhury, S. (2004). *Introduction to digital libraries.* London: Facet Publishing.

Ooghe, Bart and Moreels, Dries (2009). Analysing selection for digitisation: Current practices and common incentives. *D-Lib Magazine*, 15 (9/10).

Reza, Sarwat Masuda (2006). *Problems and prospects of digital library and library digitization in Bangladeshi institutes of higher education.* Paper presented at 4th Convention PLANNER -2006, Mizoram Univ.,Aizawl, 09-10 November, 2006.

Seshaiah, O. (2005). *Building a digital library.* Paper presented at 3rd Convention

PLANNER -2005, Assam Univ., Silchar, 10-11 Nov., 2005. Ahmedabad.

Singh, S.N. (2006). *Digitization initiatives and university libraries in India.* Paper presented at 4th Convention PLANNER -2006, Mizoram Univ.,Aizawl, 09-10 November, 2006.

Smith, Abby (2001). *Strategies for Building Digitized Collections.* Washington, D.C.: Digital Library Federation, Council on Library and Information Resources.

Verma, Maya (2008). *Digitization and New Role of Library Professionals.* Paper presented at 6th International CALIBER -2008, University of Allahabad, Allahabad, February 28-29 & March 1, 2008.

22

Importance of Information Seeking and Use Behaviour Studies in the Development of the Library and Information Centres in Digital Environment

Sobhagyawati Gupta
Madan Singh Rana

ABSTRACT

The users' information needs, information use pattern, choice of materials and preferences and information behaviour studies are very important in the context of libraries as a better service providing center. Especially, information seeking and use behaviour studies are essential for designing the library and information system and services. This paper discusses the role and importance of information seeking and use behaviour studies to develop the library and information centres in digital environment.

Keywords : User Studies, Information Seeking Behaviour, Information Use Behaviour, Library & Information Systems, Digital Environment

INTRODUCTION

The present information surge and pressure of meeting needs of users from the diversity of collection have compelled library and information centers to develop some methods to cope up with the existing situation and accordingly, plan strategies to satisfy the users. Further, this complex situation appears to be ambiguous and heterogeneous as that information need of particular groups of users and information flow from specific situations in organization are difficult to determine (Fatima and Ahmad, 2008). This kind of situation has given a boost to the growth the concept of information searching and the manner of determining the pattern of searching which is known to be information seeking behaviour. Librarians, information scientists, communication scientists, sociologists and psychologists have paid attention to the area of information seeking behaviour. This is not only helpful to understand, improve, develop and design the system, but also to expand activities, services and resources that are related to the information. The twenty-first century has witnessed remarkable progression in terms of technology ranging from print to electronic resources, bibliographic to full-text databases, traditional to digital library, physical to virtual environment and so on. This digital and virtual environment has also made profound changes in users' perception of acquiring and seeking information. Therefore, the information seeking & use behavior studies are worth to be considered while developing library & information centres & their services in the digital environment.

THE CONCEPT OF INFORMATION

Information is seen as something constructed by human beings and an important tool used in the realization of any objective or goal set by an individual. It is a valuable resource required in any society; it is the life-blood of any organization, thus acquiring and using information are critical and important activities. Uttor (1999) defined information as data value in planning, decision making and evaluation of any programme. He goes further to say that it is a data that have been subjected to some processing functions capable of answering user's query be it recorded, summarized, or simply collected that would help decision making. It is well understood in terms of books, journals, magazines, public and private sector documents of all kinds, whether published for mass circulation or unpublished and restricted or confidential in nature, results of research efforts which are made available to colleagues in form of reports, books articles and non-printed materials. From all these definitions, it is apparent that information is crucial to man's survival.

INFORMATION SEEKING & USE BEHAVIOUR

T D Wilson has been working on information seeking behavior since 1981. Information seeking behaviour is a broad term, which involves a set of actions that an individual takes to express information needs, seek information, evaluate and select information, and finally uses this information to satisfy his/her information needs. Various factors may determine the information seeking behaviour of an individual or a group of individuals. It is, therefore, desirable to understand the purpose for which information is required, the environment in which the user operates users' skills in identifying the needed information, channels and sources preferred for acquiring information, and barriers to information. According to Wilson, investigation of 'information needs' has been subject of debate and perplexity. He attempted to map the process involved in 'user needs'. Other pioneers in this area include- D Ellis, K Hall, Girija Kumar and C C Kuhlthau. On the basis of their research, they proposed models which are very popular in the field information needs and seeking behavior.

Ikoja-Odongo and Ocholla (2004) described information seeking as a process that requires an information seeker, or what might be called ''personal information structures' 'such as a person's cognitive abilities, his or her knowledge, skills in relation to the problem or task domain, knowledge and skills specific to a system and knowledge and skills regarding information seeking. Andersen (2000) in another dimension noted that research on information seeking has looked at how individuals go about finding the materials they needs. These were followed by studies of the research habits of individuals or groups that would lead to the design of appropriate information systems and services.

OBJECTIVES FOR STUDYING THE INFORMATION SEEKING & USE BEHAVIOUR

There are many objectives to study the users' information seeking and use behaviour which are directly or indirectly helpful to develop and creating an information system or services for users. After learning the models and methodologies proposed by the different scholars, the following are the objectives and purposes to study the information seeking and use behaviour:

- Evaluate the existing information resources and services of library information center: to find out what type of information resources are being used and identifying the desired information resources and services
- Study the purpose of information seeking; to find out the problems and factors affect seeking information and use behavior.
- Determine the expectation of users from libraries and information centers
- Find out the information and IT literacy levels of different categories of users
- To improve and develop the present information system or design a new information system according to users' needs and literacy levels

The above mentioned objectives of information seeking and use behavior can articulate a users' centric library and these parameters could be guiding factors for any Librarian or library professional to understand their existing library system and to improve and develop library and information system from users' perspective.

METHODS & TECHNIQUES FOR STUDYING THE INFORMATION SEEKING & USE BEHAVIOUR

Information Seeking Behavior is an important area in the library science discipline. Many researchers have studied it from different perspectives using different approaches and methodologies. Researchers such as Wilson (1981), Callison (1997), Devadason and Pratap (1997), and Ellis (1993) and many more have explored quantitative and qualitative methodologies for user studies. There are several methods to study the information seeking and use behaviour of different users' group like- Survey method by interviews or questionnaires, case study methods, observational studies, etc. These methods can be used according to scope and purpose of study.

IMPORTANCE OF STUDY THE INFORMATION SEEKING & USE BEHAVIOUR

After emergence of ICT technologies, internet, web and the information explosion, it is now more critical to acquire desired information from this flood of information. It has changed the entire information landscape from generation to its use, therefore, it is more important to study the information gathering and seeking behaviour of users for satisfying their information needs.

By studying the users' information seeking and use behaviour, libraries would be able to know the strengths and weaknesses of the whole library and information system. Libraries should do a SWOT analysis for the system and develop a plan in terms of resources, services, environment, and facilities on the basis of needs of users.

ROLE IN DEVELOPING THE LIBRARIES AND INFORMATION CENTRES

Information seeking has now become a basic activity and noticeable through a particular behavior. It is also an aspect of scholarly work of most interest to academic librarians who strive to develop collections, services, and organizational structures that facilitate information seeking (Wiberley,1989). T D Wilson (1981) expressed the view that:

> " Our concern is with uncovering the facts of the everyday life of the people being investigated; by uncovering those facts we aim to understand the needs that exist which press the individual towards information-seeking behaviour; by better understanding of those needs we are able better to understand what meaning information has in the everyday life of people; and by all of the foregoing we should have a better understanding of the use and be able to design more effective information systems."

By studying the information seeking behaviour of users, library can improve in the following areas:

COLLECTION DEVELOPMENT

One of the objectives of such kind of studies is developing the right kind of collection in the library from studying the kind of information resources are being used by the users and identifying or anticipating the kind of information resources required by them. On the basis of this, librarians can develop collection or information resources accordingly. It has been observed by many user studies that in present environment, users mostly use the internet, web, digital and electronic resources from different consortia services. Thus, it is now important to give considerable importance of e-resources in our collection development policy and develop the collection of information resources to fulfill the users' information needs all generations.

Information-seeking behavior of students, researchers, and professionals has been the focus of enquiry for decades. Initially, however, user studies were conducted primarily to evaluate library collections. Now, in the development of highly rich academic library collection, user studies can help a lot.

USER AWARENESS: FOR UNDERUTILIZED RESOURCES AND SERVICES

Understanding the actual information needs of users and then acting upon, by using different steps to satisfy those needs can lead towards successful service provision. The best way to achieve such service provision would be by conducting formal in–depth studies. Library professionals, especially those involved in bibliographic and user services should be interested in ways individuals approach the library and the methods they use to search for needed information. Accordingly, library could redesign strategies intended to improve the provision of library services especially towards information skills development and information resource awareness. Librarians can take proactive move towards orientation programmes on electronic resources, internet usage and virtual & web-based services.

Changing ICT environment is affected the information-seeking for the majority of users. It is clear that most of the users affected by the changing ICT environment. Library awareness service is essential in this regard. Library should start information literacy programme. It is important for the library to make aware to the users time to time about different forms and types of sources developed by the library.

INFORMATION LITERACY AND DIGITAL DIVIDE

Information literacy is another area to be thought properly in order to make information searching of seekers purposeful. For this it is important to learn about the characteristics of search images of successful information-seekers. Therefore, building of information literacy programmes will help seekers to clarify in their minds what they require before going into an information search on any subject.

Considering the rapid changes in information provision in the

21st century with computerized access, digitized information formats, and the plethora of resources on the internet, the access and retrieval capabilities of users who are traditionally accustomed to manual information library systems is questionable. Atkinson (1997) enumerates these as the circumstances under which it was worthwhile to re-examine issues of user behavior in academic settings. Otherwise the possibilities of creating the digital divide within information seekers would be visible in the due course. Therefore, developing the information literacy programmes would be helpful in reducing such digital and information divide in the academic environment.

USER SATISFACTION

According to Wilson '...I have tried to show that understanding the information user is a) possible, and b) highly relevant to the creation of effective libraries and information services. It is possible because we already understand so much about information needs and the behaviour people engage in to satisfy those needs, and we also know a great deal about how people work. It is also possible because, being in direct contact with the user, and having the capability to interact to an even greater degree, the librarian or information manager has in his/her own hands the capacity to discover more...'. It is relevant because creating effective information services demands knowledge of these matters - if we fail to understand users' needs and if we fail to understand the processes of satisfying those needs, information services will be ad-hoc, unsatisfactory and, eventually, ignored by the information user - when that happens the information worker had better start looking for a new job because the old one is not going to last much longer! (Wilson, 1995). According to Line (2000), new studies of information users and their needs are even more necessary in the age of the Internet.

The understanding of users' information seeking behavior also helps to address individual needs and provide users with related contents of their interests, in order to facilitate push of information in digital libraries (DLs). Finally, organizing data according to users' searching behavior may be a way to shorten information retrieval time, which is a crucial performance indicator in DLs (Chan & Kwok).

DEVELOPING THE NEW SERVICES

If you can study, understand, made satisfy the user than only you can improve, develop and plan for the future. Information seeking behavior is regarded as an important concern in the design of any information systems. Information seeking behavior is defined as "the purposive seeking for information as a consequence of a need to satisfy some goal". To cope with the growing number of Internet users and the huge amount of information, Information system designers should take account of not only the information requirements, but also users' information seeking behavior (Chan & Kwok).

It is both necessary and challenging for librarians to carry out their active role utilizing these rapidly developing technologies to design and develop new services and enhance existing library service according to the changing needs of users. Services should be planned or designed around the needs of the information user and his/her information-seeking behaviour. Understanding of the information seeking behaviour of users can help us in designing new services. The internet penetration is reasonably high, particularly in the towns and cities, as on today more than 1370 lakhs people access internet in India. Therefore, we should develop IT intensive services according to needs of users.

The question for the information manager or librarian, therefore, is not whether information is important in the organization? But how much information intensive environment is available for its operations.

CONCLUSION

The new technologies have affected every function and process in the universities, schools, libraries, and information centers and these new technologies have affected the information seeking process as well. Computers and other electronic instrumentation have provided libraries with many advantages. Storing, organizing, retrieving, and providing access to information are the main processes that have been positively affected. Computers and new information technologies have greatly enabled information specialists in performing their main tasks, especially in locating and retrieving information (Chen, 1982).

The core of the library profession remains the same, but methods and tools for information delivery continue to grow and change dramatically. Libraries must understand information seeking behavior of users to re-engineer their services and provide information efficiently. By knowing seeking behavior and needs of users, libraries and information centers can manage the contents by providing the value addition and further, it would also help in information mapping and data mining, both the explicit and tacit knowledge of library resources. Furthermore, we can implement the systems like-Document Management System (DMS), Enterprise Resource Planning (ERP) System and Information Retrieval Technologies. In other words, we can use IT into our system in such a way that suits to users optimally. Therefore, re-design, particularly organization of resources and delivery mode of services from time to time is necessary in order give the importance of pace of technological change, continuously, since the organization, its members and its functions change over time and so their information needs. The studies on information seeking behavior & needs help libraries that they should develop the state of the art infrastructure in all respects or they should upgrade existing infrastructure and services with recent advancements in technology according to present requirements of users and also prepare librarians that what type of library support services & online information skills are needed in the present environment.

Finally, information seeking and use behaviour studies are helping hands to librarians and information workers in planning their library services and resources to be acquired in the present era of digital environment.

REFERENCES

Atkinson, J.D. & M. Figueroa (1997). Information seeking behavior of business students: a research study. *Reference Librarian* 58: 59–73.

Callison, D. (1997). Evolution of methods to measure student information use. *Library and Information Science Research 19* (4): 347–357.

Devadason, F.J., & Pratap, P.L. (1997). Methodology for the identification of information needs and uses of users. *IFLA Journal 23* (1): 41–51.

Ellis, D. (1993). Modeling the information-seeking patterns of academic researchers: A grounded theory approach. *Library Quarterly 63*: 469-486.

Fatima, Nishat & Ahmad, Naved (2008). Information seeking behaviour of the students at Ajmal Khan Tibbiya College, Aligarh Muslim University: a survey. *Annals of Library and Information Studies* 55: 141-144.

Ikoja-Odogo, R & Ocholla, D.N. (2004). Information-seeking behaviour of the informal sector entrepreneurs: The Uganda Experience. *Libri 54*, pp. 54-66.

Uttor, J. (1999). The role of law libraries in a democratic culture. A paper presented at The 1999 NLA National Conference and AGM.Aug.15th-20th.

Wiberley, S.E & Jones, W.G. (1989). Patterns of information seeking in the humanities. *College & Research Libraries* 50 (6): 638–645.

Wilson, Tom (1995). Information-seeking Behaviour: Designing Information Systems to meet our Clients' Needs. ACURIL: Association of Caribbean University, Research and Institutional Libraries. XXV Conference, 1995, San Juan, Puerto Rico

Wilson, T.D. (1981). On user studies and information needs. *Journal of Documentation 37*: 3-15.

23

Copyrights Protection in Digital Environment

Vikas Asawat

ABSTRACT

We are living in the world of Internet Technology where most of the updated information is easily accessible. Thought, it facilitate easy access to information, it also eases in copying the contents and republish in other's name by some keyboard clicks. Sometimes the issues become complex as there are instances of copyright infringements. India has a specific Copyright law which regulates Copyright. Further, Copyright Amendment Act 2012 has made Indian Copyright in line with Internet Treaties, WIPO Copyright Treaty and WIPO Performance and Phonogram Treaty to make the Indian Copyright Statute in conformity with the global standard. Circumvention of content protection measures has been made punishable by introducing the amendment to make stringent digital copyright.

Keywords : Digital resources, copyright, patents

INTRODUCTION

Copyright is one of the important variants of Intellectual Property Rights which is recognized as statutory rights in the world of creativities and innovations. Copyright is an inherent right and the right takes the shape of its existence once the work is created and fixed on a tangible medium. In fact, Copyright is a bundle of rights and includes rights of reproduction, communication to the public, adaptation and translation of the work. The Copyright Act, 1957 protects original literary, dramatic, musical and artistic works and cinematograph films and sound recordings from unauthorized uses.[1] Unlike the case with patents, copyright protects the expressions and not the ideas. There is no copyright protection for ideas, procedures, and methods of operation or mathematical concepts as such. In initial days copyright was meant only for protecting the books. It was difficult to reproduce the contents of the book or work, as the copy has to be done by writing the contents manually. Later, with the advent of printing technology and with further evolution of digital and internet tools, the multiplication of original copies become a matter of a pressing a switch and a click. So, the requirement of more stringent copyright law became indispensible to prevent unauthorized reproduction of the work.

In terms of Global convention, Berne *Convention* for the Protection of Literary and Artistic Works provides for global protection for the work once the work is subject matter of Copyrights. India is one of the signatory of the Berne Convention. It is pertinent to understand the objective of the Copyright Law has been to provide due recognition and incentive to the author so that they are further motivated to create new works and literature. As the copyright protects the expressions of ideas and not the ideas itself, so we can have different works from different authors encompassing copyright to each work. The reproduction of multiple copies that are as good as original has become has become an inexpensive and easy preposition with the internet and digital systems. So, infringement of copy right becomes very handy and hassle free. At the same time, there have been introduction of new technology protection measures to minimize copying of the contents. Very often, we experience that the digital contents cannot be copied by simple commands available with the computer system due to technology protection measure also termed as anti circumvention measure. So, the organizations and persons who want to prevent their content from direct and easy copying rely on anti circumvention measures. Interestingly with the introduction of Copyright Amendment Act, 2012, Government has make circumvention of these protected works a punishable offence. In several instances, there are contract between the parties while delivering the digital contents in soft copy in way of click wrap or shrink wrap contract. Now with the growing awareness regarding copyright and promptness to enforce the copyrights, litigation also lying in Courts involving infringement of copyright either digital or non digital plain contents. Even the case related to shrink wrap and click wrap contract has also been decided by the Indian Court and these Contracts are recognized as valid contracts.

DIGITAL PERIPHERY AND COPYRIGHT

It is evident that the information in Digital form has become an indispensible phenomenon in today internet world. It is next to impossible that information and content being accessible to all without the internet. So, internet becomes the most preferred platform to launch the contents so as to make it available to large number of reader. We are also aware that now we can access many journals online on our computer system without the need of procurement of hard copy. At the same time we certainly need appropriate Laws and regulation so that the misuse of content by other can be prevented and if there is free riding penal provisions can be invoked. In recent times, we can see the users collecting information of specific topic from various sources available of internet without need to arrange the hard copy. Dissemination of information available over the internet is just a matter of sharing the hyperlink on email, blogs etc. So, mass dissemination is possible with respect to conventional methods of photocopying.

COPYRIGHT AND INFRINGEMENT

Section 14 of the Indian Copyright Act provides exclusive rights to the copyright holder, authorizing the copyright holder to reproduce, distribute, perform, and translate the work, along with other rights. Section 51 of the Copyright Act, 1957 talks about the infringement of copyright. The section is very broad and does not specifically categorize as to whether such infringement occurred in internet/ digital or in physical world. Section 51 when read in consonance with Section 14 gives an insight that reproducing any copyright protected work, issuing and distributing copies of the work to the public or communicating the work to the public would amount to the copyright infringement under the Act.

INTERNET AND INTELLECTUAL PROPERTY

The Laws, regulations and court Judgments in India provides for legal protection of Intellectual property Rights over the internet. There are definitely some issues that make enforceable of the rights difficult, when we are protecting these rights over the net. It is difficult to identify the infringer as there is a problem of anonymous (no identification of the user) over the net, access of the net via cyber cafe, disclosure of false identity, deletion and removal of hyperlinks by infringer. So, once the contents have been put over the net, it is suspected of copying and mass dissemination via email, news blog, webpage, social networking sites etc without actually disclosing the identity of actual person.

Even using the similar or misleading domain name and publishing or using the trade name and trade mark or proprietary artistic work also comes under infringement and passing off of the rights. So, care should be taken while putting the work on internet and disseminating it, otherwise it may attract penalty and criminal liability. Prior to advent of internet technology, the distribution of original look like copy was very cumbersome, so the copyright holders have some sort of assurance that their rights would not be misused. Now that sense of assurance has been diminishing with the easy reproduction and dissemination of original look like copy of the copyrighted work. The ease with which digital technologies allow for copying and distribution challenges copyright law enforcement. So the equilibrium that existed before the internet technology seems disturbed and issue regarding how to stop unlawful transactions on the Internet becomes a challenge. A new issue with respect to Intell1ectual Property in Open Source Software (OSS).[2] There is a general misconception regarding OSS that they are in public domain. The fact is that OSS are equally protected by IP laws, but distributed in such a way that it ease and promote access to the code rather than restricting the access. This approach helps the software developer across the world to freely use, share and modify the software and helps to get the most updated and advanced software.

COPYRIGHT NOTICE ON THE WORK

Copyright notice on works can put by using copyright symbol i.e. c in circle © Followed by name of Author and then Comma and then followed by year of publications. The notice indicates the intention of the author or published of having claimed copyrights and have both economic rights as well as moral rights reserved with them.

Registration under the Copyright Act of a copyright is not compulsory or mandatory and the prominent reason for holding so was that Section 45 providing for registration uses the word may and Section 13 and Section 17 and the scheme of the said Act does not provide for any compulsory registration. Section 48 of the Copyright Act provides a presumption to an extent only to indicate the rule of evidence provided for rebuttable presumption and for prima facie proof and nothing more.[3]

COPYRIGHTS ISSUES IN INFORMATION CENTRES/ LIBRARIES

Information Centres/ Libraries involves many issues regarding copyrights viz-

1. Sometimes Printed Materials including Books have limited copies and their further prints are not available. The Libraries in such situation have to make copies of the work in order to provide easy availability of the work to the requisite readers. In such cases the permission of copyright holder may be obtained

to make multiple copies to be used for Library purpose.

2. Many Libraries subscribe to Online Journal and Consortia which provide reader and member of libraries to access these journal and works only at designated system. Sometimes these journals are not available on general terminal but are available specific terminals having desired Internet Protocol address. Many a times the contents are copy protected and can only be printed and saved on the system. There is an increasing trend that the online journal and e books are copy protected to avoid misuse of the copyright in the work.
3. Compact Discs and DVDs are also procured in library as a soft copy of various hard covers or their modified short versions for use in Library. Sometimes these CDs and DVDs cover oral and visual presentation of information. These all are copyright protected and cannot be used for use other than purely library reading activity.

FAIR USE AND DIGITAL WORK

Copyright laws provides for certain exceptions where the use of Copyright material for certain purpose does not come under the purview of copyright infringement. Some of the exception includes the following - For the purpose of research or private/ personal study; For learning and teaching instructions in a classroom; For criticism or review; For reporting current events and current affairs, including reporting of lecture delivered in public ; in connection with Judicial Proceedings; Performance by amateur[4] club or society if the performance is given to a non-paying audience; the making of sound recordings of literary, dramatic or musical work under certain conditions.[5] Copyright Amendment Act 2012, extends fair use provisions to the Copyright in Digital Environment. Concept of Caching on internet is a well known concept where the webpage once visited/browsed will be easily opened subsequently as the storage facility is available in cache memory for recently viewed pages. The Act provides for exception for any transient and incidental storage of any work through caching. The provision has been made considering international practice of keeping cache as an exception of copyrights. At the same time, any deliberate storing of such works and reproduction and distribution of such works without duly authorization will lead to an offence of infringement and will attract both civil and criminal prosecution. Though for the purpose of education, academic and research purpose as the copyrighted works will be available in web form or in internet, the exception under this section will prevail and there will be no liability of infringement.

The explanation to Section 52 (1) (a) has been substituted as - -The storing of any work in any electronic medium for the purposes mentioned in this clause[6], including the incidental storage of any computer programme which is not itself an infringing copy for the said purposes, shall not constitute infringement of copyright. So the fair use provisions have been extended to the tech savvy reader and user with educational and research intent.

Clause (b) has been substituted as- the transient or incidental storage of a work or performance purely in the technical process of electronic transmission or communication to the public. So, the said activity has also been excluded from the purview of infringement.

Clause (c) has been substituted as transient or incidental storage of a work or performance for the purpose of providing electronic links, access or integration, where such links, access or integration has not been expressly prohibited by the right holder, will not come under purview of infringement.[77]

FAIR USE PROVISION AND DIGITIZATION OF LIBRARIES

The new Amendment to the Copyright Act has introduced a new clause (n) that facilitate the digitization of libraries. Clause (n) reads as- the storing of a work in any medium by electronic means by a noncommercial public library, for preservation if the library already possesses a non-digital copy of the work. So "non-commercial public libraries" are allowed to store an electronic copy of a work if it already has a physical copy of the work. However, the provision in first reading seems having limited implication as it says that the storage shall be "for preservation". As infringement under section 51 talks about infringement in case of commercial lending, so a constructive interpretation will allow library administration to legally scan and lend electronic copies of works in the same manner that they lend physical copies.

While Clause (o) which also provides exception to Library and they are allowed to make maximum three copies of a book (including a pamphlet, sheet of music, map, chart or plan) by or under the direction of the person in charge of a "non commercial public library"[8] for the use of the library if such book is not available for sale in India. So, a library can make three copies of the work solely for the purpose of use of the Library and solely for non commercial purpose.

GUIDELINES TO PREVENT COPYRIGHT INFRINGEMENT IN DIGITAL WORK

There are some guidelines that can be followed to avoid infringement of work in digital format-

1. The computer or access system should be password protected and any unauthorized use should not be allowed. Sometimes the authorization is by way of IP address and only certain systems have accesses which are under control of Library. These protection measures will help to minimize misuse or unauthorized use of library resources.
2. Practice of filling the request form for paper printing of electronic copy should be strictly adhered to and should be given for research and privates study. The number of pages and number of chapter printing at a time can be limited depending on the nature of the work.
3. The system having electronic resource should have access to limited web pages and other websites like personal email etc. may not be allowed access so as to prevent misuse of work.
4. There should be no provision of using CD, USB memory etc on the system having electronic resource, so that misuse can be prevented.
5. Now a days digital watermarking is also used as a tool to indicate

the original source of the work even in printed copies of the work.

6. Use of software that prevents cut copy paste options and thus prevents easy copying of the work from one format to another. This option encourage reader to develop his own expression and views rather than simply copying some other's work.

CONCLUSION

With the newly introduced amendment of 2012 in Copyright Act, the Government has clearly shown its stand toward digital copyright. The amendment has given due consideration to non commercial public libraries and they can store a digital copy of non digital work provided it is solely for the purpose of library and for purely non commercial use. At the same time users of Library must be oriented to the issues of copyright infringement, so that they can understand the value of rights of the owner of the work. Some of the electronic resource provider have used anti circumvention measures so that the misuse of the work can be prevented. India has taken a big step by making the Circumvention of content protection measures punishable under the act to make stringent digital copyright. So we have both option i.e. law and technology to prevent the unauthorized use of the work. But the need of the hour is to create a culture of respecting other creativity and use in the manner as prescribed by the law.

REFERENCES

1. Section 13 of The Copyright Act, 1957
2. Open-source software refers to software for which the source code (underlying programming code) is made freely available for use, reading the code, changing it or developing further versions of the software, including adding amendments to it. (Definition from WIPO website http://www.wipo.int/patent law/en/developments/open_source.html)
3. AIR 1976 Madras 2
4. A person who engages in an art, science, study, or athletic activity as a pastime rather than as a profession (Source- http://www.thefreedictionary.com/amateur, last visited on 28th December 2012)

5. Section 52 of The Copyright Act, 1957
6. private or personal use, including research; (ii) criticism or review, whether of that work or of any other work; (iii) the reporting of current events and current affairs, including the reporting of a lecture delivered in public.
7. Proviso to the Clause (c) unless the person responsible is aware or has reasonable grounds for believing that such storage is of an infringing copy: Provided that if the person responsible for the storage of the copy has received a written complaint from the owner of copyright in the work, complaining that such transient or incidental storage is an infringement, such person responsible for the storage shall refrain from facilitating such access for a period of twenty-one days or till be receives an order from the competent court refraining from facilitating access and in case no such order is received before the expiry of such period of twenty-one days, be may continue to provide the facility of such access.
8. The Copyright Amendment Act, 2012 has introduced the words "non-commercial public library". Before amendment the word was "Public Library".

24

Usage Pattern of Internet Based Library Services in University Libraries of Rajasthan: A Study

Dr. Praveen Babel

ABSTRACT

The development of computers and communication technology has brought radical changes in the mode and methods of information, storage retrieval and transmission. The advent of Internet has created greater impact on the Library and Information Centres to have access to various information sources and disseminate it to its users. The services available on Internet can be utilized by the Library and Information Centres for acquisition, collection development and various services like CAS, SDI, ILL, Reference service etc. through the various types of resources that are available on Internet. The article lists the various databases, websites available for utilization in Library and Information Centres.

Keywords: Usage pattern, Internet, library services

INTRODUCTION

Libraries have the major responsibility of managing information resources enabling their users quick and convenient access to these resources and to provide variety of on-demand and in-anticipation information services. Increasing use of information technology in the production of information has resulted in an explosion of electronic information sources. The Internet and the World Wide Web (WWW) have enabled seamless access to these sources from any corner of the globe. While many libraries could afford to ignore Online and CD-ROM revolutions, it is doubtful if any library today can remain untouched by the ongoing network information revolution brought about by the Internet and WWW. In a networked environment, the challenges and opportunities for the information professional are manifold. Firstly, Internet needs to be exploited as an information source. Information sources residing on the Internet need to be taken into account in the collection development strategy and in rendering information services. These sources also need to be reflected in the catalogues and indices prepared by the library. Users need to be trained in using effective Internet information access strategies. Secondly, the collection and services of the library need to be made available on the Internet (and intranets), through the library web site. Information may be delivered using e-mail and web browsers, which have emerged as the preferred information access mechanisms. Internet can also be used for information resource sharing among libraries in a city or region. Thirdly, Internet can be used to improve the productivity of operations in different library units, by virtue of being able to quickly reach people, publishers and vendors; carry out business transactions; and access related information sources. Finally, Internet offers a great opportunity for professional development and skills upgrading of the library staff through discussion forms, courseware and tutorials, professional journals and newsletters and current awareness services. In this paper we have made an attempt to indicate how the Internet can be used to improve functioning of different library activities, including library management; acquisitions; cataloguing and classification; reference and information services;

serials management; training and user orientation; and professional development of library staff. For each of these activities, we briefly describe Internet usage, and provide a list of related sources and sample case studies. Key to the effective use of Internet in Libraries is the Library Home Page. The home page has to be designed keeping in view the needs of the library users and also the library staff. Library professionals need to keep themselves up-to-date with new developments in Internet applications. We provide a list of key sources for this.

LITERATURE REVIEW

The Internet is a global system of interconnected computer network of networks that use the standard Internet Protocol Suite (TCP/IP) to serve billions of users worldwide. It consists of millions of private, public, academic, business, and government networks of local to global scope that are linked by a broad array of electronic and optical networking technologies. The Internet carries a vast array of information resources and services, most notably the inter-linked hypertext documents of the World Wide Web (WWW) and the infrastructure to support electronic mail.

S. Das (1999) points out that Internet access is useful for resource sharing among different libraries. Internet offered an innovative and rich electronic environment where users could locate the information they need, quickly and easily. M. Hopkins (2000) clarifies that Web-based Information (or the Internet) is a major force for changing the role of Libraries and Information Centers. R. Kumar and A. Kaur (2004) conducted a case study on Use of Internet by Teachers and students at Shaheed Bhagat Singh College of Engineering & Technology, New Delhi and suggested that the use of Internet among the teachers and students in the college need to be improved. However majority of users used the Internet for educational purposes.

Luambano and J. Nawe (2004) determined that the students used Internet for communication with friends and relatives less than for academic purposes and the level of students' access to the Internet was low because at the time of the study, computers with Internet facilities were inadequate. P. Genoni, and others (2006) suggest that Internet and e-research are changing the nature of scholarly communities. Research scholars are positive regarding the usefulness of the Internet for research purposes and for expanding their scholarly community. R. Hinson (2006) postulates Internet Adoption Model for Academics. The Internet Adoption Model for Academics (IAMA) is conceptualized as an abstract object with five main components: Internet for teaching, Internet for research, Internet for consultancy, Internet for administration, and Internet for policy making. A. Manimekailai, and others (2006) reveal that the use of Internet at Annamalai University, is inevitable part and the perceived usefulness is an important driver of Internet usage. S.Y. Bansode and S. M. Pujar (2008) find that the research scholars of Shivaji University, Kohlapur use the Internet for their research and communication purposes. More awareness about Internet resources, and training in use of the some needs to be provided by library professionals. Feng-Kwei Wang and John Wedman (2001) observe that many studies indicate that computer technology has the potential of changing teachers' pedagogical practices. This paper describes a major initiative to support teachers in integrating Internet resources into the instructional process while shifting their instruction to a more constructivist approach. Referred to as eThemes, this service accepts requests from teachers, finds Web sites that meet the requirements specified in the requests, and creates an archive of quality Internet resources for easy access and searching. It minimizes teachers' resource-seeking time and maximizes their resource-using time in their instruction to enhance teaching practice and student performance.

OBJECTIVES AND METHODOLOGY

The study aims at identifying the Usage of Internet Based Library services in university of Rajasthan. The objectives of the study are the following.

- To know the application of various IT resources and services in deemed university libraries of Rajasthan

- To know the purpose of utilization of Internet services in deemed university libraries of Rajasthan.
- To study the level of satisfaction of the users pertaining to the use of Internet by deemed university libraries of Rajasthan, and
- To find out the various hindrances faced by the users while accessing and using the Internet Services

The study has used questionnaire-based survey methods. Questionnaire and observations represent the most common methods of data collection in social sciences research. These techniques enable us to checking of data for its validity, reliability and consistency. We selected a random sample of 312 research scholars and faculty members from the following seven deemed university libraries. Questionnaires were personally distributed to the research scholars and faculty members of the various disciplines. Out of 312 distributed questionnaires 285 (91.34 per cent) respondents responded. The responded data were analyzed from the SPSS software. Simple percentage and chi-square are used for the analysis of data.

The following are the Deemed Universities:

1. Banasthali University (1983), Banasthali, (BUB).
2. Birla Institute of Technology and Science (1964), Pilani, (BITS).
3. Jain Vishwa Bharti Institute (1991), Ladnun, (JVBI).
4. Malavia National Institute of Technology (2002), Jaipur, (MNIT).
5. Rajasthan Vidyapith (1987), Udaipur, (RVU).
6. Institute of Advanced in Education Deemed university, Sardarsahar, (IASE).
7. Mody Institute of Technology and Science, Laxmangarh, (MITS).

ANALYSIS AND INTERPRETATION OF THE DATA

The analysis and interpretations of the data collected through questionnaires distributed to the research scholars and faculty members have been tabulated by the SPSS (A Statistical Software Package)

SELECTION OF THE SAMPLE OF USERS FROM THE DEEMED UNIVERSITIES

Table 1

Research Scholars				Teachers				Total	
Sciences		Social Sciences/ Humanities		Sciences		Social Sciences/ Humanities			
a	b	a	b	a	b	a	b	a	b
72	67	60	53	80	71	100	94	312	285
93.06 %		88.75 %		88.75 %		94%		91.34%	

Note :a. Served; b. Responded

Table 1 indicates that 93.06 per cent research scholars of sciences and 88.33 per cent research scholars of social science have responded whereas 88.75 per cent teachers of science and 94 per cent teachers of social science have responded.

PURPOSE OF INTERNET USE

Table 2

S. No.	Purpose	Users	Percentage
1.	Research	237	83.16
2.	Study	230	80.7
3.	Communicat ion	166	58.25
4.	Any other	101	35.44

Pearson Chi-Square: 3.574 df-3 p- .311

In this information era, computers have paved the way for advancement in technology, which ease the day-to-day activities of the users. Use of computers serves many purposes. Academic users use Internet for different purposes. Analysis of the above table 2 shows that a high majority of respondents (83.16 per cent) use Internet for research work. The second important reason for accessing Internet is for study (80.70 per cent), On the other hand, 58.25 per cent users access Internet for communication purpose.

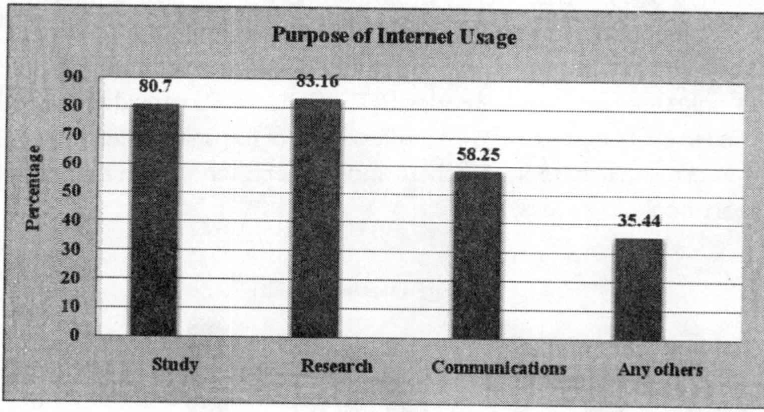

Fig. 1. Purposes of Internet Use

AVAILABILITY OF INTERNET FACILITY IN UNIVERSITY LIBRARIES

Table 3

S.No.	Places	Users	Percentage
1.	Computer Center	132	46.32
2.	Depar tment	132	46.32
3.	Home	115	40.35
4.	University Library	74	25.96
5.	Internet Caf	36	12.63
6.	Any other	12	4.21

Pearson Chi-Square: 14.885 df- 5 p- .011

As the use of Internet trend is growing fast, there are many venues available to access Internet. Today every office, institutes and homes are equipped with Internet facility. A person who does not own computer or Internet facility can access Internet at other places. Table 10 examines the access to Internet at different places. The highest number of respondents indicate that they access Internet at computer center and departments. 40.35 per cent users respond that they use Internet facility at home and 36 per cent at Internet café. A few users (25.96 per cent) indicate that they use Internet in library. During his visit to university libraries, the investigator found that only three university libraries BITS, BUB, MITS provide Internet facility to users for browsing e-journals. Most of the universities provide the Internet facility to the teachers and research scholars in their own departments to access.

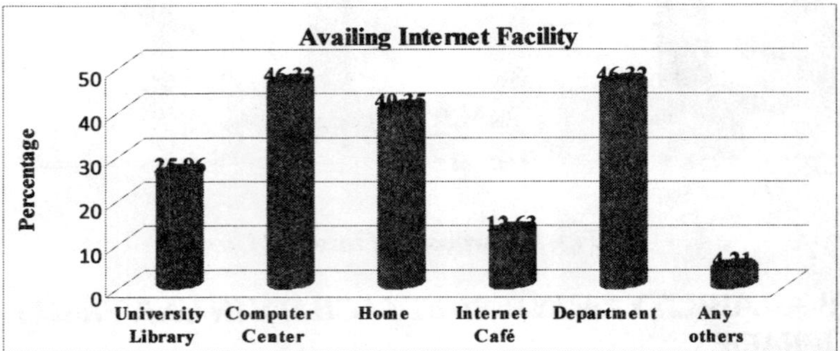

Fig. 2. Availability of Internet Facility

FREQUENCY OF INTERNET ACCESSING

Table 4

S.No.	*Frequency*	*Users*	*Percentage*
1.	Daily	195	68.42
2.	Once a Week	47	16.49
3.	Rarely	17	5.96
4.	Once a Fortnight	13	4.56
5.	Once a Month	4	1.4

Pearson Chi-Square: 11.850 df-4 p- .019

Respondents are asked about the frequency of accessing

Internet. 68.42 per cent of the respondents use Internet daily, while 16.49 per cent users point out that they use them once a week and 5.96 per cent of users use Internet rarely. The main reason of less access to Internet is that they do not find relevant matter related to research. Chi-square test shows that frequency of using internet in library does not depend on the category of users i.e. research scholars and teachers in the universities.

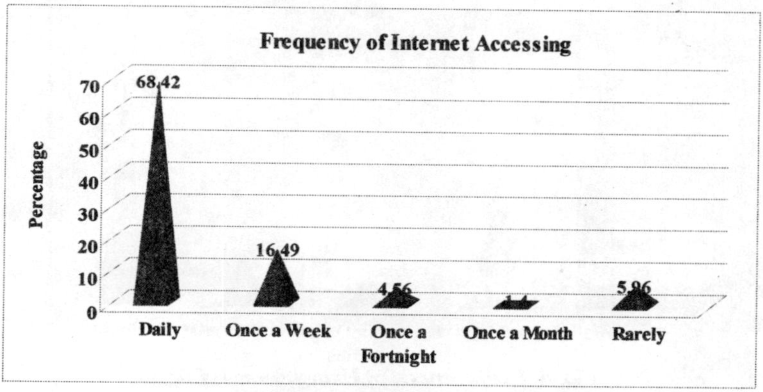

Fig. 3. Frequency of Internet Accessing

PREFERENCE OF USING SEARCH ENGINES

Table 5

S.No.	Search Engines	Users	Percentage
1.	Google.com	240	84.21
2.	Yahoo.com	133	46.67
3.	MSN.com	20	7.02
4.	Alta Vista.com	17	5.96
5.	Lycos.com	2	0.7
6.	Any other	35	12.28

Pearson Chi-Square: 5.543 df- 5 p- .353

The most important search engine tool is Google. The above table 13 shows that majority of the respondents (84.21 per cent) use Google, while 46.67 per cent respondents use Yahoo. Small percentage (5.96 per cent) of the users use Alta-vista. Lycos is used by (0.07 per cent). The analysis and interpretation of the above data indicates that, majority of the respondents access through Google search engine. Chi-square test shows that at 5% level of significance. The preferences of using search engines at university libraries are independent among the teachers and research scholars.

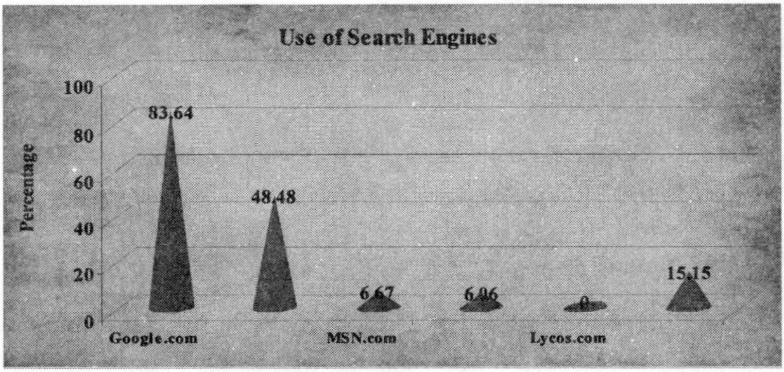

Fig. 4. Preferences of Using Search Engines

USERS PROBLEMS IN ACCESSING INTERNET SERVICES

Table 6

S.No.	Services and Resources	Users	Percentage
1.	Slow Speed of Internet	166	58.25
2.	Inadequate ICT Infrastructure	146	51.23
3.	Limited Computer Literacy	76	26.67
4.	Not Suited to my Research/Teaching	37	12.98

Pearson Chi-Square: 6.169 df-4 p- .187

The above four possible problems of users indicate the reasons of their dissatisfaction level. A good number (58.25 per cent) of them indicate "slow speed of internet" as the reason of dissatisfaction. Other reasons indicated are "inadequate ICT infrastructure" by 51.23 per cent, 'limited computer literacy" by 26.67 per cent and "not suited to my research/teaching by 12.98 per cent.

Chi-square test shows that reasons for their users dissatisfaction with ICT application in libraries is independent among the different universities.

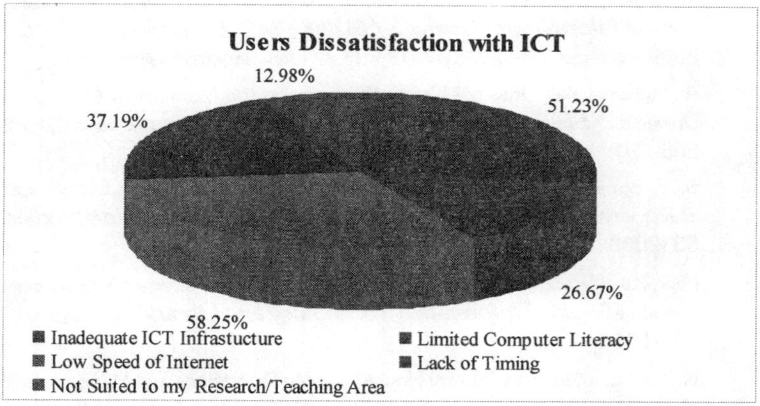

Fig. 5. Users Problems in Accessing IT

CONCLUSION

This study provides usage patterns of internet basede library services among university libraries of Rajasthan and results of this study show that majority of users used internet for research purpose on daily basis, google search engine used highest level.

REFERENCE

1. S. Das, "Access to Internet in R&D Libraries and Information Centers." ***Library Progress (International)***, 19, (1-2) (1999): 13-14.
2. M Hopkins. (2000). Managing the future growth of Library collections. Discussion document. Retrieved on 15 May 2009 from the World Wide ***Web: http:// www.inf.aber.ac.ok\central\quest.asp***
3. R. Kumar and A. Kaur, "Use of Internet by Teachers and Students in Shaheed Bhagat Singh College of Engineering & Technology: A Case Study." ***Journal of Library and Information Science.*** 29, 1-2 (2004): 81-94.
4. I. Luambano and J. Nawe, "Internet Use by Students of the University of Dar es Salaam." ***Library Hi Tech.*** 21, 10 (2004): 13-17. Retrieved on 15 May 2009 World Wide Web: http:// www.emeraldinsight.com

5. P. Genoni and others, "Scholarly Communities, E Research Literacy and the Academic Libraries." ***The Electronic Library***, 24, 6 (2006): 734-746. Retrieved on 15 May 2009 World Wide Web: http:// www.emeraldinsight.com

6. R. Hinson, "The Internet for Academics: Towards a Holistic Adoption Model." ***Online Information Review***. 30, 5 (2006): 542-554. Retrieved on 15 May 2009 from the World Wide Web: http:// www.emeraldinsight.com

7. A. Manimekalai, "Internet Use Pattern among the Students in Annamalai University." ***SRELS Journal of Information Management***. 43, 3 (2006): 265-270.

8. S. Y. Bansode and S M. Pujar, "Use of Internet by Research Scholars at Shivaji University, Kolhapur." ***Annals of Library and Information Studies***. 53 (2008): 123-126.

9. Feng-Kwei Wang and John Wedman, "e-Themes: An Internet Instructional Resource Service, " ***Information Technology and Libraries***. 20, 4 (2001): 179-184.

10. K. Thulasi Internet for Library House Keeping Operations and Management. National Centre for Science Information (NCSI) Indian Institute of Science Bangalore - 560 012

25

Evaluation Criteria for Judging the Quality of Online Information

Dr Fayaz Ahmad Loan

ABSTRACT

There are many types of online information available on internet. People seek online information to satisfy their information needs but one doesn't know that information available on internet is true or false, therefore, it is necessary to evaluate online information prior to use for various purposes. This paper presents evaluation criteria for online information and resources available on the internet.

Keywords : Evaluation criteria, online information, Information quality.

INTRODUCTION

The web is the ever expanding information universe. It is the greatest treasure of information containing information on all branches of knowledge under the Sun. It has become a hub of information seekers who off and on dives in this ocean to find information of interest. It has freed the scholar from the limitations of a physical library. There are visible evidences of departure from total reliance on print based information to the use of online information (Agalo, 1998). The modern information seekers visit the physical library less, rarely use library websites and mostly begin searches with a commercial search engine (Kenneway, 2007). The majority of people use search engines rather than library resources for seeking information and only two percent (2%) of university students begin their research by using a library website (OCLC, 2005). However, the credibility of online information has been under scanner since long. In fact, there is taxonomy of at least ten (10) identified forms of "misinformation" or "disinformation" presented on or via the Internet, and no one knows how much misinformation is actually promulgated in this way (Floridi, 1996; Fitzgerald, 1997). According to Burbules, "the Web is not an ordinary reference system; it poses some unique and, in many respects, unprecedented conditions that complicate the task of sorting out dependable from undependable information". With the emergence of the Web 2.0 tools and services like wikis, blogs and social networking sites, a flood of information is published on the Web. Some of this information is fact, some dubious, some false and some is opinion, some propaganda while some for persuasion. Filters of information typically present in a print environment like publishers, editors, reviewers, librarians and subject experts are often not present on the Internet (Fritch and Cromwell, 2001). Any *Tom, Dick and Harry* can publish anything on the Web at a very low cost and distribute virtually worldwide. In many cases there is no peer review system or any other kind of review mechanism involved to determine the credibility, quality and accuracy of information. The information seekers blindly rely upon information of unknown pedigree and dubious quality. According to Gorman, "The net is even worse than a vandalized library because thousands of additional unorganized fragments are added daily by the myriad of cranks, sages, and persons with time on their hands who launch their unfiltered messages into cyberspace." Hence as more and more information is published on the Web without any peer review system, it is important to know how to evaluate online information to judge the credibility of information.

EVALUATION CRITERIA

There are numerous guides and checklists available on the subject of evaluating Internet resources. Many authors have stated that the evaluation of Internet information is similar to the evaluation of print materials, and that many of the same evaluative criteria apply in both media (Brandt, 1996; Tate & Alexander, 1996; Katz, 1997; McMurdo, 1998). The three popular methods for evaluation of credibility of traditional sources are reputation of publisher, credentials of the author and writing style (Standler, 2004). University of Alberta Libraries (2011) selected a list of criteria that a Web page should meet for credibility. A checklist of evaluation criteria includes scope and subject matter, authority, currency and completeness, design, and ease of use, as well as an annotated list of links to other Internet Evaluation Sites, including some targeted to elementary and secondary school educators and students. The UCLA College Library (2008) recommended content, source, currency and structure criteria for evaluation of online information. The Duke University Libraries (2007) offered a criteria checklist including authority, purpose, current, objective versus bias, and support. The Ohio State University Libraries (2008) introduced various techniques for judging the value of Web sites for research purposes. The techniques include purpose, author, publisher, content, recognitions and review. Elizabeth Kirk (2012) selected authorship, publishing body, point of view/bias, knowledge of other sources, accuracy or verifiability and currency as checklist for evaluation of web resources. Grassian (1995) found content, source, date and structure more appropriate for verifying the credibility of online information. Harris (2010) recommended checklist of four points which include credibility, accuracy, reasonableness and support. Kapoun (1998) advocated for accuracy, authority objectivity, currency and coverage as the deciding factors for judging the quality of information. Susan (2009) found authority, accuracy, objectivity, currency and coverage as standard criteria for evaluation of online information. The available literature shows that various checklists are available for verifying the credibility of online information. However, all are based on personal opinions of the authors. The present study is an attempt to select standard criteria for critical evaluation of online information by including the most common points recommended by the majority of authors and institutions. The standard criteria include of the following points:

1. Authority

> "Reading the information before knowing the authority of information is like an attempt to suicide"

In the literary world, authority refers to an expert whose works are taken as definite and free from doubt. There are two levels of authority for the online information - *viz-* author and publisher. The website/ document should provide full information so that legitimacy of the information can be proved. The following queries can depict the authority of the online information.

- Is there any information about the author(s) of the information? If yes, is there contact information like e-mail address?
- What is the profession of the author(s)? With what organization or institution is the author associated?
- What are the author's qualifications, credentials and connections to the subject?
- What is the *h-index* of the author(s)? Have you seen the author's name cited in other sources or bibliographies?
- Who is the publisher(s) of the information and what is his reputation in scholarly world?

2. Accuracy

The accuracy means the trueness of information. When the online information is verified from other sources, it can be considered as accurate or factual information. Ideally, the information should be checked through the primary sources. The cited references and links should be consulted to find out the accuracy of information. This is especially important for openly-edited sources like blogs and wikis.

The following questions are helpful for finding out the accuracy of information:

- Is the information based on logic, reason and sense?
- Is the information verified by other noteworthy sources/ documents?
- Is the information provided supports or contradicts with the existing knowledge?
- What are the credentials of the sources on which information is based?

3. Objectivity

Literary, objectivity means judgement based on observable phenomena and uninfluenced by emotions and personal prejudices. Objectivity is opposite to bias and bias is reflected by misleading statements, outrageous and unsupported claims. The author should provide detailed information about the depth of the study. Limitations of the information should be clearly pointed out. Read the information and grasp the meaning to determine the author's intentions.

- Is information provided based on research (factual), opinion or propaganda?
- Is information on all sides of a subject provided including limitations?
- Does the information appear to be valid and well-researched, or is it questionable and unsupported by evidences?
- Is the author's point of view objective and impartial? Is the language free of emotion-rousing words or bias?
- Is the information reviewed by any subject expert and verified its objectivity?

4. Currency

The idea of currency is a bit complex. It means that information is still valid and not obsolete. The concept of currency relates to both information and website. It does not only mean newly updated website but the information on the webpage is current as well. Otherwise, *old wine in new bottles* cannot be considered current. For example, a webpage upgraded today provides information about Indian population based on 2001 census cannot be considered current. Hence, the date of information and up gradation of website should be provided regularly. The currency of information is judged through various queries like:

- When the data was collected and when it was published?
- When the information was last revised?
- Do the references of the information are based on current data?
- How often is the website updated?
- When the website was last updated?

5. Source

Source is defined as a document from which information is obtained. Information can be obtained from an online book, journal, dictionary, magazine, etc. or any website, blog, wiki and the like. The information from online journal can be considered as qualitative because the scholarly journals mostly contain information about original research. However, for assessing the level of quality, journals with International Standard Serial Number (ISSN), high impact factor, peer review system and expert editorial board with reputed publisher are taken into consideration. In order to assess the quality of book its authority should be evaluated and readers should not rely on preface and blurbs. The information found on blogs and wikis must be cross checked from other sources. The websites can be personal, special, professional, academic, governmental, organisational, news and commercial sites. On personal websites, individuals post their resumes and showcase their interests, opinions and ideas. The special interest sites maintained by non-profit organizations or political activists dealing with special issues, such as environmental problems are always under scanner. These sites can be relatively mainstream or radical in interests and vary widely in credibility of information. Special interest sites are, by their nature, biased. Professional sites are maintained by professional institutions/organizations or sometimes by individuals. The credentials of the professional sites give clues to the reliability of the information. Majority of the academic and governmental websites provide reliable information, however, the purpose and mission of these organisations should be critically evaluated. The information obtained from news and commercial sites is mostly misleading as most of the news sites want to provide fascinating news based on propaganda to catch the attention of readers. The commercial sites want to sell their products and very often mislead the readers.

- What is the source of information- journal, book, magazine or any other web page?
- What is the authority of book, journal or magazine?
- What is the impact factor of journal or magazine?
- What is the type of website on which information is obtained?
- What is the purpose of website?

6. Documentation

Documentation is one of the basic criteria for judging the credibility of information. It relates to the design and presentation of the information. Web resources should have the same criteria for documentation that print resources meet. The basic principles of documentation are layout, appropriate graphic use, editing control, general attractiveness and usability. The inaccurate and hasty preparation of the article is evidence of misleading information. Spelling, grammar, and text errors may indicate sloppy preparation and sloppy information. The information should be well documented and standards should be followed for spelling, citations and references. The points listed below can depict the quality of documentation on information:

- Are there spelling, grammatical or text errors in the information?
- Is the information edited by any editorial staff and language expert?
- Has the author(s) used simple and understandable words and terms?
- Has the author(s) followed the standards for spelling like

American or British?

- Has the author(s) followed the standards for citations and references like American Psychological Association?

7. Ask an expert

The consultation of an expert- *subject or information* is necessary as the user cannot be a master of all things. The subject expert can judge the quality of text in terms of accuracy and objectivity and the information expert *(librarian)* can check the authority, currency and documentation part of the information.

FUTURES AREAS

The Web isn't only a treasure of information but a dustbin of information as well. The user can retrieve the information from both sources through search tools; however, the *seven star evaluation criteria* (SSEC) can help in differentiating the qualitative from the fraudulent. The future course of action is to provide artificial intelligence to crawlers *(Spiders or Robots)* of web search tools so that they can differentiate between the good and bad information on the Web.

REFERENCES

Agalo, J. (1998). *Emerging developments of audio-visual and multimedia use in national and academic libraries*, in Kenya, paper presented at the 64th IFLA General Conference, Amsterdam, 16-21 August, 1998, Retrieved January 20, 2012 from: www.ifla.org/v/ifla64/105-117e.htm.

Burbules, N. C. (2001). Paradoxes of the Web: The Ethical Dimensions of Credibility, *Library Trends*, 49(3), 441-453

Brandt, D.S. (1996). Evaluating information on the Internet, *Computers in Libraries*, 16(5), 44–46

Duke University Libraries (2007). *Evaluating Web Pages*. Retrieved January 20, 2012 from: http://library.duke.edu/services/instruction/libraryguide/evalwebpages.html

Elizabeth Kirk (2012). *Evaluating information found on the Internet*. Retrieved January 20, 2012 from: http://guides.library.jhu.edu/evaluatinginformation

Esther Grassian (1995). *Thinking critically about World Wide Web resources*. Retrieved January 20, 2012 from: http://www.library.ucla.edu/libraries/college/11605_12337.cfm

Fitzgerald, M.A. (1997). Misinformation on the Internet: Applying evaluation skills to online information, *Emergency Librarian,* 24(3), 9–15.

Fritch, J.W., & Cromwell, R. L. (2001). Evaluating Web Resources: Identity, Affiliation, and Cognitive Authority in a Networked World, Journal of the American Society for Information Science and Technology, 52, 499-507

Floridi, L. (1996). Brave.net.world: The Internet as a disinformation superhighway?, *Electronic Library,* 14, 509–514.

Harris, R. (2010). *Evaluating Internet Research Sources.* Retrieved January 20, 2012 from: http://www.virtualsalt.com/evalu8it.htm

Kapoun, J. (1998). Teaching undergrads WEB evaluation: A guide for library instruction, *C&RL News,* (July/August 1998), 522-523.

Katz, W.A. (1997). *The Internet and reference services.* In W.A. Katz, Introduction to reference work: Reference services and reference processes (Vol. 2; 7th ed.). New York: McGraw-Hill, 89–118.

Kenneway, M. (2007). Marketing the library: using technology to increase visibility, impact and reader engagement. *Serials,* 20(2), 92-97.

McMurdo, G. (1998). Evaluating Web information and design, *Journal of Information Science,* 24(3), 192–204

Online Computer Library Centre (2005). *Perceptions of Libraries and Information Resources: A Report to the OCLC Membership.* Dublin, Ohio. Retrieved January 24, 2012 from: http://www.oclc.org/reports/2005perceptions.htm

Ohio State University Libraries (2008). *Net.Tutor: Evaluation of Web Sites.* Retrieved January 22, 2012 from http://liblearn.osu.edu/tutor/les1/

Standler, R. B. (2004). *Evaluating credibility of information on the Internet,* Retrieved 22 January 2012 from www.rbs0.com/credible.pdf

Susan, E. B. (2009). The Good, the Bad, and the Ugly or, Why It's a Good Idea to Evaluate Web Sources. Retrieved January 25, 2012 from: http://lib.nmsu.edu/instruction/eval.html

Tate, M., & Alexander, J. (1996). Teaching critical evaluation skills for World Wide Web resources, *Internet Librarian,* 16(10), 49–55.

University of Alberta Libraries (2011). *Critical Evaluation of Resources on the Internet,* Retrieved January 25, 2012 from: http://guides.library.ualberta.ca/eval_internet

UCLA college library (2008). *Thinking Critically about World Wide Web Resources,* Retrieved January 25, 2012 from: http://www.library.ucla.edu/libraries/college/11605_12337.cfm

26

Combating the Occupational Stress of Academic Librarians with Different Strategies

K. Anuradha

ABSTRACT

Any career in academic environment is generally considered to be stress-free, decent and safe with high social standing and job security. On the contrary, many surveys and findings exhibit the fact that "Librarians suffer the most stress" [BBC; 2006] compared to other risky occupation. Though the technological advancements have reduced the routine work, it has many adverse effects on the role of the academic librarian. The pressing need for an academic librarian is to be technology-savvy at the same time, service minded with great perseverance and job skill. The role of the librarian in any academic institution is pivotal and the expectations from them are expanding exponentially.

1. INTRODUCTION

In this technology-driven, information era the stakeholders of any educational institution are still dependent on the librarians to satisfy their information needs. The work load is ever-increasing, resulting in a dire situation of demand exceeding the availability of resources which in turn renders excessive stress to the library personnel. The stress which is experienced by any person due to their occupational demands may be categorized as "occupational stress". Occupational stress may be caused by poor remuneration, unexciting routines and inadequacy of the basic work tools of librarianship. The negative impact is decreased job satisfaction, reduced morale, ill- health and many more problems depending on personal characteristics.

There are four types of stress faced by librarians in a digital environment they are technological stress or the techno-stress, physical stress, mental stress and situational stress. Many technical works in library is always short of man power and increasing work load but never receive acknowledgement from the upper management on the work done . Rocco, house and French (1980); said that a librarian's stress is buffered with social support from colleagues, but this support did not help alleviate work related stressors such as job dissatisfaction, boredom and workload.

2. STRESS

According to Richard S Lazarus, Stress may be defined as "A condition or feeling; experienced when a person perceives that demands exceed the personal and social resources the individual is able to mobilize".

Stress is inevitable and everyone experience stress in all situations. If the situation is manageable with ease, the stress perceived is within limits and it has positive implications like an urge to complete the task efficiently and effectively in time. If the situation is not manageable, the stress level is beyond the limits, contributing innumerable psychological and physical adverse impact on the mind and the body.

In the simplest language stress can be defined as lack of mental and physical well- being caused by unhappy situations or stimuli not under control. Stress can be caused by pleasant situations as well. For example- unexpected increments, promotions, applause from the parent organization etc. The concept of stress was introduced in life science by Selye Hans in 1936.The word stress is derived from a Latin word "stringere" which means physical hardship, starvation, torture or pain.

2.1. Pressure and stress

Pressures and stress are the terms confused by people. Pressure is a contributing factor for stress. Continuous pressure in work place without a chance to recover leads to occupational stress

2.2. Stressors

The factors which increase the stress level are called as stressors. Stressors may be categorized into two types, extrinsic stressors and intrinsic stressors. The personal values, self-concept and attitudes are the intrinsic whereas job related factors like job control, work load, work scheduling, role conflict are some of the extrinsic factors.

2.3. The General Adaptation Syndrome [GAS]

Dr. Hans Selye the pioneer investigator of stress has identified three stages of response to stressor as alarm, resistance and exhaustion.

2.3.1. Alarm

The person may feel some degree of panic and tries to cope with it. In the academic LIS professionals the stressors are 1.inadequate resources.2.reorganisations 3.work load 4.Management's poor communication 5.retrenchment 6.visit of any assessment bodies like NAAC, AICTE and NBA etc 7.lack of deserving identity 8.technological ignorance 9.job control 10.lack of remuneration.

2.3.2. Resistance

The effort of the librarian to cope or the strength he gathers to face the stressors is the next stage. The academic librarian may take steps and correlate the staff and assign their duties, seeks the help of management, maintains the records perfectly, being technologically-savvy, completion of all clerical works punctually to have a smooth work flow; all these activities come under the resistance stage.

2.3.3. Exhaustion

Prolonged exposure to stressor may cause exhaustion. If the librarian could not cope with the stressors and the work pressure continues to disturb psychologically and physically beyond a certain level and time, it leads to complete exhaustion or burn out.

3. THE OUTCOMES OF STRESS ARE

3.1. Physiological

Head ache, sleep disruption, digestive problems or ulcers. The symptoms may vary depending on each individual.

3.2. Psychological

Emotional instability or exhaustion, affective commitment, moodiness, nervousness and tension, chronic worry, depersonalization, dissatisfaction.

3.3. Behavior

Frequent Absenteeism, Aggression, performance problems, safety problems, unpleasant relationship with the management/parent organization. Poor rapport of the library personnel with the users of the library are the behavioral outcomes.

4. DIFFERENT APPROACHES FOR STRESS MANAGEMENT

4.1. Action based approach

The action-based approach helps us to

4.1.1. Deal the stress in work place

4.1.2. Face the problematic jobs

4.1.3. Cope with problematic people

4.1.4. Overcome the environmental stress

4.1.5. Manage the performance stress

4.1.6. Avoid complete exhaustion.

4.2. Emotional-based approach

Compromising with the situation emotionally. The interpretations or the outlook regarding a situation can be changed. Lack of power to change the situation can be handled this way.

4.3. Acceptance-based approach

Accepting the situation as it comes and trying to survive the difficulties is the other approach.

5. DIFFERENT STRATEGIES TO COMBAT STRESS

Many strategies have been developed to manage the stress in the work place

5.1. Physical Strategies

The best method to manage the stress is to have physical activities like walk, run, and do yogasanas, exercises and domestic chores. One of the best methods to manage stress on the physical level is to dissipate the energy by working vigorously

5.1.1. Physical activities/exercises

A morning refreshing walk or exercises can boost up energy at work

5.1.2. Aerobics

Tends to bring down the stiffness of muscles and gears the day with positive energy

5.1.3. Yoga

No other activities could match with yoga. Each and every asana contribute to the wellness of at least one external/internal organ. The mind is purified and focused.

5.1.4. Sports

Sports personalities are always overwhelming with energy so, sports activities infuse a lot of positive energy and clear outlook on different issues.

5.1.5. Domestic chores

In Indian context the domestic chores are always meant for fairer sex, but only a few understand that it has positive implications of good focusing and reducing the stress by dissipating the energy in a useful way.

5.1.6. Art

Practicing any form of art like dance, painting and music etc.

5.1.7. Breathing practices

This method helps to focus on one and only activity at a time and helps to tackle the problem more efficiently.

6. IMAGINATIVE STRATEGIES

1. Take a break in the work schedule for two to three minutes and imagine a pleasant experience
2. Develop imaginations of living in the most beautiful place with most near and dear ones .Imaginations should be very realistic so that even the sounds and scent could be felt
3. Visualizing the dreams and vision of oneself more vividly
4. Listing out all the expectations and imagining them to be realistic
5. Decrease the anxiety, depression and boosting self confidence by recounting all the positive happenings in one's life.

Such practices will lessen the stress in day to day activities and brings peace to the mind instantly. This method also gives optimism in life.

7. EMOTION-BASED STRATEGIES

7.1. Keen observation

Observing the stress and the factors causing the stress in one, should be watched and analyzed. Assessing the feedback received by observation gives more data relating the emotions and its causative factors.

7.2. Control of emotions

The knowledge of causative factors and its root cause will help to combat the stress. Emotions controlling techniques can be learnt and practiced. This renders to the better management of stress in the future.

8. MENTAL STRATEGIES

8.1. Positive approach or optimistic approach

The difficulty or the problem can be taken in a more optimistic way which will change the way we deal and solve it.

8.2. Brain storm practical sessions

For stress management which will discover many ways to deal the stress hours in a multi dimensional approach

8.3. Expanding the options and horizons

For stress management is another relevant technique.

8.4. Analyze, evaluate and clarify about stress management

Set the pattern of working for the stress hours before hand, this will help the real critical situations to be handled with ease. Focus on gratitude and share the burden of work with co-workers rather than shouldering it alone.

8.5. Develop self-efficacy

The degree to which a person believes that he/she can attain their goals. Observational learning and social experience will develop the personality and self confidence. Persons with self efficacy are found to be more enthusiastic in facing challenges. Self efficacy depends on wellness of a person which in turn relies on one's awareness regarding their physical, mental, social, spiritual and environmental status.

8.6. Meta-cognitive skills

This can be developed.Assesing the thought process and controlling the thoughts and thereby emotions are the best possible ways.

9. SPIRITUAL STRATEGIES

9.1. Contemplations

Prayer and similar exercises are some methods to combat stress. Being active in your faith and volunteering in spiritual activities is highly recommended. Nurture the spiritual connection with nature as it will be appealing and improving the health status and stress management.

9.2. Habit inculcation

Regular prayers and consistently spending at least five to ten minutes can definitely be helpful in coping with stress.

9.3. Meditation- a stress buster

Beside cognitive intelligence, people of this era require intelligence and that is emotional intelligence. The emotional intelligence is attained by meditation. There are two types of meditation1.active 2.passive

9.4. Passive meditation

Sitting in one position and concentrating entirely on one entity is passive meditation. Meditating on daily basis especially in early morning hours will contribute for better control of mind. This will gradually lead to active meditation

9.5. Active meditation

Active meditation is nothing but working with 100% concentration which gives excellent results. Any work done with complete dedication is sure to be rewarded so, active meditation is good for any professional.

10. CONCLUSION

Stress management is the hot topic in any organization because of high competition in each and every field of this technology-driven era. The academicians and especially librarian are the most vulnerable group as it requires confronting with the users to satisfy their information necessity in the required manner. The parent organization must give positive orientation to their employees. The academic librarians must also learn and follow the different strategies to tackle their problem on their own.

REFERENCES

1. M.B, Landry. (2000).The effects of life satisfaction and job satisfaction on reference librarians and their work. *Reference and Users Services Quaterly*, 40(2),166-177.
2. La Rocco.J. House,,M. J.S and French,Jr, J.R(1980). Social support, occupational stress and health. *Journal of Health and Social Behaviour*, 21 (3), 202-218.
3. Parasuraman.S., & Hansen, D (1987).coping with work stressors in nursing: effect of adaptive and maladaptive strategies. *Work and Occupations*, 14(1), 88-105.
4. Sundararajan,S. (2010) Multidimensional strategies for successful stress management. *Journal of Modern Science*, 2(1), 24.
5. Aggarwal, R. (2001). Stress in life and at work. Response books, Sage publications India Pvt ltd., New Delhi.
6. Geetha A.(2007). Stress management and value education. *Edutracks* 6(8).
7. Basu, S. (2009). Stress among teacher educators. *University News*, 47(49).

27

Awareness Level of Understanding the Need of Information Among the Faculty Members and Students of Banasthali Vidyapith and University of Rajasthan: A Critical Study

Shesh Mishra

ABSTRACT

The study contributed to the knowledge base of higher education practice and the teachers' and students' continuing education in the following ways : pertaining to cognitive abilities related to information ; re – cognition of the value of information – empirical information – to higher education practice ; increased awareness of the need for research based information ; promotion of seamless synthesis of research and practice ; and contribution to the process of both information seeking and information gathering, which are vital for the lifelong learning of the teacher and student both. During 2009-2010 surveyed the faculty members, research scholars and post graduating students of Banasthali University, Rajasthan and University of Rajasthan, Jaipur through self administered questionnaire. The paper finds that the assessment method had real strengths especially in terms of validity. University libraries knew what they were expected to do and where they needed to put in effort. The assessment method has been carried out once with faculty members, research scholars and post graduating students of Banasthali University and University of Rajasthan, so the findings can only be regarded as interim.

Keywords: Information literacy, Assessment, Higher education, Information need.

INTRODUCTION

It is a universal goal of higher education to produce graduates who are knowledgeable in their disciplines and are able to adjust and advance in life after their tertiary education. Lifelong learning is an inherent desire of the educational mission of any institution of higher learning. Therefore, to prepare themselves for the future, students of higher learning institutions should acquire the ability to be rational and creative, and to solve problems. In relation to this, they should be able to retrieve, evaluate, use, manage and disseminate information effectively. An 'educated graduate' will no longer be defined as a person who has absorbed a certain body of factual information, but also one who knows how to find, evaluate and apply needed information [1]. According to Wilson[2] the amount of information encountered by a student in the final year of a teacher education program is equivalent to the experience of their grandparents over their life rate growth. It is further projected that by the year 2020, knowledge would double every 73 days.

Toffler[3] coined the phrase 'information overload' to describe the feeling of being overwhelmed, frustrated and even defeated. Wurman[4] explained the process that led to information overload; he called it 'information anxiety'. It is produced by the widening gap between what we understand and what we think we should understand. He reiterated questions such as, how many journals in your field do your regularly review? How do you keep up with the world news? Wurman warned that information anxiety limits people to be only seekers of knowledge because no time is left for them to be reflectors of knowledge. He also emphasized that no one in higher education can escape from this information overload.

Students' ability to navigate, retrieve and use information effectively becomes central to educational, professional and civic success[5]. University graduates should be confident in making judgments in an ever-changing information needs situation. Within the information society, students must be multi-skilled in problem solving, in using ICT tools, and able to be independent lifelong learners – factors which form the basis of an information literate person. Academic libraries are expected to play an important role in developing students' information literacy. Within its role in making the academic library a centre for teaching, learning and research, it should ensure that the students acquire the appropriate information literacy competencies to enable the graduates to be productive members of society and lifelong learners. The academic library then is the perfect setting and catalyst for information literacy initiatives, due to the abundance of information available, as well as that the academic libraries have made huge investments in its print collection, databases, electronic journals and library systems[6]. Academic libraries have attempted to bridge the gap between classrooms and the library and information resources through information literacy initiatives for undergraduates.

Due to the information overload and sophistication of information technology for access, students are faced with the difficulty of finding effective ways to access, evaluate and use the various formats and channels of information. Information can be retrieved from the library shelves or from home or office workstation. However, retrieving information from any source requires an understanding of how information is organized, followed by the skills to retrieve and use it effectively. An individual's working, studying or running daily life essentially involves learning situations, where one makes use of what one has been taught or trained in, but where one also has to learn to formulate answers to the issues and challenges encountered. Many scholars and educationists reiterate the importance of information literacy in facing information overload and advancement in technology[7].

INFORMATION LITERACY

The term "information literacy" was introduced in 1974 by Paul Zurkowski, the President of the Information Industry Association in a proposal which he submitted to the National Commission on Librarians and Information Science (NCLIS). He described information literates as people who are trained in the application of information resources to their work. He stated that these people "have learned techniques and skills for utilizing the wide range of information tools as well as primary sources providing information solution"[2]. Information Literacy is about information in all forms.

The term has now flourished and throughout the literature, one comes across various definitions, alternative terminologies, explanations and clarifications for information literacy[8].

The current definition of information literacy began to take shape in the mid 1980s. Irving[9] defined information skills within the educational context as skills that students require in order to complete their classroom task. The earliest recorded definition of information literacy which is endorsed by an association was documented in 1989 in a report from the American Library Association (ALA) Presidential Committee on Information Literacy. It brought forth the significance of information literacy to individuals, businesses and citizenship in the context of the Information Age. The report not only defined information literacy, but also identified schools and colleges as the major players in producing information literate students. It stressed on the need for institutions of higher education to equip their graduates with information literacy skills that would enable them to succeed academically and help them to develop critical, problem-solving and lifelong learning skills. This report described that, "To be information literate, a person must be able to recognize when information is needed and have the ability to locate, evaluate, and use effectively the needed information. Producing such a citizenry will require that schools and colleges appreciate and integrate the concept of information literacy into their learning programs and that they play a leadership role in equipping individuals and institutions to take advantage of the opportunities inherent within the information society. Ultimately, information literate people are those who know how to learn, how knowledge is organized, how to find information, and how to use information in such a way that others can learn from them. They are prepared for lifelong learning, because they can always find the information needed for any task or decision at hand [10]."

METHODOLOGY

The survey instrument designed by the author as outlined above served as the primary method of data collection for this study. The survey method was chosen because of its ease of distribution and the facility with which response data could be retrieved and analyzed. It also enabled the author to ask specific questions relevant to this study. Author has personally distributed printed questionnaire to the faculty members, research scholars and post graduating students. Some questionnaire also sent through e-mails. In order to analyze the survey data, the author created a database using Excel software. The creation of a database allowed the author to sort the data along a number of axes as well as to conduct appropriate statistical tests on the data. Statistics is mathematical technique or a process of arranging, analyzing and interrelating numerical data obtained in any quantitative research. It is a tool of measurement and evaluating.

The statistical techniques used for the analysis of the obtained data were percentage and Chi-Square Test.

ANALYSIS

The purpose of the study was to assess Information Literacy of faculty members, research scholars and post graduate students of Banasthali Vidyapith and University of Rajasthan. Information Literacy is necessary to support successful implementation of teaching/ learning in higher education institutions.

The analysis begins with profiles of the faculty members (FM), research scholars (RS) and post-graduating students (PG) of both the universities. Following the group profiles are the results from the investigation that address the research questions. The focus of the study was on describing the levels of awareness of information literacy and the skills & resources for information related to facilitating the initiation of information literacy programs to support higher education practice and enhance other learning strategies.

It is helpful to understand the structure and organization of the results. The focus is first on the demographic data and profiles of each of the three Higher Education Groups (FM, RS, PG) participating in the study. The profile of each group is presented as a part of the demographic description. Table 1.0 displays the demographic data represented by frequency and/or percent of each of the three Higher Education Groups.

DATA COLLECTION AND MANAGEMENT

Seven Hundred and Ninety Five questionnaires were distributed personally during the days between February 5, 2009 and December 22, 2009, to assure that all data were collected within the same timeframe. All data collected were returned to the researcher by December 22, 2009. The data were coded, analyzed, and entered into a Microsoft Excel spreadsheet program for maintenance and manipulation by the researcher.

DESCRIPTION OF EACH STUDY GROUP

Two Hundred and forty One (241) self-administered questionnaires were distributed to faculty members of Banasthali Vidypith (BV), and University of Rajasthan (UR). The faculty surveyed Eighty-Eight or 37% responded to the questionnaire. The faculty surveyed were 53% (n=46) Banasthali Vidyapith and 47% (n=42) University of Rajasthan. Faculty surveyed for gender-wise were 74% (n=65) female and 26% (n=23) male. Faculty surveyed for qualification were 35% (n=31) Post-Graduate, 59% (n=52) Ph.D. and 6% (n=5) others. Faculty members surveyed for faculty-wise were 10% (n=10) Arts & Humanities, 34% (n=15) Social Sciences, 42% (n=37) Pure & Applied Sciences and 14% (n=26) Music & Fine Arts.

One Hundred and Sixty Eight (168) self-administered questionnaires were distributed to research scholars of both the

Population Sample Table 1.0

Uni	Banasthali Vidyapith																								University of Rajasthan																							
	201																								106																							
Sta	Faculty Member								Research Scholars								Post Graduate Student								Faculty Member								Research Scholars								Post Graduate Student							
	46								48								107								42								22								42							
Fac.	AH		SS		PA		FM		AH		SS		PA		FM		AH		SS		PA		FM		AH		SS		PA		FM		AH		SS		PA		FM		AH		SS		PA		FM	
	5		5		23		13		10		14		18		6		24		44		23		16		5		10		14		13		6		3		10		3		8		24		3		7	
Gen	M	F	M	F	M	F	M	F	M	F	M	F	M	F	M	F	M	F	M	F	M	F	M	F	M	F	M	F	M	F	M	F	M	F	F		M	F	M	F	M	F	M	F	M	F	M	F
	1	4	0	5	3	20	1	12	0	10	4	10	0	18	0	6	0	24	0	44	0	23	0	16	3	2	7	3	7	7	1	12	4	2	0	3	8	2	1	2	5	3	7	17	2	1	1	6

universities. The research scholars surveyed seventy or 42% responded to the questionnaire. The research scholars surveyed were 24% (n=17) (4 BV + 13 UR) male and 76% (n=53) (44 BV + 9 (UR) female. Research scholars surveyed for faculty-wise were 23% (n=16) (10 BV + 6 UR) Arts & Humanities, 25% (n=17) (14 BV + 3 UR) Social Sciences, 40% (n=28) (18 BV + 10 UR) Pure & Applied Sciences and 13% (n=9) (6 BV + 3 UR) Music & Fine Arts. The research scholars surveyed for university-wise were 69% (n=48) Banasthali Vidyapith and 31% (n=22) University of Rajasthan.

Three hundred and eighty six (386) self-administered questionnaires were distributed to post graduating (PG) students of both the universities. The PG students surveys one hundred and forty nine or (39%) responded to the questionnaire. The post graduating students surveyed gender-wise were 90% (n=134) female and 10% (n=15) male. The post graduate students surveyed university-wise were 28% or n = 42 University of Rajasthan and 72% or n = 107 Banasthali Vidyapith. The post graduate students surveyed faculty-wise were 21% or (n=32) Arts & Humanities, 46% (n=68) Social Sciences, 17% (n=26) Pure & Applied Sciences and 15% (n=23) Music & Fine Arts.

The analysis and interpretation of the collected data in the following three ways:

- Status-wise or Designation-wise i.e. Among the Faculty Members, Research Scholars and Post graduating Students.
- University-wise i.e. Between Banasthali Vidyapith and University of Rajasthan.
- Faculty-wise i.e. Among the Arts & Humanities, Social Sciences, Pure & Applied Sciences and Fine Arts and Music.

UNDERSTANDING THE NEED OF INFORMATION

Objective: To study in the context of understanding the need of information among the users.

STATUS-WISE

Table 1.1. Awareness of understanding the need of information among the users status-wise

	Yes	No	Chi-square Test
Faculty Members	22.72%	77.27%	df = 2
Research Scholar	15.71%	84.28%	χ^2 *Tab* = 5.991
Post Graduate Students	22.81%	77.81%	χ^2 *Cal* = 1.619
			p Value = 0.445091

Table 1.1 shows the percent distribution in context of understanding the need of information among the users status-wise. 22.72% faculty members, 15.71% research scholars and 22.81% post graduating students were aware of the understanding the need of information, while 77.27% faculty members, 84.28% research scholars and 77.81% post graduating students were not. Fig. 1.1 also shows the bar diagram of distribution understanding the need of information among users status-wise.

Table 1.1 also depicts the Chi-square test for independence of attributes at 5% level of significance. The value of Chi-square calculated is less than Chi-square tabulated and the degree of freedom (df) is 2. The value of p shows statistically non-significant (p e" 0.05). This implies that there is a non-significant variation among the users in context of understanding the need of information. It means variation of understanding the need of information is not affected by the level of users. Hence the attributes are independent.

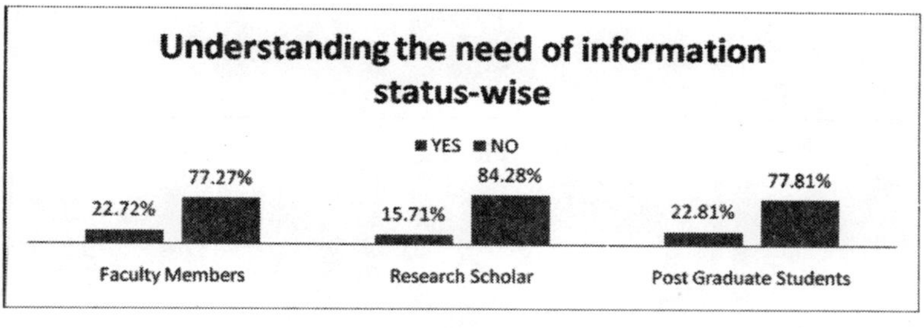

Fig. 1.1

Table 1.2. University-wise

	Yes	No	Chi-square Test
Banasthali Vidyapith	23.38%	76.61%	df = 1
University of Rajasthan	16.98%	83.01%	χ^2 *Tab* = 3.841
			χ^2 *Cal* = 1.704
			p Value = 0.191732

Table 1.2 shows the percent distribution in the context of understanding the need of information among the users universities-wise. Regarding understanding the need of information both the universities had very low need of information. Banasthali Vidyapith university users are more enthusiastic in context of understanding the need of information.

Table 1.2 also shows the Chi-square test for independence of attributes at 5% level of significance. The value of Chi-square calculated is less than chi-square tabulated and the degree of freedom (df) is 1. The value of p shows statistically non-significant (pe" 0.05). This implies that there is a non-significant variation in the context of understanding the need of information. It means the variation in the understanding the need of information is not affected by both the universities users. Hence the attributes are independent. Fig. 1.2 also shows the bar diagram of distribution of understanding the need of information among the user university-wise.

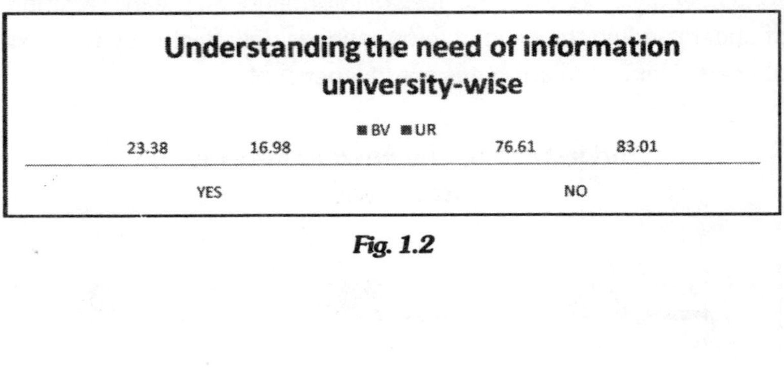

Fig. 1.2

Table 1.3. Faculty-wise

	Yes	No	Chi-square Test
Arts & Humanities	25.86%	74.13%	df = 3
Social Sciences	22%	78%	χ^2 *Tab* = 7.815
Pure & Applied Sciences	20.87%	79.12%	χ^2 *Cal* = 1.921
Fine Arts & Music	15.51%	84.48%	p Value = 0.588878

Table 1.3 shows the percent distribution in the context of the understanding the need of information among the users faculty-wise. Faculty of Arts & Humanities users were most enthusiastic regarding understanding the need of information, while faculty of Fine Arts & Music were least. Table 1.3 also shows the Chi-square test for independence of attributes at 5% level of significance. The value of Chi-square calculated is less than Chi-square tabulated and the degree of freedom (df) is 3. The value of p shows statistically non-significant (pe" 0.05). This implies that there is a non-significant variation in understanding the need of information among the users faculty-wise. It means there is no variation in the context of understanding the need of information among the users of all the faculties. Fig. 1.3 also shows the bar diagram of distribution of understanding the need of information among the users faculty-wise.

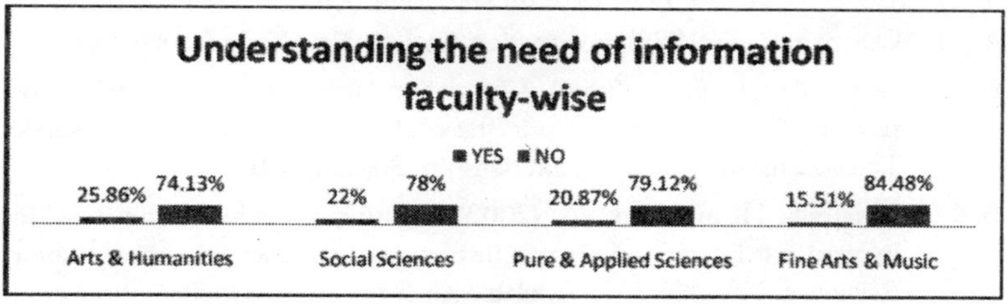

Fig. 1.3

CONCLUSION

It is found that there were no significant differences found in understanding the need of information among the users status-wise. It is found that faculty members & post graduating students were almost equally aware of the understanding the need of information, while research scholars were least aware. There were no significant differences found in understanding the need of information among the users university-wise. It is found that users of Banasthali Vidyapith were more aware of the understanding the need of information in comparison to users of University of Rajasthan.There were no significant differences found in understanding the need of information among the users faculty-wise. It is found that users of Arts & Humanities were most aware of the understanding the need of information, second were users of Social Sciences, third were Pure & Applied Sciences and last and least were users of Fine Arts & Music. In last there is need of IL program or library orientation for the users of both the universities specially RS & PG students. Also library can design specific user education program faculty-wise.

REFERENCES

1. Breivik, P. S. (1998). Student Learning In The Information Age. Phoenix, Arizona: American Council on Education and ORYX Press.
2. Wilson, T. D. (1999). Models in information behaviour research. The Journal of documentation, 55(3), 249-260. Available at http://www.emeraldinsight.com/Insight/viewPDF.jsp?contentType=Article&Filename=html/Output/Published/EmeraldAbstractOnlyArticle/Pdf/2780550301.pdf (Accessed on 29 August, 2009)
3. Toffler, A. (1970). Future Shock. New York: Boston Books.
4. Wurman, R. S. (1989). Information Anxiety. New York: Doubleday
5. Owusu-Ansah, E. K. (2004). Information literacy and higher education: placing The academic library in the center of a comprehensive solution. The Journal of Academic Librarianship, 30(Jan), 3-16.
6. Skaerbak, H. and Skov, A. (2003). Fighting an uphill battle: teaching information Literacy in Danish institutions of higher education. Library Review, 52(7), 326-332. Available at: http://www.emeraldinsight.com/Insight/viewPDF.jsp?contentType=Article&Filename=html/Output/Published/EmeraldFullTextArticle/Pdf/0350520704.pdf (Accessed on 29 August, 2009)
7. Hancock, V. E. (1993). Information literacy for lifelong learning, ERIC Digest (ED358870). Syracuse, NY: ERIC. Available at: http://www.eric.ed.gov/ERICDocs/data/ericdocs2sql/content_storage_01/0000019b/80/13/e7/6c.pdf (Accessed on 29 August, 2009)

8 http://www.educause.edu/pub/er/review/reviewartcles/31231.html

9 Irving, A. (1985). Study and Information Skills Across the Curriculum. London: Heinneman Educational Books. Available at: http://www.ericdigests.org/pre-9218/information.htm (Accessed on 21 July, 2009)

10 American Library Association. Presidential Committee on Information Literacy. (1989). Final Report. Chicago: ALA. Accessed on 29 March 2009 from: http://www.ala.org/ala/acrl/acrlpubs/whitepapers/presidential.htm

28

User Education in 21st Century: Indian Perspective

Dr. Shabir Ahmad Ganaie

ABSTRACT

Libraries are dynamic institution established in a society with multifold objectives and missions. The mission is to produce well informed individuals who can contribute positively for the overall growth and development of their societies. Individuals using libraries must be well aware about the techniques adopted by libraries for organizing the information resources and must have knowledge about the services provided by libraries. They need awareness about the libraries and this awareness is created among the users through user education. Present paper highlights the concept of user education, elaborates the techniques adopted for organizing user education programs and suggests some new ways and means where by users are made aware about the techniques , tools, resources and all such facilities that can be availed by users in virtual environment of 21st century.

Keywords: user education, library

1. INTRODUCTION

Libraries and information centers from time immemorial are devoted to the cause of uplifting the human societies as these not only preserve knowledge of the present and past but also make this rich resource of knowledge accessible to those who are willing to gain and use it for the growth and prosperity of nations.History bears testimony to the fact that each and every civilization has established libraries and India is not an exception. Whether it is the library at Nalanda or the libraries in the great palaces of Mughlas and Maharajas, it is evident that everybody at the helm of affairs in ancient Indian civilizations were giving due attention to the libraries. There are evidences in the literature that in ancient periods when compiling the manuscripts was a time consuming and laborious job, libraries were established by the royal families only as these families were treating the libraries as the "entities of respect". Libraries were not accessible to all but only to a few – usually to people belonging to higher castes. However, with the passage of time more and more people were accessing libraries and doors of libraries also got opened for the masses because of developments that took place in the societies. Some of these developments were associated with:

a) Universalization of education

b) Democratization of societies

c) Awareness of people about their rights and duties.

d) Increase in research and developmental activities

e) Invention of printing press

f) Availability of information sources in huge quantities

g) Advent of information and communication technologies

Thus there has been an increase in the number of libraries and also there is increase in the number of the users who are using the resources and services provided by these libraries.

2. LIBRARIES IN 21ST CENTURY: A CURSORY LOOK

In the 21st century lot of changes are occurring in all the

institutions established by the societies and libraries are not an exception. There is a paradigm shift in the concept of libraries and Librarianship. Some of the changes that occurred in the libraries are shown in table 1.

Table 1 : Paradigm shift in Libraries

From	To
1. Books were for preservation.	1. Books / documents/ information are for use.
2. Books/ Documents were only for few.	2. Books/ documents / information are for all.
3. Bigger the collection, better the library.	3. Better the collection, best is the library.
4. Librarians were acting as storekeepers.	4. Librarians are acting as intermediaries.
5. Libraries were operating in isolation.	5. Cooperation among libraries leading to consortium is the main feature.
6. Library activities either were manually performed or were partially automated.	6. Libraries are adoptingdifferent software packages and the result is the creation of digital libraries/ virtual libraries or institutional repositories. Use of metadata, ontologies etc are used frequently.
7. Libraries were focusing on fulfilling the information demands of users.	7. Libraries are proactively playing a role by which anticipatory information services are tailored for providing pinpointed, exhaustive and expeditious information to the users.

Thus we find today libraries have become institutions trying their level best to provide right information to the right user in the right amount and at right time by the application of all modern electronic gadgets. Libraries use RFID, social networking, digital and electronic information sources, computer hardware and software and are involved in the consortium formulations with other libraries and information centers at national and at global level. Library and information professionals apply their competencies for separating the relevant information from the junk information available in multiple formats like CD-ROMS, E-books, E-journals or in their print formats. All these developments led to the metamorphosis of the traditional libraries into electronic, digital or virtual libraries. These different forms of libraries have posed some challenges to the users of these libraries. How users can be educated about the access, retrieval and use of information is the concern of user education.

3. USER EDUCATION- WHAT IT MEANS?

Usereducation has been defined in different ways by different authors. Fleming has defined user education "as various programs of instruction, education and exploration provided by libraries to users to enable them to make more effective, efficient and independent use of information sources and services to which these libraries provide access" (Fleming,1990).

Thus, user education is a process of activities involved in making the users of the library conscious about tremendous value of information in day to day life and to develop interest among the users to seek information as and when they requires.

4. IMPORTANCE OF USER EDUCATION IN 21ST CENTURY

Libraries are facing challenges posed by the information and communication technology. ICT has changed the information landscape and thus we find library information resources in multiple formats. Ubiquitous internet has made it possible to create lot of information in audio, visual, text or in graphic formats. Thus we in the present information landscape find information in multimedia mediums. In the contemporary world, libraries are having wide range of materials like

- Digitized (scanned) books, journal articles, newspapers, manuscripts etc.
- Digital text
- Audio files (mp3)
- Video files (mp4)
- Photographic images (jpeg)

- Data sets
- Thesis and dissertations.

Libraries are adopting the technologies for increasing the quality of the information services provided to the library patrons. Technologies adopted by libraries include:

- Social Networking Tools likeFacebook, twitter, blogs etc.
- Mobile technologies
- RSS feeds
- Cloud Computing
- RFID Technology
- Search engines and meta search engines
- World Wide Web
- Library software packages etc.

Libraries are adopting technologies in order to become the part of library networks, consortia etc in order to have access to wide range of information resources available at different places. With the aid of technological gadgets, users of libraries are availing the opportunities to use these resources remotely as well as within their work places. It is because of these technologies that libraries are reaching to the doorsteps of their patrons instead of patrons to visit the libraries. Libraries by adopting these technologies have revolutionized their activities of collection building, organizing the resources, preserving these resources and ultimately the services to the library patrons. This whole situation demands that library patrons must be equipped with the knowledge and skills necessary for making effective and efficient use of information resources. These skills and knowledge are related to:

- Discover information
- Search information
- Retrieve information
- Use information and ultimately to
- Generate information.

This information is to be exploited maximally in order to generate more information for increasing the quality and standard of life.

5. TECHNIQUES APPLIED IN USER EDUCATION

Library professionals can adopt a number of methodologies for instructing library patrons about different facets of libraries and information centers. These facets may range from showing an individual how to use the library's online catalogue and basic print reference sources to formal classroom sessions about conducting research in laboratories. The basic component of user education includes demonstrating how, when and why to use different resources available in libraries and services offered by these library and information centers. Library professionals can use any of the following methods for educating the users:

a) Library tour where library patrons can be taken by the librarian to different sections of the library and will provide practical demonstrations of different tools applied for acquiring and organizing different information sources in the library. Patrons will get information about different reference sources available in reference section of the library. These sources include

- Bibliographic sources
- Encyclopedias
- Dictionaries
- Biographical sources
- Government information sources
- Ready reference sources

b) Virtual tour of the library where librarian introduces users about the library through the website created by the library professionals for the library. Different links available on the website are discussed by librarian to the users in detail.

c) By delivering lectures to the library patrons, however, library profession while delivering lectures should avoid technical jargons.

d) Library professionals can utilize mass media channels to disseminate information to the library patrons about the tools, techniques applied in the libraries and information centers. These channels include radio talks, television telecasts, newsletters, pamphlets etc.

While planning user education program it is essential that library professionals think about their audience. What are their interests, technological knowhow, academic and professional background,their information needs, their approach to information etc are the factors that can assist the librarian in devising the strategy for conducting user education programs.

Ultimate aim of user education is to ensure that users of libraries are turned into information literate individuals who can independently use information for concrete purposes. They are able to evaluate information sources available in print or digital / electronic formats. Information literate persons definitely will contribute more and more knowledge assets because of their following features:

- They know how to formulate their information needs.
- They would be aware of wide range of sources (including open access sources) available for finding information and select the sources which will best meet users needs;
- They would be aware of appropriate indexing and abstracting services and databases and understand the principles of their use;
- They would develop database searching techniques for accessing both web-based and CD-ROM databases;
- They would be able to use current awareness methods to keep up-to-date with the published literature;
- They would be able to use national and international academic networks for getting information;
- They would be able to use discussion forums, list servers, online chat services and blocks for obtaining and disseminating information;

- They would be able to use local library network for obtaining documents through inter-library loan and document delivery services;
- They would be able to compare and critically evaluate information obtained from various sources;
- They would be able to cite bibliographic references in their academic projects, papers, articles, reports or theses; and
- They would be able to construct a personal bibliographic system

LIBRARIAN AND USER EDUCATION

In order to conduct user education in an effective and efficient way library professional must be competent enough in terms of his knowledge and skills. A professional conducting user education must possess

a) Professional competencies including
   - Functional literacy
   - Scientific literacy
   - Technological literacy
   - Information literacy
   - Cultural literacy
   - Global awareness

b) Personal competencies including
   - insight,
   - creativity,
   - risk-accepting,
   - responsibility, and
   - public relations (Fatahiyan, 2004).

Library professionals who themselves are competent enough can help others to become competent enough. It is this spirit that compels library professional to keep themselves aware about the latest developments occurring in the profession.

CONCLUSION

User education has gained importance in the 21st century because users of libraries are facing the challenges posed by information explosion on one hand and application of information technology in libraries on the other hand. Users of libraries in the 21st century must be equipped with multiple literacies. These literacies are

- Computer literacy having focus on developing basic skills for operating computer technologies.
- Network literacy focusing on developing skills for accessing and scrutinizing the information available on networks like internet, inflibnetetc
- Library instructions in order to develop awareness among the library users to make maximum use of the library resources like catalogue, OPAC, WebOPAC etc.
- Media literacy is concerned with developing skills among users of information about the use of information sources available in different formats like text, audio, video, graphic, cartographic etc like documents.
- Digital literacy takes into consideration skills required for making effective use of digital information available usually on World Wide Web (WWW).

These literacy's are to be developed among the users of libraries through user education programmes. Success of any library depends upon the satisfaction of users. Users are satisfied if there information needs are fulfilled promptly and exhaustively. It is possible through user education programme. One must remember that through user education programmes , we are producing lifelong learners. As the old saying is that "giving a man a fish feeds him for a day while teaching him to fish feeds him for a life time". Users who know how to use the resources of libraries will provide opportunity to the library professionals to think on other lines whereby users are empowered with knowledge and wisdom. It is through user education that we can fulfill the message of the following five laws of library and information science profession in an effective and efficient manner:

Information is for use

Every reader his / her information.

Every bit of information its user.

Save the time of the user

Library is a growing organism.

Keeping in view the dynamic nature of library and information science profession, it is the need of hour that library professional experts and experts from other related disciplines like computer sciences, management etc join hands with each other and must devise a strategy where by users of information are empowered with skills and knowledge which they can use for exploiting information positively for fulfilling their own interests and for achieving the national interests.

REFERENCES

Fatahiyan, H. (2004). Role of ICT in education. Nama: Electronic Magazine of the Iranian Documentation Center 4 (1): 1-18.

Fleming, Hugh. (1990). User education in Academic libraries. London: Library Association.